MW00800233

INTRODUCING COMPARATIVE LITERATURE

Introducing Comparative Literature is a comprehensive guide to the field offering clear, concise information alongside useful analysis and examples. It frames the introduction within recent theoretical debates and shifts in the discipline whilst also addressing the history of the field and its practical application. Looking at comparative literature within the context of globalization, cosmopolitanism, and post- or transnationalism, the book also offers engagement and comparison with other visual media such as cinema and e-literature.

The first four chapters address the broad theoretical issues within the field such as interliterary theory, decoloniality, and world literature, while the next four are more applied, looking at themes, translation, literary history, and comparison with other arts.

This engaging guide also contains a glossary of terms and concepts as well as a detailed guide to further reading.

César Domínguez is Associate Professor of Comparative Literature and Jean Monnet Chair at the University of Santiago de Compostela, Spain.

Haun Saussy is University Professor in the Department of Comparative Literature at the University of Chicago, USA.

Darío Villanueva is Professor of Literary Theory and Comparative Literature at the University of Santiago de Compostela, Spain.

"Bound to engage the professional academic as well as the common reader, *Introducing Comparative Literature* calls on the insights of a remarkable range of theorists, historians, anthropologists, artists and philosophers to present—and at the same time rethink—the field. In a series of clear, concise chapters dedicated to inter-literary theory, decoloniality, world literature, themes and images, translation, literary history and interartistic comparisons, the authors deftly open up new ways of thinking about comparative literature as they effectively display its much-needed contributions to a pluralist, cosmopolitan education. This lively volume should soon become required reading in the literary classroom."

Sandra Bermann, Cotsen Professor of the Humanities; Professor of Comparative Literature, Princeton University, USA

"This excellent book is an essential guide to the field of comparative literature, introducing students to its key concepts and techniques in a lively and engaging way. Combining a lucid introduction to theoretical debates with useful outlines of the key contexts of the discipline, it also opens up the fascinating field of inter-artistic comparison and engages with exciting developments in adjacent fields such as comparative philosophy. An indispensable book for comparative literature students and teachers alike."

Javed Majeed, Head of Comparative Literature, King's College London, UK

"*Introducing Comparative Literature* is a useful and refreshing book that provides both a thorough overview of the discipline's historically diverse definitions and some intriguing propositions concerning the directions in which Comparative Literature is evolving in the present, and may evolve in the future. It is a fine volume that should be on the bookshelves and the syllabi of professors engaged in the work of maintaining and rejuvenating the practices of Comparative Literature."

David LaGuardia, Professor of French and Comparative Literature, Dartmouth College, USA

"This book offers a provocative and refreshing alternative to the old familiar Anglo-American theories of comparative literature."

Susan Bassnett, Professor of Comparative Literature, University of Warwick, UK

INTRODUCING COMPARATIVE LITERATURE

New Trends and Applications

César Domínguez, Haun Saussy and Darío Villanueva

Routledge
Taylor & Francis Group

LONDON AND NEW YORK

First published 2015
by Routledge
2 Park Square, Milton Park, Abingdon, Oxon OX14 4RN

and by Routledge
711 Third Avenue, New York, NY 10017

Routledge is an imprint of the Taylor & Francis Group, an informa business

© 2015 César Domínguez, Haun Saussy and Darío Villanueva

The right of César Domínguez, Haun Saussy and Darío Villanueva to be
identified as authors of this work has been asserted by them in accordance with
sections 77 and 78 of the Copyright, Designs and Patents Act 1988.

All rights reserved. No part of this book may be reprinted or reproduced or
utilised in any form or by any electronic, mechanical, or other means, now
known or hereafter invented, including photocopying and recording, or in any
information storage or retrieval system, without permission in writing from the
publishers.

Trademark notice: Product or corporate names may be trademarks or registered
trademarks, and are used only for identification and explanation without intent to
infringe.

British Library Cataloguing-in-Publication Data
A catalogue record for this book is available from the British Library

Library of Congress Cataloging in Publication Data
Domínguez, César.
Introducing comparative literature : new trends and applications /
César Domínguez, Haun Saussy, Darío Villanueva.
Includes bibliographical references and index.
I. Saussy, Haun, 1960- II. Villanueva, Darío. III. Title.
PN865.D66 2015
809--dc23
2014022341

ISBN: 978-0-415-70267-6 (hbk)
ISBN: 978-0-415-70268-3 (pbk)
ISBN: 978-1-315-77098-7 (ebk)

Typeset in Bembo
by Taylor & Francis Books

CONTENTS

FIGURES AND TABLES

List of figures

List of tables

PREFACE

As one usually gets acquainted with comparative literature for the first time during BA and MA seminars (if not later), after a long, previous period of having been a "common reader" in one's first language and having been exposed to other kinds of literary training, it is quite accurate to say that for many people comparative literature represents an exciting discovery that may change the direction of their academic career. Quite often, such a change takes place, in accordance with the current organization of university curricula, while being a graduate student. The excitement of the discovery lies in two main factors. First, one realizes there is a big world beyond the limits of the "national" literature that has provided the sheer bulk of *compulsory* readings during primary and secondary school. And second—and not less importantly—one realizes that the excitement about comparative literature has much to do with the fact that it is another form of reading—neither better, nor worse, just *different*—that has striking similarities with the way one reads just for fun. In other words, comparative literature scientifically endorses some of the intuitions we have as common readers.

A literary example may illustrate this point quite well. In David Lodge's 1984 novel *Small World*, the young Irish academic Persse McGarrigle says his MA thesis is "about the influence of T.S. Eliot on Shakespeare," to which Professor Dempsey replies "with a loud guffaw," "That sounds rather Irish, if I may say so" (Lodge 51). Dempsey's burlesque reaction is due to the fact that one would expect a study of the opposite influence—that of Shakespeare on T.S. Eliot—for a twentieth-century writer cannot influence one who died in the seventeenth century. Or, can s/he?

> "Well, what I try to show," said Persse, "is that we can't avoid reading Shakespeare through the lens of T.S. Eliot's poetry. I mean, who can read *Hamlet* today without thinking of 'Prufrock'? Who can hear the speeches of Ferdinand in *The Tempest* without being reminded of 'The Fire Sermon' section of *The Waste Land*?"

> *(Lodge 52)*

While Dempsey's approach is author-based, meaning that the influence moves from writer A's present to writer B's future, McGarrigle's approach is reader-based, meaning that the reader's experience may move in all directions, even in those which are alien to the creative process. Our mind cannot approach literary works, as well as other artistic artifacts, as if it were a *tabula rasa*; it cannot erase all the knowledge and events that took place after the literary work was composed. Both knowledge and events will mediate our reading, and hence we cannot read the work as it was composed by its author, neither can we read it as it was read by its most immediate readers. The reader of this book may think this is a loss. And it is. But it is also a gain. Neither approach—author-based or reader-based—is better or worse in itself, but either may be more appropriate for a specific research aim. What is undeniable, however, is that research based on the reader-approach replicates the experience of the common reader.

McGarrigle's examples on the influence of Eliot on Shakespeare may be easily multiplied. Since Jorge Luis Borges's writings are known to be a realm of paradoxes, it is understandable that this "paradox of influences" also attracted his attention. In his 1951 short story/essay *Kafka y sus precursores* (Kafka and his Precursors), Borges argues that Kafka's works help us to understand works by previous writers, so much so that some of these previous works would not exist without Kafka: "if Kafka had never written a line, we would not perceive this quality; in other words, it would not exist. The poem 'Fears and Scruples' by Browning foretells Kafka's work. Kafka perceptibly sharpens our reading of the poem. Browning did not read it as we do now" (Borges 201). Both Lodge's and Borges's examples deal with the influence of a "future" (from the writer's point of view) literary work on a "past" literary work. Let us replace *influence*—a technical concept in literary studies whose meaning is debatable, as this book will show—with rewriting, both in a metaphorical sense (while reading Shakespeare/Browning, we rewrite them through Eliot/Kafka) and a literal one. Borges also imagined this literal paradox in his 1939 "Pierre Menard, autor del *Quijote*" (Pierre Menard, Author of the *Quixote*). The (imaginary) late nineteenth-century/early twentieth-century French writer Pierre Menard aims to write *Don Quijote* again, exactly as it was written by Cervantes in the seventeenth century. Though Menard's *Quijote* is an exact replica of Cervantes's *Quijote*—line for line, word for word—it is not the *Quijote* of Cervantes, for many reasons. Suffice it to mention here only one. "The contrast in style is also vivid. The archaic style of Menard—quite foreign, after all—suffers from a certain affectation. Not so that of his forerunner, who handles with ease the current Spanish of his time" (Borges 43).

As common readers, our reading experience is mediated by artifacts quite similar to Menard's. Many readers of this book may never have read Dante's *Inferno*, but many will have played the action-adventure video game *Dante's Inferno*. (Notice how the title of the video game tells its users it is faithfully based on Dante's work.) Others may have not read any of Jane Austen's novels, but know their plots and characters very well thanks to movies based on them. And most readers enjoy reading literary works that were not initially written in the language they are reading them in, that is, they are reading a translation (another kind of rewriting)—and this fact often goes unnoticed. We read a book because either something from it has attracted our attention (topic, plot, characters, etc.) or somebody has recommended it to us, and we read it in the language we feel comfortable with—whether our first or "second" language, it does not matter. And writers—at least, good writers—are compulsive common readers and, therefore, these and other kinds of rewritings also get into the texture of their own works.

The reader may have noticed that we have already used the phrase "common reader" several times. *The Common Reader* is the title of two essay collections by Virginia Woolf. Woolf, in her turn, took it from Samuel Johnson, who in his *Life of Gray* says that he rejoices "to concur with the common reader; for by the common sense of readers, uncorrupted by literary prejudices, after all the refinements of subtilty and the dogmatism of learning, must be finally decided all claim to poetical honours" (cited in Woolf 1). While Woolf's view of the common reader is somewhat elitist—"He is worse educated, and nature has not gifted him so generously"—nonetheless her characterization of the common reader fits quite well with our own view: the common reader is someone "who reads for his own pleasure rather than to impart knowledge or correct the opinions of others. Above all, he is guided by an instinct to create for himself, out of whatever odds and ends he can come by, some kind of whole" (1).

In short, a common reader tries to make sense of what s/he is reading, creates "some kind of whole," which is made up of the fabric of words as rewoven in her/his mental encyclopedia. Within this mental encyclopedia, connections are made among literary works, most of these connections consisting of comparisons across languages, time, space, cultures, arts, discourses. By comparing we build sense, for comparison is a cognitive operation, and a connection between at least two elements transforms both elements. A literary comparison is, therefore, reading a work through other works, and reading those other works through the work at hand.

The reader of this book may already have some *a priori* ideas about what comparative literature entails. A standard definition says that comparative literature is about comparing works in different languages. If this is so, what is the relevance of some of the examples mentioned above? In Lodge's example a comparison was made between two writers who write in English—Shakespeare and Eliot. Likewise, the narrator of "Pierre Menard" compares "two" works in Spanish, a seventeenth-century work and its twentieth-century replica. In other cases we are comparing a literary work with its video game or movie rewriting. Only in the case of Borges's example of Browning and Kafka, we seem to be dealing with a comparison across languages, provided the reader is not reading Browning in the original and Kafka in English translation, or Kafka in the original and Browning in German translation. If we stick to such a conventional definition of comparative literature as comparing works in different languages, then only the Browning/Kafka case would qualify as comparison.

The issue of crossing linguistic borders was implicit in the initial definitions of the discipline, for the emphasis was placed on the fact that the field of comparative literature consisted of studying "the *relationships* between *different* literatures" (Texte 253; emphasis added), where "relationships" was understood as "influences" and "different" as "in different languages." In fact, this definition was included in the first lecture of a seminar taught by Joseph Texte at the Université de Dijon under the title "L'Influence des littératures germaniques sur la littérature française depuis la Renaissance" (The Influence of German Literatures on French Literature after the Renaissance) in the early 1890s. And yet, such a definition may also include comparisons between works in a single language (Eliot/Shakespeare and Cervantes's *Quijote*/Menard's *Quijote* would then fit here). For it is starting from such a common-sense notion—linguistic borders—that comparative literature poses its challenging questions. If comparison is a matter of reading across linguistic borders, what counts as a language? Is twentieth-century English or Spanish a different language from seventeenth-century English or Spanish? Is Argentinean literature a literary "whole" distinct from other literary wholes that also use Spanish? Is T.S. Eliot an American or British writer? Are not cinema, painting, opera, comics, etc., also kinds of language, so that, for instance, a comparison between a novel and a film qualifies as reading across language borders?

Whatever the answers to these questions may be, the truth is that comparative literature tightened its initial definition more and more as a result of its aim to make a place for itself among other literary disciplines. Around forty years after Texte's definition, in 1931 Paul Van Tieghem defined comparative literature in the most influential university textbook in the discipline as "the study of literary works of different literatures through their mutual relationships" (Van Tieghem 5), a definition in which the concept of influence was understood as a *rapport de fait* (factual connection), meaning not only that influences take place between only two works (binary comparison), but also that an influence proper requires that the writer of "work B" has read "work A" (in another language) and integrated it into her/his own work, an integration that the comparatist makes visible through analysis. It is worth mentioning that Van Tieghem acknowledged that many writers read "work A" not in its original language but in translation, or "read" that work only through allusions included in other works or summaries in journals, just to mention two types of mediation. This implies an implicit acknowledgement of the writer as a "common reader" and, therefore, a vision of comparative literature as a kind of scientific replica of the common reader's experience. Though this issue has never been discussed as definitional of comparative literature, it remains with us as the usual understanding of the discipline. It will be qualified further below.

But let us come back to the restrictions. By the late 1950s, the long period of accumulation of binary, factual connections was experienced by some comparatists as an asphyxiating atmosphere that had led the discipline into a cul-de-sac or, as it was termed, a "crisis." In 1958, an exiled Czech scholar trained in the Central European philological tradition, active among the Prague School linguists and founder of the Department of Comparative Literature at Yale University, René Wellek, presented at the second conference of the International Comparative Literature Association a paper titled "The Crisis of Comparative Literature." That very same year, the French professor and promoter of Middle Eastern and Asian languages and cultures, René Étiemble, published an essay titled "Littérature comparée ou comparaison n'est pas raison" (*Hygiène* 154–73), which would be the prologue for another diagnosis of comparative literature's crisis, his own 1963 *Comparaison n'est pas raison. La crise de la littérature comparée* (Comparison Is Not Proof. The Crisis of Comparative Literature). The effects of Wellek's diagnosis were immediate, and his paper has been directly or indirectly discussed by comparatists during the second half of the twentieth century, while Étiemble's had a somehow inferior and later influence.

For Wellek, comparative literature was suffering a major crisis because neither the object of study (influences between literatures), nor the method (comparison) was discipline-specific. As a matter of fact, there was no difference at all, argued Wellek, between studying how a writer influences another writer within one single literature and studying the process in distinct literatures. Another European exile, the German-Jewish Henry H.H. Remak, professor at Indiana University, faced the crisis of the discipline by offering a "new" definition, which has become standard. In its shorter version, it reads as follows: Comparative literature is "the comparison of one literature with another or others, and the comparison of literature with other spheres of human expression" ("Comparative Literature" 3). But, as is evident, such a new definition does not address either problem—object or method—but merely expands the field from the interliterary (the traditional comparison of different literatures) to the interartistic (the comparison of literature and other arts) and the interdiscursive (the comparison of literature and other discourses).

Though generally accepted, such a new definition proved unable to solve the crisis, so much so that the past twenty years have seen many well known comparatists (e.g. Susan Bassnett in 1993 and Gayatri Chakravorty Spivak in 2003) affirming that the discipline is dead. The tone of such statements is clearly provocative; what they want to stress really is that some forms of practicing comparative literature are not valid any longer. For some scholars, like Bassnett, the invalidity is method-related (one of the issues pinpointed by Wellek) and their solutions consist of dissolving comparative literature in other disciplines (translation studies in Bassnett's case). For others, like Spivak, the problem lies in the typically Eurocentric object of the discipline (comparative literature as the comparison of works within some five or six "major" European literatures—an issue addressed by Étiemble), and their solutions consist of both learning *other* languages (e.g. non-Western languages) and merging comparative literature with other fields (area studies in Spivak's case).

Now that ten or twenty years have passed since these death certificates were issued, the reader may think that the writers of this book must be perverse necrophiliacs seeking to infect their readers with their attraction to a corpse, namely, comparative literature. In a way, it is true, for we want our readers to become infected with our excitement about comparative literature. But in a larger sense it is not true, for we, like many scholars and students across the world, do not think comparative literature is a dying or dead discipline. The very fact of your reading this book supports our point of view. It may well be the case that you are reading this introductory textbook because you are attending a BA or MA seminar on comparative literature. Or you have heard about something called comparative literature and you want to know what it is. If this is so, this book will fulfill its aims, provided it succeeds in infecting you with the excitement comparative literature conceals, which would mean that, after reading this textbook, you will be willing to read further books on the discipline.

For us, the excitement is a combination of at least three factors—the common reader's experience, enthusiasm about human diversity, and the allure of risk and crisis. Indeed, comparative literature is the replication, under methodologically stringent conditions, of the common reader's experience, that is, a reading experience that crosses all kinds of borders (temporal, spatial, linguistic, cultural, etc.) in order to build meaning, which is highly dependent on comparisons with other artifacts, literary/artistic or not.

As for human diversity, is there a more important proof of human beings' creativity than the number of languages that have existed, exist, and will exist? With a material so fragile and limited in number as sounds, human beings have created thousands of languages for purposes of communication and, not satisfied with that, they have reserved a part of their linguistic interactions to carry out further experiments with language. This part is to a large extent what we call *literature* today, so one can say that literature is a metalanguage, language reflecting on the creativity of language. As no human group is deprived of language, likewise, no human group is deprived of literature, in the sense we give to the word today. In fact, semioticians have argued that languages are possible precisely because a part of them is reserved for the above-mentioned metalinguistic experimentation. There is no literature without language; but it is equally true that there is no language without literature, that is, verbal creativity and reflection on communication. Another requirement for languages to exist, semioticians and linguists say, is *contact*, so that languages evolve thanks to contact with other languages. And such a contact is realized when speakers mix languages, some speakers become proficient in several languages, and some speakers (translators) become specialized in mediating between linguistic communities. No language exists in a linguistic or semiotic vacuum. And this is equally true for literatures. Literatures come into contact with other literatures because either some readers have put them in contact (a bi- or pluri-literary reader, the equivalent of a bi- or pluri-lingual speaker), or some mediators have deliberately promoted such contacts (literary translators, for instance). An acute awareness about literatures influencing each other promoted the emergence of comparative literature during the early nineteenth century as a specific field of research. The conditions of the field's emergence were, to be sure, biased culturally (with comparison restricted to literatures in some European languages) and nationally (with comparison most often aiming at endorsing a privileged role for some countries due to their massive literary exports). But enthusiasm about human diversity should not be a naïve stance. Like biodiversity, linguistic ecosystems are also in danger. According to Peter K. Austin and Julia Sallabank, "there are about 7,000 languages spoken around the world; and […] at least half of these may no longer continue to exist after a few more generations as they are not being learnt by children as first languages" (1). It is then ironic that while some scholars state that comparative literature is dead, languages—the material of which the object of study of comparative literature is made—are becoming extinct at an alarming rate and, hence, the discipline may before long find itself having turned into a kind of comparative archeology.

Last but not least, we agree with both Wellek and Étiemble that comparative literature is in a state of crisis, though for different reasons from theirs. In fact, one may say that the crisis as diagnosed by them has been overcome more than fifty years later. The exploration of new and exciting directions, most notably East/West studies, has tempered somewhat the discipline's Eurocentrism and answered Étiemble's critique. Further, the 1980s' "new paradigm" made possible a fruitful collaboration between comparative literature and literary theory, resulting in a remarkable improvement of its methodology in answer to Wellek's critique. Our perception of comparative literature as a discipline in crisis is closer to Charles Bernheimer's when he says, "Comparative literature is anxiogenic" ("Anxieties" 1). For us, the crisis of comparative literature is neither a positive nor a negative aspect, but simply the result of its development within an ontological insecurity, which is due to its object of study. Comparative literature is the only discipline within literary studies that acknowledges literature without borders (Goethe's *Weltliteratur*, in a sense) as its object of research. While, on the one hand, literary history and literary criticism traditionally operate within national/linguistic borders and, on the other hand, literary theory, despite its universal aims, is remarkably Eurocentric and monolingual, comparative literature aims to study world literature. We share, therefore, Claudio Guillén's vision of the comparatist's task as a *project*.

> the comparatist nowadays has discovered that the object of her/his research may and should emerge, as a newborn baby, from her/his experience, initiative, and imagination. S/he has to demarcate a field of research among the many virtualities offered by literature. [...] When starting, [...] the comparatist cannot rely on some given realities, a priori delimited. The object of her/his study, as well as its definition and demarcation, is but a project.
>
> (Entre el saber *103*)

The problematic nature of world literature—from both an ontological (What is world literature?) and epistemic (Is world literature knowable?) perspective, which poses comparative literature in a critical position as constantly confronting new problems—mirrors the problematic nature of its methodology. There exist two opposing views in this regard. For some scholars, comparison is accepted straightforwardly *qua* method. For others, like Benedetto Croce and Wellek, inasmuch as the method of comparison is shared by several disciplines, it does not qualify for delimiting a distinctive discipline. Our view differs in that we consider that comparison should be approached from three different perspectives—predisciplinary, disciplinary, and transdisciplinary. By "predisciplinary perspective," we make reference to the fact that comparison is a mental operation that consists of establishing a minimal intellectual correlation of analogy between two (or more) elements, whereby both similarities and differences are investigated. Comparison is a logical-formal act, a dialectical relationship between a differentiating way of thinking (induction) and a totalizing attitude that looks for what is constant (deduction). It implies a way of relating to the Other, what Guy Jucquois (*Le Comparatisme*) has called *décentration* (decentering), a questioning of certainties and a suspension of security. By "disciplinary perspective," we mean that this method prevails in some disciplines, such as comparative literature, comparative linguistics, comparative religion, comparative philosophy, comparative anatomy, comparative law, comparative politics, and so forth. And by "trans-disciplinary perspective," we argue that a cross-exploration of problems shared by all these disciplines would be extremely fruitful when it comes to addressing methodological problems and fostering interdisciplinary collaboration.

Despite a frequent disclaimer ("what we do isn't really comparing"), our work on this volume has convinced us of the centrality of the act of comparison to international literary research. It is not as an end in itself, but as a means of discovery, that comparison enables us to discover relations, differences, hidden causes, questions not before asked. And the wider the field of things to be linked through comparison, the richer the results.

It is worth noting that the number of comparative disciplines is bigger in the humanities and social sciences than in other sciences, a fact that pinpoints the multifaceted and heterogeneous nature of human beings' creations, language and literature included. As other comparative disciplines, the starting point for comparative literature is to acknowledge that the phenomenon one aims to explain is problematic. Once again we should recall that, in contrast to other definitions of comparative literature, Guillén's precisely underlines the importance of the word *problem*: "comparative literature has been and is an intellectual discipline characterized by the posing of certain problems that only comparative literature is in a position to confront" (*The Challenge* 104). Facing such a problem and with the aim of solving it, the comparatist formulates a hypothesis from which some consequences may be derived. These consequences, in turn, are inductively examined so that the passage from homogeneous facts to their causes operates by way of what Charles S. Peirce called <u>abduction</u>. Abduction consists of "examining a mass of facts and in allowing these facts to suggest a theory. In this way, we gain new ideas; but there is no force in the reasoning" (C.S. Peirce, "Letter to Calderoni," cited in Nesher 178). Comparison as abduction shows that scientific statements are fallible, for experimental testing may prove consequences are false. Similarly, in the case of comparative literature, a hypothesis is always provisional, for world literature is an object yet to be known.

This particular combination of the common reader's experience, enthusiasm about human diversity, and the allure of crisis makes comparative literature an exciting and demanding discipline. There is a big literary world out there and, though one tries as hard as possible to learn new languages (both living and dead) so as to read literary works in their original languages, human capabilities are limited. A partial solution is, of course, reading in translation, something that comparatists held to be anathema some years ago, while now it is generally accepted that it is better to read in translation than not to read at all, not to mention that writers themselves read in translation, and translation puts literatures into contact. So, "though we cannot make our sun / Stand still, yet we will make him run."

This book is an introduction to an exciting and demanding discipline. In a limited space, we have tried to provide an informative overview of the discipline by stressing *new* trends and applications. The adjective "new" should be understood as both the latest topics discussed by comparatists, and methods that, though not new in the previous sense, are not very familiar to global academia. No new handbook on comparative literature has been published in English in the past twenty years. There are, of course, quite a few many-authored books in which several contributors participate and discuss their fields of expertise separately, a sign of the growing complexity of the discipline. Though co-authored by three comparatists, this book is meant to provide the reader with a coherent vision of the current state of the discipline and future applicabilities. Coherence is not its only virtue. At times, discrepancies and nuances have been introduced in footnotes, for where the co-authors were not entirely in accord, we took this to be a sign of the vitality of the discipline and of its locally inflected dynamism, and therefore anything but a drawback. Though all three of us read and contributed to all chapters, the main responsibility for chapters 1, 8, and 9 was Villanueva's; that for chapters 2, 3, and 7 was Domínguez's; that for chapters 4, 5, and 6 was Saussy's. Domínguez had the task of synthesizing drafts from all three and composing the present Preface.

Introducing Comparative Literature: New Trends and Applications is divided into nine chapters. Chapter 1 discusses the position of comparative literature within literary studies and quickly surveys the history of the discipline from its origins to the present moment. It is directly related to Chapter 9, for the short-sighted insistence on the crisis of the discipline needs to be recontextualized within a more worrying crisis, that of the humanities in general and the role of literary education. It is obvious that the Humboldtian–Kantian university is being replaced in many places across the world by what one may call the "corporate university," an institution of higher learning that is organized around what neoliberalism classifies as disciplines that bring an immediate profit. In both Canada and the US, many departments of comparative literature have been closed down. And yet, what has been read as another proof of the discipline's death may transform into a unique opportunity, the search for new structures that make interdepartmental and interdisciplinary collaboration the rule rather than the exception. Between the initial and the final chapter, seven chapters address seven approaches we consider most relevant at the present moment for a scientific systematization of the research on the common reader's experience. Chapter 2 reviews the theory of the interliterary process. Its relevance is due to at least three factors. First, it questions the conventional division of comparative literature between two schools—"French" and "American." Second, it questions the basic tenet of the discipline, namely, that literary development stops at either side of the national/international divide in accordance with the division of labor between national literary study and comparative literature. And third, it addresses world literature as the proper object of study of comparative literature. Chapter 3 explores the links between comparative literature and decolonial studies, a field closely associated with Latin America that aims to show how, though imperialism and colonialism may be over as a political order, coloniality is still active as the most widespread method of domination across our world. Though some statements by decolonial thinkers are highly debatable, we argue that decolonial studies represent a valuable contribution to continue the process of overcoming comparative literature's Eurocentrism. From interliterary theory, which poses world literature as the research object of comparative literature, and decolonial studies, which challenges the Western concept of literature, Chapter 4 follows, in which the concept of world literature is thoroughly discussed, including the renewed interest in world literature during the past ten years and its re-emergence as either a new paradigm of comparative literature or even a new discipline. Be this as it may, what is undeniable is that our interest in literature, both culturally close or distant, is thematic. If literature is a use of language that testifies to humans' creativity, its creation is intimately linked to the aim of overcoming our mortality. Literature speaks about the topics that concern us as human beings across time and space, the most perfect means for listening to people long dead, to languages that have become extinct, to worlds that no longer exist, and, last but not least, to distant views that both challenge and enrich ours. This is what Chapter 5 aims to present. Chapter 6 is devoted to translation, the medium through which literary works circulate across time and space, literatures get into contact, and writers, like other common readers, read and even train themselves. Once we have a clearer picture of this immense interliterary network, Chapter 7 interrogates the possibility of building transnational literary histories. Comparative literary history has become the most experimental field within the discipline during the past three decades and deserves to be discussed in detail due to the relevance of its alternative view on literature-in-time in contrast to the typical restriction according to national lines. And Chapter 8 explores the interartistic axis of comparative literature, which, though posed as new by Remak's definition, has contributed to the development of the discipline since its nineteenth-century foundation. Two sections follow after Chapter 9—a glossary with key words for comparative literature, and a list of further reading.

It is obvious that many other contents might have been included. But this is an introductory handbook that aims to provide BA and MA students who have no (or at best limited) previous knowledge of comparative literature, as well as any reader interested in the topic, with a clear and concise approach to the discipline that may be easily read during a typical one-semester seminar. This book will achieve its aims only if it is successful in showing that neither is comparative literature dead, nor are comparisons odious, despite John Lydgate. Unless by "odious" one means that comparisons lead to problems (in Guillén's sense), in which case we would in fact agree that comparisons are both odious and—as Dogberry puts it in *Much Ado about Nothing*—odorous.

ACKNOWLEDGEMENTS

The authors are especially indebted to two groups of people, our colleagues in the profession and our students. As for the former, three forums stand out—the American Comparative Literature Association, the Sociedad Española de Literatura General y Comparada, and the International Comparative Literature Association. Equally rewarding is the intellectual atmosphere of the Academia Europaea and the Stockholm Collegium for World Literary History, as well as the Hermes Consortium for Literary & Cultural Studies. As for students, their excitement and participation in our BA, MA, and doctoral seminars—from survey courses on premodern world literature and introductory courses, to comparative literature, to monographic seminars on comparative European literature, and literature and cinema—are a constant, refreshing challenge. Our editor, Ruth Moody, has given us encouragement and patience, as needed. Last but not least, both activities and funding by the Jean Monnet Chair "The Culture of European Integration" (no. 528689) have been of key importance.

1

COMPARATIVE LITERATURE AND THE FUTURE OF LITERARY STUDIES

Before the actuality of comparative literature can be discussed, its possibility must be established. The first ground of its possibility is the fact that human beings, of whatever time, country and culture, have used language. But language: what is that?

It is worth noting the distinction drawn in French between the terms *langage* and *langue*, both of which translate to the single English word, "language." This distinction is not made in all languages. Ferdinand de Saussure elucidates it in his foundational text of modern linguistics, *Cours de linguistique générale* (published by his students from notes in 1916).

Langage is an innate faculty possessed by all humans in virtue of their anatomy and neuronal configuration. There has never been a human community made up of individuals without the capacity to communicate. But for the linguistic potential to be fully realized, the existence of a *langue* is also necessary. This could be defined as the aggregate of conventions adopted by the social body that allows the exercise of the linguistic faculty on the part of each individual: a "language," in the sense that we speak of English or Chinese or one of the varieties of sign language as a "language."

We are thus confronted with a complex system, which requires the insights of biology, sociology, and psychology to be unraveled. Language seems almost miraculous and, above all, radically egalitarian and democratic, since no one lacks a share in it. On the other hand, the most sublime expressions of human language are the preserve of those gifted with a special sensibility and competence and who produce language as art, seeking to give, to cite the well known verse from Mallarmé's "Le Tombeau d'Edgar Poe," *"un sens plus pur aux mots de la tribu"* (a purer sense to the words of the tribe). If language is a universal faculty, so too is its expression as art. Since the eighteenth century, the European world has described this expression as literature.[1]

Language and poetry are two strong arguments in favor of the existence of a universal human condition. To a large degree, both Goethe and the founders of *Littérature comparée* (comparative literature) are representatives of the spirit of enlightenment rationalism, which inspired, among other achievements, the recognition of universal human rights. Literature expresses the deepest, most universal, and lasting elements of human experience, those that survive the particularity of individual passions and sentiments. The same is true of the reality that surrounds us, whose four basic elements (earth, water, air, and fire) are also invariable. If, as Aristotle intuited, the basic foundation of all the arts is imitation, then human beings are essentially mimetic creatures (*Poetics* 1447a12–16 and 1448b4–8).[2] To satisfy our mimetic impulses, we have the arts. All arts are mimetic, and their object is the same: human and natural reality. But each art goes about its work with different instruments. The art that imitates with words is that for which Aristotle has no specific name (*Poetics* 1447b9), but to which he dedicates his *Poetics*, the first work of literary theory.

Johann Peter Eckermann informs us that in May 1827 Goethe received at his home the erudite French scholar Jean-Jacques Ampère, and that they spoke profusely of literature. A few months previously the German writer had formulated his ideas on national literature, which for him was no longer a relevant distinction, bound to give way to a cosmopolitan *Weltliteratur* (world literature). In fact, between 1827 and 1831 Goethe mentioned several times the concept of *Weltliteratur*, which he at times terms "Universal World Literature," or "General World Literature." On another occasion he refers to "European, in other words, World Literature" (Goethe, "On World Literature" 14).[3]

Ampère, for his part, belongs to the circle of the French founders of the new discipline of *Littérature comparée*, which had been taking form in the years 1815–30 under the influence of Abel-François Villemain. We have, then, at the start of the nineteenth century, two concepts—world literature and comparative literature—that are very closely linked.

The first of these, *Weltliteratur*, is part of the prophetic vision of a poet who used the term to define a new territory, a literature without boundaries. This would be the object of a new discipline, based on the comparative method, which at that time was coming to the fore in various scientific disciplines, from Wilhelm von Humboldt's comparative anthropology, which dates from 1795, to Georges Cuvier's comparative anatomy (1800–05), to Jean-Jacques M.C.V. Coste's embryology, to the comparative linguistics of Franz Bopp, Friedrich Diez, August Schleicher, Kristian Rask, or A.W. Schlegel.

Almost two centuries later, the concept of *Weltliteratur* is gaining renewed prominence. Its content is periodically revised. David Damrosch (*What Is World Literature?* 15) insists that the term does not refer to a chaotic library of works of diverse provenance, but a functional network, established in the context of a universal system. His definition is threefold (281): world literature as "an elliptical refraction of national literatures," as "writing that gains in translation," and as "not a set canon of texts but a mode of reading, a form of detached engagement with worlds beyond our own place and time."

The concept of *literary system* is integral to Damrosch's approach. Such a concept is implicit in the thought of T.S. Eliot, Dionýz Ďurišin's theory of interliterary processes (see Chapter 2), Claudio Guillén's early work ("Literatura como sistema" and *Literature as System*), and the "new paradigm" of comparative literature that we will refer to in greater detail at a later stage in this first chapter. For Damrosch (*What Is World Literature?* 173), also, "a work only has an effective life as world literature whenever, and wherever, it is actively present within a literary system beyond that of its original culture."

The spirit that animated the birth of comparatism, and which survives in those who practice it today, is the same as that which T.S. Eliot describes in his well known "Tradition and the Individual Talent" (1920). According to this Harvard alumnus—and we should remember that Harvard was a pioneering university in the study of comparative literature—an ideal order is constituted by the totality of the works that have been written, an order partially modified with the appearance of every new work.[4] Not only is the significance of each work in the ideal order changed with the addition of each new text, but also the significance of the ideal totality they constitute. The past influences the present of literature, but the present also influences the past (see the Preface). If this is the case in terms of time, it is also true in terms of space. It is absurd to think that literature written in a given language or culture exists in a self-sufficient vacuum. The classics of Greco-Roman, Chinese, and Arabic culture, no less than contemporary works in diverse languages and nationalities, all contribute to the creation of every individual literary artifact, which can only be understood and valued through comparison.

The study of literature

Literary study is constituted by the combination and collaboration of four distinct disciplines: poetics or literary theory, literary criticism, literary history, and comparative literature. For the last 150 years, however, literary history has been the dominant approach—a legacy of German Romanticism and its involvement in the emergence of the concept of the nation-state.

The paradoxical truth of the matter is that literary nationalism both enables and limits the practice of comparative literature. Literary history as a discipline broke with previous approaches that did not distinguish among literatures according to the languages in which they were written, but posited the existence of a literary continuum in which works were understood in terms of supranational systems of poetics and rhetoric. From this perspective there was simply Literature, which took on different manifestations in different linguistic codes, but which belonged to one common country, a Parnassus of letters in which Rhetoric and Poetics, though originating in Greece and Rome, founded a tradition not bound to any single national culture. As Guillén comments, "the unity of the poetic always triumphed over the diversity of the poetry" (*The Challenge* 25).

Once the predominance of this approach was broken at the start of the nineteenth century, comparative literature came to restore continuity, though this time from a perspective not based on "literary universals" but through the "literary particulars" of each language as realized in its artistic expression, and through the comparison and evaluation of these different manifestations in terms of their similarities and divergences.

Within the totality of the "literary sciences"—a term derived from the German *Literaturwissenschaft*—comparative literature is one of four main approaches to the literary phenomenon. These approaches are linked in a clear chronological order. The first approach analyzes and evaluates texts, a tendency already visible in pre-Socratic literary criticism. Once this operation is carried out on a sufficiently wide scale, profound similarities appear among different texts. Hence arises the impulse to generalization and the outlining of laws—what we could term the theoretical leap. When a given culture begins to take on a historical sense of itself, especially with the development of a sense of nationhood, literary history comes to the fore. Comparative literature appears when the literary history of particular nations begins to seem limiting or inadequate: it considers national literary history as an element within a plural literary history.

Eugenio Coseriu maintained that a good linguist should be both botanist and gardener, theoretician and practitioner, a determined seeker of concrete data but also attentive to the invariants that underlie them. The same is true in the study of literature: we have to be attentive to the particularities of a given text, but also capable of seeing it in context, in order to glean from it richer meanings. The study of literature requires a balanced and fertile harmony of these four approaches. Neither literary criticism nor literary theory can then be separated from comparative and historical approaches. A literary theory that does not base itself on an analytic criticism that is sufficiently developed will be a weakened theory; it will be equally weak if it does not sufficiently take into account the historical panorama. What comparative literature brings, however, is an absolutely necessary contrastive approach, which, diffracting the historical sequence of literary production into various linguistic areas, allows for their juxtaposition. What comparative literature ultimately gives us is the ratification of conclusions that the other three areas of literary science suggest. It consolidates the hypotheses of literary theory every time it identifies invariants or general laws common to diverse traditions. It grants the literary history of a determined nation or language a deeper resonance in its capacity to contrast a given tradition with others. It enriches literary criticism, providing it with a wide panorama on which to refine its instruments.

Origins

Comparative literature was conceived as a variant of literary history since its consolidation in the 1820s and 1830s, after its initial formulations in the work of precursors such as the Spanish Jesuit, Juan Andrés, author of the foundational *Dell'origine, progressi e stato attuale d'ogni letteratura* (1782–99; On the Origin, Progress and Present State of All Literature), whom Goethe planned to visit during Andrés's exile in Mantua (D'haen, Domínguez and Thomsen 1–8).

Its founders are French, with major figures such as the aforementioned Villemain, who after his first lectures from 1816–26, between 1828 and 1849 published courses on French literature in which he established comparisons between authors and movements in other literatures and who employed the term "*Littérature comparée*."[5] But in his first writings there were already the beginnings of a duality that it is important to note. We have already remarked the close relationship between comparative literature and literary history. Villemain, however, in the editorial introduction to the second volume of his *Tableau de la littérature au XVIIIe siècle* (1827–28) states that "this comparative study of literatures" is the *philosophy of criticism*. This is the equivalent of our literary theory, the continuation of what Aristotle had begun: a *Poetics*, consisting of the formulation of the basic principles that underlie literary phenomena.

Definition and utopia *intrinsically*

Definitions of comparative literature are multiple, and their multiplication has not ceased since Fernand Baldensperger (1921) opened the *Revue de Littérature Comparée* with an inquiry into "*le mot et la chose*" (the name and the thing).

But the proposal of Henry H.H. Remak, which Roland Mortier (12) at the ninth congress (1979) of the Association Internationale de Littérature Comparée/International Comparative Literature Association (AILC/ICLA) argued was "*la meilleure définition de la littérature comparée*" (the best definition of comparative literature), continues to have validity:

> Comparative Literature is the study of literature beyond the confines of one particular country and the study of the relationships between literature on one hand and other areas of knowledge and belief, such as the (fine) arts, philosophy, history, the social sciences, the sciences, religion, etc. on the other. In brief, it is the comparison of one literature with another or others, and the comparison of literature with other spheres of human expression.
>
> *(Remak, "Comparative Literature" 3)*

The essence of this definition is also at the heart of what A. Owen Aldridge (1) sees as the specificity of comparative literature: "Comparative Literature can be considered the study of any literary phenomenon from the perspective of more than one national literature or in conjunction with another intellectual discipline or even several."

As the youngest of the disciplines dedicated to the study of literature, comparative literature has been sensitive to the provocations and contradictions that confront historical research, derived from the evolution of thought, ideology, and culture in modernity and postmodernity, but it is also intrinsically subject to tensions that are difficult to overcome. We refer to the fact that comparative literature inherently implies certain utopic components, born of the vastness of the field that it attempts to cover and the natural human limitations of those of us who take the discipline as our vocation.

It is true that some comparatists are, due to their family or geographical origins, privileged in the breadth of their range. Hugo Meltzl de Lomnitz, the creator in 1877–79 of the discipline's first journal, was a German-speaking Hungarian who lived in Transylvania as a citizen of the Austro–Hungarian empire, was trained in Heidelberg and taught in the Franz-Joseph-Universität of Cluj/Clausenbourg/Kolozsvár. Similarly international profiles are repeated among the great comparatists. We may mention as indicative Louis Betz, a New Yorker with German parents who studied and taught in Zürich, as well as Edward W. Said (*Out of Place*), a Palestinian born in Jerusalem in 1935 who later moved with his family to Lebanon, and from there to Egypt in 1948, and studied at Princeton and Harvard before teaching English and comparative literature at Columbia.

Immediately, however, the limitations of even such gifted persons are revealed. Meltzl, for example, modeled his *Weltliteratur* as a *Dekaglottismus*, consisting of German, English, Spanish, Dutch, Hungarian, Icelandic, Italian, Portuguese, Swedish, and French, as well as Latin. Apart from the obvious omission of Greek and Arabic, all the Eastern and African languages are excluded, as are certain European languages with rich literary traditions. (Russian was intentionally excluded by Meltzl in reproof of tsarist censorship.) In practice, the "decaglottism" of the journal he founded, the *Acta Comparationis Litterarum Universarum*, was more fictitious than real. In percentage terms, the predominant languages during its eleven years of existence were Hungarian and German, with almost half of the articles written in the latter.

Meltzl defended his "principle of polyglottism" against the "principle of translation," insisting that "true comparison is possible only when we have before us the objects of our comparison in their original form" (20). Such an ambition for authenticity would constitute the aura of the "true" comparatists up until contemporary debates. In some ways, comparative literature has from its origins been the reserve of the virtuosos of literary studies: a restricted terrain, conceived as a space where the happy few, capable of mastering a wide variety of languages and open to the most cosmopolitan horizons, could show their brilliance. But even for the most gifted comparatists the demands of comparative literature are always utopian, consisting as they do in the mastery of all the historical and contemporary literatures and languages.

Comparative literature has, with some reason, been accused of elitism and Eurocentrism. Furthermore, as a discipline it has from its beginnings disturbed the professional advocates of national literary histories, especially when comparison aspired to the rank of an independent, and prestigious, discipline. As a consequence comparatists have always had to defend themselves against the hostility of colleagues in related disciplines, against the monolingual or monocausal versions of history that have incessantly tried to influence its development, and against the discipline's own methodological and intellectual porosity, which has made it overly susceptible to passing fashions and paradigms in literary and humanistic studies.

Comparative literature has always tended towards history, but at the same time it has, since its beginnings, had the potential for theoretical elaboration, which, in time, would give rise to the development of two orientations. The first, chronologically speaking, is marked by a fundamentally historical emphasis, and pays more attention to *rapports de fait* (factual connections), to the direct and causal relations

{ factual
{ theory

between works and authors, to the circulation of schools, genres, tendencies, styles, motifs, etc.; whereas the second is more inclined towards theory.

For more than a century the former orientation, which derives from positivism, considered the essential object of study the transmission of themes (see Trousson), motifs, characters, schools, etc. from one country to another, or, more accurately, from one language to another, approaches that have led it to be caricatured as the study of the "international trading of literatures." The model, in this case, is PhD dissertations such as Fernando Baldensperger's 1904 *Goethe en France*, which has its sequels in J.M. Carré's 1920 *Goethe en Angleterre*, or Robert Pageard's 1958 *Goethe en Espagne*.

As opposed to this, the other tendency attends above all to convergences, without necessarily searching for causal relations. This approach answers the questions provoked by polygenesis, the fact that in distant parts of the world, extraordinarily similar literary expressions take place without our necessarily being able to confirm a direct relationship between them.

When William Faulkner, for example, was questioned as to the influence of James Joyce on his writing, an obvious question as his narrative technique seems so similar to that created by Joyce in *Ulysses* and *Finnegan's Wake*, his response was to admit the similarities between the works, but to protest that he had achieved his style before having read Joyce. The key, according to Faulkner, lay in the fact that "there must be a sort of pollen of ideas floating in the air, which fertilizes similarly minds here and there which have not had direct contact" (cited in Villanueva 7; see Villanueva for discussion).

Or consider the motif of the "double," found in myths and legends across the world. Its abrupt rise in prominence in the early to mid-nineteenth century (Hoffmann, Poe, Baudelaire, Dostoevsky, and so forth) could be *documented* by tracing the links of influence connecting these and other writers, but to *explain* or *situate* it, other kinds of causes would need to be invoked: the experience of modern big cities, the sensitivity to hypocrisy, new discourses of both individualism and collectivism, for example. "Influences" and "parallels" are working hypotheses that help us gain understanding; they have no business turning into exclusive dogmas.

Hugo /Meltzl
Historical vicissitudes   *Juan Andrés*

As we have already pointed out, from its very origins it is easy to perceive a very direct relationship between the vicissitudes of our most recent history and the development of comparative literature. From the middle of the nineteenth century, the growth of comparative literature depends on individual achievements. After the work of Meltzl and some important eighteenth-century precursors such as Juan Andrés, in 1849 Louis Benloews entitled his inaugural speech to the Université de Dijon "Introduction à l'histoire comparée des littératures" (Introduction to the Comparative History of Literatures), and in 1886 an Irishman living in Auckland, Hutcheson Macaulay Posnett, published the first textbook specifically dedicated to the study of comparative literature, and seeking to frame the nascent discipline in the evolutionism of Tylor or Spencer.

But the twentieth century would be the most important time for the consolidation of comparative literature. It is at this moment that comparative literature not only becomes a subject taught within universities, but also is articulated institutionally in the creation of national and international associations. But also very important is the historical context here as, after World War I and the Treaty of Versailles, the idea grew that conflict could be avoided through a greater understanding between nations; mutual cultural and artistic understanding were seen as central to this endeavor.

We could document this openness to the need of an intercultural understanding through the works of certain interwar comparatists, such as Albert Léon Guérard, who was a prominent world-government activist. Conspicuous writers who worked toward this ideal would include Romain Rolland, Thomas Mann, Heinrich Mann, and many writers in the pro-Soviet camp.[6] But at least in the 1930s these initiatives of a small élite were not echoed in the wider public, where nationalist agendas dominated. Some para-academic organizations like the *Centre de synthèse* led by Henri Berr, or the *Collège de sociologie*, or the alliances of left-wing writers often led by the USSR, were active, but did not strike institutional roots. Expressions of this idea of "international understanding" would be institutionalized and become common currency only after World War II in UNESCO and related bodies. Between the wars, the traditions of *Völkerpsychologie* (the "psychology of peoples") were alive and well. And in fact comparative literature became institutionally solid only after World War II. Ernst Robert Curtius, Leo Spitzer, and Erich Auerbach were trained as Romance studies scholars; Charles du Bos and Ramón Fernández were critics writing for magazines. Among writers, paradox abounds: Ezra Pound, who was cosmopolitan in his tastes, adhered to Mussolinian fascism, while Eliot, who believed in channeling the "mind of Europe," went from sympathizing with Charles Maurras to a form of Christian conservatism.

World War II temporarily halted the progress of comparative literature. The war brought a great deal of nationalistic, triumphant, egocentric comparison, intended to show one's own country as triumphing over intellectual rivals. One has only to dip into the literary journals of the time to see *l'esprit germanique* (German spirit), *der franzözische Geist* (French spirit), etc. reified into the actors of history. And such reifications are always comparative—the German *Geist* exists in contrast to French rationalism, Anglo-Saxon practicality, or whatever other stereotype is current. However, such comparisons aiming at consolidating an essential identity are inherently futile. Some people learned this even without having to go through a terrible war.

But in the US, because of the country's isolationist past and tendency to "wash clean" immigrants of their old-country past, World War II brought a new wave of interest about cultural differences that could be fed by the universities' expansion, as Robert J. Clements reminds us in his research on the development of comparative studies within the US. Clements notes that comparative literature even came to be expressly encouraged by UNESCO, which in 1976 went to the length of establishing a university syllabus for its study at both doctoral and postdoctoral levels.

Clearly peacetime conditions favor literary interchanges and the desire to discover similarities between literatures of different languages and cultures. In the second half of the twentieth century, the Cold War was a major hindrance to the development of comparative literature, especially in the countries behind the Iron Curtain, such as Hungary and Czechoslovakia, which had been pioneers in the development of the discipline. The break-up of the Soviet Union and the fall of the Berlin Wall at the end of the 1980s coincided with visions of a new Europe that would be both economically and politically integrated, a vision in which the recognition of common cultural roots was key. (The definition of these roots would be tested by Turkey's application for membership in the European Union.) The rise of world literature can be seen as responding to similar impulses in the context of economic globalization, a tendency already identified by Karl Marx and Friedrich Engels in 1848 (see Chapter 4), when they announced the emergence of a "world literature" "from the numerous national and local literatures" as a side effect of the emerging "world market" (13). *economic globalization*

It remains the case, however, that comparative literature as a discipline must abandon an ideological Eurocentrism, to which an equally ideological "anti-Eurocentrism" would oppose itself. Though the concept of an exhaustive comparative or world literature must be recognized as chimerical, it is perfectly legitimate to promote the comparative study of European literature, for instance, as one "regionalization" among others of the vast field of literary studies, an initiative that César Domínguez (*Literatura europea* 25) links with Gayatri Chakravorty Spivak's proposal to combine area studies with the "traditional linguistic sophistication of Comparative Literature" (*Death* 8).

Spivak

Theoretical and ideological vicissitudes

Comparative literature has experienced moments of crisis in the past thirty years, due both to the growth of nationalist sentiment and also to the growth of multiculturalism, the latter becoming extremely dominant within university departments far removed from the sphere of cultural anthropology from which it developed. From this perspective, the literary phenomenon can only be seen in the context of imperialism and colonization. Western culture here comes to be seen as a tool of oppressive power, and comparative literature a fundamentally Eurocentric discourse that imposes literary values that are both elitist and class based. For scholars from this field, any literature can be compared to another, and those works which have been understood as canonic or "classic" are only perceived as such as they are accompanied by power structures that minimize peripheral cultural expression. In every case, it is evident that literature flourished for centuries before there was any such thing as "Western culture," in Chinese, Japanese, Arabic, Sanskrit, Persian, etc. For if no single culture is by right "privileged" over any other, and if all existing literary works are potentially comparable with one another, then the designation of some works as "classics," as "core" or "canonical," can only be a matter of cultural politics, of unilateral action by power structures seeking to minimize cultural expressions from the "margins."

The unstable equilibrium between the historic and the theoretical that we have underlined above provokes recurrent crises in the discipline. One such conflict was made explicit in René Wellek's lecture at the second conference of the AILC/ICLA that took place in 1958, which he titled "The Crisis of Comparative Literature." Wellek there argued against a predominantly historical, influence-based version of comparative literature, relegating that style of research for being "a stagnant backwater" of intellectual life (167). In order to avoid such stagnation, Wellek urged, practitioners of comparative literature, literary theory, literary history, and literary criticism should take as the object of their study the literary work in itself, not its historical envelope, and in order to do that they would have to confront "the problem of 'literariness,' the central issue of aesthetics, the nature of art and literature" (169). Wellek may have seemed, in terms of the polemics of the time, to embrace an "American" model of comparative literature (as distinguished from the more historicist "French" one), but his putting "the problem of 'literariness'" at the center of the discipline harked back to the 1930s structuralism of his university city, Prague.

The relationship between Wellek's 1958 position and the literary phenomenology of the Polish disciple of Edmund Husserl, Roman Ingarden, is clear, especially if we take into account the significant Slavic elements that Wellek himself included in his 1948 *Theory of Literature*, which he had published with his Iowa colleague Austin Warren. But the most determined support for a reorientation of comparative literature, changing it from an exclusively positivist discipline into an integrally theoretical one, was to come from France.

The initial impetus for this reorientation was the work of René Étiemble, who in 1963 published *Comparaison n'est pas raison. La crise de la littérature comparée*. This was a decidedly polemical text, which for Étiemble had significance not just in terms of literary disciplines, but in terms of a political affirmation of universalism and an historic and intellectual openness. Such ideas, like those of Wellek, continue to be relevant to the contemporary study of the role of comparative literature in the future of literary studies. For a comparatist of the generation of Baldensperger, the practical knowledge of German, English, Spanish, French, and Italian was sufficient. For Étiemble this was no longer the case; ignorance of Russian and Japanese, not to mention Chinese and Arabic, was absolutely unacceptable. Despite his advocacy of language study, he does not disregard—in fact the opposite is the case—the fundamental importance that translations should have in his project for a new comparatism. What is clear is his rejection of an exclusively positivist comparative literature and his interest in the aesthetic, the integrated study of forms, and the comparative analysis of metrical systems and symbols, an interest that would lead to the "comparative poetics" of his disciple Earl Miner (*Comparative Poetics* 238).

Postmodern crisis

At the end of the twentieth century Susan Bassnett would affirm that "[t]oday, comparative literature in one sense is dead" (47). Ten years later, the no less influential Gayatri Chakravorty Spivak consummated this process with her *Death of a Discipline.* Had the discipline died? Were then the self-critical and innovating voices within comparative literature inconsequential?

The symptoms that Bassnett described to justify her pessimism were, variously: English literature's replacement of literary theory in American universities, the impact of cultural studies, the reduction of specific chairs dedicated to comparative literature, and, in general, the critiques from postcolonial and multicultural perspectives. Spivak (*Death* xii), for her part, conceives of her book as "the last gasp of a dying discipline," an agony she attributes to the same general conditions which her British colleague had already described. She argues that comparatists must not only dare to "cross borders," but also attempt to recuperate meaningful readings (*Death* 72).

It is true that comparative literature does constitute a type of political ideology. It is a system of ideas that is accompanied by a wide vision of literature, humanism, and history, for it is claimed that by researching and teaching literatures cross-culturally, comparatists aim at increasing mutual understanding by stressing common human values beyond borders. In support of this claim, the history of comparative literature exhibits striking parallels with the history of international law, as far as to share some foundational texts, for instance, Immanuel Kant's *Idee zu einer allgemeinen Geschichte in weltbürgerlicher Absicht* (1784; Idea for a Universal History with a Cosmopolitan Purpose) and *Zum ewigen Frieden. Ein philosophischer Entwurf* (1795; Perpetual Peace. A Philosophical Sketch).

In the second edition of his *Entre lo uno y lo diverso. Introducción a la literatura comparada,* Claudio Guillén echoes to some degree the pessimism of Bassnett and Spivak, describing the atmosphere within which contemporary comparatists work as one defined by uncertainty, especially compared with the forty years between 1945 and 1985, which constitute the golden age of the systematic critical and historical study of literature in a context of a cosmopolitan literary space. What most concerned Guillén, and accounted for his pessimism, was the unprecedented politicization of the humanities. He focused particularly on the increasing prevalence of cultural and postcolonial studies to the detriment of more traditional approaches to the study of literature. But it is also important here to take into account the evolution of literary theory, especially in the US.

Despite the intellectual rigor of the thought of Jacques Derrida and Paul de Man, it must be admitted that the triumph of reductionist readings of deconstruction had a negative effect on the prestige of literature in academic curricula, which had until then conceived of *belles-lettres* as a necessary element in a general humanistic education in the spheres of ethics, expression, aesthetics, and general knowledge. Literature was considered as intrinsically meaningful, a guide to fundamental—what Northrop Frye (*The Critical Path*) would call "incumbent"—human concerns.

These reductionist readings of deconstruction seem to suggest that literature is precisely the lack of fundamental meaning, that it is more of an echo chamber in which one cannot trust in the ultimate validity of the voice, and in which stable meaning is dissolved. If the book signifies, it signifies that which the reader desires it signify. But it is a large step from this hermeneutical relativism, in which, according to the phenomenological approach of the already cited Ingarden, the literary work becomes a schema whose indeterminacies should be "filled in" by the reader, to the radical negative hermeneutics of deconstructive approaches, which would deny the capacity of literature to express any meaning whatsoever.

It was in this direction that deconstructionists moved, with negative consequences for the status of literary studies in the university. For many, deconstruction created a vacuum, a barren terrain in which approaches such as cultural studies took root. A response to such reductionist readings is already suggested by certain texts by Derrida in relation to comparative literature, such as, for instance, "Who or What is Compared?". Derrida's seven theses are instrumental for rethinking the role of (comparative) literature within the humanities ("The Future of the Profession"; see also Cohen). But simultaneously with the rise of these reductionist interpretations, and perhaps due to them and to external factors (the exact proportions will be long debated), literary tradition lost its central role, and along with it the academic and philological tradition of literary study within which comparative literature had its place.[7] Said recognized this, noting that the new disciplines were diverting "the humanities from its rightful concern with the critical investigation of values, history, and freedom, turning it, it would seem, into a whole factory of word-spinning and insouciant specialities, many of them identity-based, that in their jargon and special pleading address only like-minded people, acolytes, and other academics" (*Humanism* 14). On the other hand, the "varieties of deconstructive Derridean readings" end "in undecidability and uncertainty" (Said, *Humanism* 66). It should not surprise us, then, that the solution that Said (34) proposes in his posthumous work is "a return to a philological-interpretative model that is older and more widely based than the one that has prevailed in America since the introduction of humanistic study in the American university 150 years ago."

It is hard to avoid apportioning some blame to theoretical excess in this debacle, an excess which, as George Steiner (*Real Presences* 7) notes, contributes to the construction of an academic culture with a predominant register that is "secondary and parasitic." This reaction to theoretical bloat can be seen among many academics in the US, with Karen J. Winkler's "Scholars Mark the Beginning of the Age of Post-Theory" marking an important sea-change.[8]

This is the context of the Bernheimer Report of the American Comparative Literature Associaton (ACLA), which was critical of the deconstructive turn in the humanities. Bernheimer ("The Bernheimer Report" 5) described a tendency to give "priority to theory over literature, to method over matter" because of the destructive influence of "the inevitable aporia of deconstructive undecidability." Likewise, Bernheimer deliberately gave a very narrow picture of deconstruction, in order to make cultural studies appear as a savior. To this devaluation of the specificity of literature and the possibility of meaning in the text was added the politics of multiculturalism and its rejection of the Western canon and the eradication from syllabi of writers that had until then been considered classic, a tendency that Harold Bloom (*The Western Canon*) lamented as a consequence of the predominance of the "School of Resentment."[9] From the moment that a "work's value is perceived as residing primarily in the authenticity of the image it conveys of the culture it is taken to represent, politically and mimetically" ("The Bernheimer Report" 8), each literature becomes absolutely equivalent to any other, and therefore each work is essentialized, perceived without the recognition of any contextual primacy or prevalence. In consequence, any possibility of comparative judgment is neutralized, and the rejected Eurocentric canon is not substituted for by any African or Asian alternative. Along this path we reach another aporia, in which "multiculturalist comparatism begins at home with a comparison of oneself to oneself" ("The Bernheimer Report" 11). But what Bernheimer terms "the anxieties of comparison" offers a vast field of possibilities for the collaborative approach between the youngest of the literary disciplines and the multiple facets of cultural studies.

Since the final decades of the twentieth century, we have heard of the possibilities of a "new paradigm" for comparative literature, to use the phrase which Pierre Swiggers, and Douwe W. Fokkema ("Comparative Literature and the New Paradigm"), drawing on the works of Thomas S. Kuhn, have made theirs. Can we say that this "new paradigm" still has validity thirty years since its first formulations?

Among the ideas that were formulated at that time, some are of undeniable value even today. The most important of these is the proposal to move from a consideration of the singular literary text as the central focus of study to a wider consideration of the literary phenomenon. The literary scholar should consider the system of literary communication, which would include the text itself, the determining features and context of its production, reception, and postprocess, with the different codes that are enacted throughout this entire process. The supernational aspects of this literary system would be the object of concern for comparative literature. It would be necessary then, following Fokkema, to rely on tools of analysis that would complement traditional methodologies, especially those that take from psychological, sociological, and experimental approaches. It is our task to reconstruct different literary situations throughout history, and for this, knowledge of historical readers' reactions is necessary, for from them we can deduce the codes that determined the historical reception of texts as literary or non-literary. These codes should be compared with codes of different types. Ultimately, the aim is to compare literary systems with a view to understanding the effects that they continue to produce in readers, and to analyze the conditions of production and reception of literature from a perspective wider than a semiotic pragmatics of the theory of communication.

In any case, Kuhn's notion of "paradigm" might need to be adjusted and made more relevant in this domain, because, unlike the physical sciences, literary studies do very little *explaining* and a lot more *interpreting* (to use Dilthey's terms) and *evaluating*. The literary version of "paradigm" answers the question, "What is important?" rather than the question, "How can this be explained?", "importance" being more obviously a matter of consensus than is causality; a Kuhnian story about *Literaturwissenschaft* would end up emphasizing social determinants even more than when Kuhn wrote about scientific revolutions.

In the light of Fokkema's proposals ("Comparative Literature and the New Paradigm" 13), the ascendency of those theorists who, in the latter third of the twentieth century, have made a contribution to the new comparative paradigm, in fact a "cultural paradigm," is unmistakable. These include, after Viktor Shklovsky and

Yury Tynyanov, Jan Mukařovský, Felix Vodicka, Hans Robert Jauss, Yuri Lotman, Norbert Groeben, Siegfried J. Schmidt, and most especially, Dionýz Ďurišin and Itamar Even-Zohar. That is to say, as well as the Circle of Prague, which achieved such a rich harmony of formalism with historical and social considerations of literature, we find here representatives from German reception theory, the Cultural Semiotics of Tartu, pragmatic and empirical theories of literature and, finally, polysystems theory.

It is in this tradition that we should place the latest proposal for a new comparative literature, that of Steven Tötösy de Zepetnek, who from the 1990s has formulated approaches that could be placed under the general rubric of "The Systemic and Empirical Approach to Literature and Culture."

For Siegfried J. Schmidt, the literary system includes four fundamental spheres: the production of texts, the mediation which these undergo in order to be disseminated, reception, and, finally, their postprocessing or transformation in non-literary products. From this theoretical construction it is possible to make comparisons not just between literatures but between literary systems, which would form part of a universal system. This is the procedure of Itamar Even-Zohar in his theorization of the "polysystem," an approach that is also that of the notable Belgian scholar José Lambert.

These theories allow us to study the complex network of relations between interrelated and interdependent systems and work with heuristic constructions such as "canonic and non-canonic texts," "dominant and dominated models," "repertoire," "primary and secondary systems," "center and periphery," "intra- and interrelations," "production, tradition, and importation," and the "stability and instability" of a system. From this short enumeration we can infer the importance to systems theory of the study of interference or dependence between literary polysystems, and of no little significance in this regard is the provenance of Even-Zohar and Lambert from, respectively, Israel and Belgium—both countries characterized by a rich history of multilingual and multicultural overlapping. Both thinkers also pay attention, from the same theoretical presuppositions, to the relations between literary or artistic systems and other symbolic systems, which come to form an integrated macrosystem, and in this macrovision they are close to certain aspects of the thought of the Tartu school. It also worth pointing out the special attention these systemic theories give to the role of translation.

A "literary system" is defined as a totality of writers, works, and readers related through a series of common norms and models that do not coincide exactly with those of other systems. This definition allows us to see past rigid national profiles, as the frontiers of each system are mobile, depending on the greater or lesser stability of each system. In any case, no system can exist in isolation, and the connections between them are very variable, allowing for an inexhaustible field for comparative and systemic research.

In this regard, Even-Zohar ("Laws of Literary Interference" 58–60) posits as a working hypothesis the existence of laws of interference that regulate literary relations: literatures are never in a position of non-contact, and literary interference is almost always unilateral, and not necessarily accompanied by interferences of a different order. The source-literature is such because of prestige and power, and the target-literature looks to it for those elements that are lacking in its own repertoire. The contacts that are referred to here can be established between only one sector of both systems, and later extend (or not) to others. The imported elements need not play the same role in the receiving system as they did in the system of origin, and in fact the appropriation of elements generally implies their simplification, regularization, and schematization. For Even-Zohar, Hebrew literature is a perfect case study, as throughout history its relations of dependence and symbiosis have pointed to two distinct poles, with Yiddish literature functioning, until recently, as "the noncanonised system of Hebrew literature" ("Interference" 620).

Tötösy de Zepetnek's research could also be included among these new systemic approaches to comparative literature. A Hungarian who spent much of his career in Austria, Switzerland, and Canada, and currently based in the US, has not only formulated a systemic approach to literature, but has applied it to a field with which he is personally well acquainted because of his personal origins: Central European culture. There has been, however, significant change in Tötösy de Zepetnek's perspective in recent years, as he has become ever more inclined towards comparative cultural studies (Tötösy de Zepetnek and Sywenky).

Current relevance of the "new paradigm"

There is another dimension to the "new paradigm" of comparative literature that seems to us incontestable. It consists, basically, in the imperative of abandoning of any supposed genetic relation to justify comparative analysis, and attending to the empirical evidence that is available to us. If, between two distinct literary systems, or between a literary work and that of another artistic medium, whether it be plastic or musical, there appears a common element, without there being a relationship of dependency between one work to the other, then a fundamental theoretical element will appear; that is, an invariant of literature.

Jonathan Culler ("Comparative Literature") was one of the influential figures who argued for a privileged, if not exclusive, relationship between literary theory and comparative literature in 1979. Almost forty years later, in the wake of all the ideological and methodological storms that have rocked the discipline, obliging it to navigate between the Scylla of deconstruction and the Charybdis of cultural, postcolonial, and globalization studies, he continues to defend "the centrality of literature" and argues that, though we may read texts of various types, it is important to engage in a practice of "reading literarily" ("Comparative Literature, at Last" 241). Culler adds that research in comparative literature "can focus on theoretical questions about possible approaches to world literature, their dangers and virtues" (246), complementing the positive declarations of Haun Saussy—the editor of the volume *Comparative Literature in an Age of Globalization*, where Culler's contribution is included—in affirming that "as with theory, so with comparative literature: our triumphs seem destined to be triumphs without triumph" (247).

Comparative Literature in an Age of Globalization was published at the behest of the ACLA in 2006. Though comparative literature is by definition an international discipline, the majority of the aforementioned theoretical storms that fundamentally changed the humanities were played out in the American academia; the 2006 volume is the latest in a tradition of reports published by the ACLA that attempt to examine the relevance and standing of comparative literature, starting with the "Levin Report" in 1965, the "Greene Report" in 1975, and the volume coordinated by Bernheimer in 1993—*Comparative Literature in the Age of Multiculturalism*.

The Romanian scholar Adrian Marino (*Comparatisme* 141–46) also discusses this "*nouveau paradigme*." For Marino, to speak of literature necessarily implies a universal, as opposed to a supranational, dimension. Marino conflates the totality of all world literatures with "*la littérature pure et simple*" (144; pure and simple literature), and it is only through this "*approche globale de la littérature*" (global approach to literature)— later practiced by Pascale Casanova's "*république mondiale des lettres*"—that a solidly based poetics can be achieved, as all general criteria and typologies are inseparable from the universal. It follows from this that a literary theory constructed from elements that are at the same time widespread and creative of general categories, elements that are usually called invariants, is proved more valid on every occasion that these same invariants appear among literatures that have not been in regular or close contact, for example European and Asian literatures (Marino, *Comparatisme* 92).

invariant

Earl Miner (*Comparative Poetics*) follows this path from the formal perspective of poetics. According to this line of reasoning, when in Chinese literature we discover a type of lyric composition that is similar to the *alba* of medieval Romance languages, one can claim, with all legitimacy, that this type of composition is an invariant that transcends the contingency of the purely historic. Miner states unequivocally that there is an intimate link between genres and explicit poetics upon the *a priori* that genres are identical despite their different names across cultures: "The thesis of this essay is that an originative poetics develops when a critic or critics of insight defines the nature and conditions of literature in terms of the then most esteemed genre. By 'genre' is meant drama, lyric, and narrative. These 'foundation genres' may be termed by other names" (*Comparative Poetics* 7). But a simply nominal variation is a principle difficult to accept for a comparative approach to genres. Let us recall the argument by the Polish comparatist Stefania Skwarczynska: "it is not possible to deny that for a European it is difficult to agree with an Indian or Chinese regarding the nature of genres: one usually doubts whether they are talking about the same thing" (cited in Navarro, "*Un ejemplo de lucha*" 86). Furthermore, Miner's argument is in contradiction with his own second canon of comparability, for it states that two genres may have identical functions in their respective literary systems. In any case, it seems obvious that it is impossible to construct a solid theory of literary genres from a number of works taken exclusively from the history of European literature.

Comparative methodology

Comparative literature has often been accused of a certain methodological indefinition, and comparatists often seem reluctant to clarify these issues. But though it is obvious that comparative literature, because of the sheer vastness of the areas it covers, implies a certain utopian ambition, this is not to say that the discipline does not rely on methodologies that are capable of producing concrete results.

Manfred Schmeling paid special attention to the methodological difficulties of comparatism, and proposed various types of strategy to overcome these. Earl Miner, for his part, elaborated a *Comparative Poetics,* which he subtitled *An Intercultural Essay on Theories of Literature.* For Miner, it was a case of comparing the different "conceptions or theories or systems of literature" (*Comparative Poetics* 4), genres, and the invariants that are expressed discursively by creators and thinkers throughout history, both in the West and in the East. It is no coincidence that Miner would cite as major figures of inspiration Étiemble and Wellek, nor that he would dedicate his work, *in memoriam,* to James J.Y. Liu, the author of *Chinese Theories of Literature.* Perhaps Miner's major conclusion is that the generic trilogy of epic–lyric–drama is obligatory in all literary systems, as the only difference between the European Aristotelian tradition and the Eastern Sino-Japanese tradition is that in the former, lyric is initially formulated only implicitly, whereas in the latter, it is exactly the reverse, with the poetics of drama and narration deriving from a consideration of lyric.

Marino (*Comparatisme* 214), on the other hand, frames his new comparative literature in terms of a phenomenological approach, and is faithful to the Husserlian return to the "things themselves" (*zu den Sachen selbst*), as opposed to more superficial morphological descriptions of literary phenomena. The analysis of analogies and similarities would, from this perspective, resist the construction of supposed genetic relations in order to discover fundamental theoretical invariants.

With regard to parallels, which Marino understands as objective phenomena, he proposes that we distinguish between two major groups, which can themselves be further divided into two distinct possibilities (*Comparatisme* 224–32). On one hand, there are those that can be understood historically but without positing contacts or influence (what he terms "parallel polygenesis") and those that can be understood as the result of contact and influence, as Goethe and Carlyle understood the process of literary interchange. The first model of parallelism is completely removed from genetic relations, and seeks contrasting parallels between authors and works of distinct languages and historical moments, with the aim of revealing singularities and differences, or, moving in the opposite direction, proposing general parallels between literatures.

★

Sufficient time has passed since the Bernheimer Report of 1993 to allow us to respond with certainty as to whether the porosity and flexibility of comparative literature has allowed it to retain its status as an academic discipline in the face of the diversity and range of cultural studies. We argue that comparative literature has risen to the challenge, showing itself to have enough resources to grow out of its contradictions, integrate new perspectives, and progress along the path of interdisciplinarity.

Saussy's report confirms this diagnosis, and Saussy ("Exquisite Cadavers") goes so far as to declare the "triumph of comparative literature," which not only has recovered from its end-of-the-century crisis, but currently is invested with a new legitimation and authority, playing a role in literary studies not dissimilar to that of the first violin in an orchestra. Departments of Comparative Literature have even demonstrated a generous hospitality "to the miscellaneous, disfavored, outmoded, or too-good-to-be-true approaches" ("Exquisite Cadavers" 34). The basic cosmo-politanism of comparative literature has allowed it to surpass the limitations of cultural studies, and to correct its own Eurocentric biases. At the same time, it has helped in framing debates about the canon and opened itself to new models of canonicity. In its relationship to world literature, it seems as if we have almost returned to the moment of the encounter of Goethe and Ampère, where that discipline has become not so much a rival but "an object, even a project, of comparative literature" (11).

Saussy's verdict is neither fanciful nor self-interested. It is founded on strong foundations, not least of which are "the universality of human experience" (12), and the fact that "no human culture is without verbal art" (17). The terrain that comparative literature explores is as solid as that special use of language to create beauty that we call literature. For these reasons, Saussy argues for "the centrality of literariness to the discipline," a focus that should also be central to the three other branches of literary studies, and especially, without disdaining history and criticism, the theory of literature. As Saussy notes, "Everyone who made or applied Theory became a comparatist" (18).

To study literature is to read texts, to practice "close reading," so as to discover an aesthetic unity from linguistic organization. These texts form part of a system of actions at the heart of society, the most important of these actions being literary creation and reading, but the distinct forms of mediation of literary texts and the derivation of secondary texts from these are also of interest. This does not inevitably lead to the consideration of other discourses and codes, rather to the consideration of the role that new communication technologies play, not only in the diffusion of literature, but also in the transformation of creative practices and in their influence on the cultural make-up and "acts of reading" (Iser) of the new generations of "digital natives" (Prensky).

Perhaps more than ever, to gain an in-depth knowledge of the literary phenom-enon requires a comparative perspective, a perspective that can be achieved only with the outlook, attitude, and methodology of an academic discipline which has for two centuries gone under the name of comparative literature.

Notes

1 On the parallels to "literature" and "*belles-lettres*" in other civilizations, see for example Miner, *Comparative Poetics*.
2 A comparison of explicit poetics, that is, works that aim to explain how "literature" works, as carried out by Miner, shows that Western literary theory is the only one across the world based upon the genre of drama (as in Aristotle's *Poetics*) and, hence, the rele-vance of the concept of *mimesis*. Miner's conclusions, of course, are debatable. In any case, "imitation" is used here in a sense broader than the Aristotelian as including the imitation and representation of feelings.

3 The equation between *Weltliteratur* and European literature by Goethe is good proof of the limitations of his concept. Though the coinage of the term seems to be associated to the reading of a Chinese "novel," his discussion ends by placing Greek and Latin writers at the core of world literature.

4 However, and very much like in the case of Goethe, one cannot overlook that T.S. Eliot acknowledges a central position for the Latin poet Virgil.

5 Also, we must not forget Mme de Staël, who is implicitly a comparatist throughout *De l'Allemagne* (1810–13) though she does not use the word.

6 The *Congrès international des écrivains pour la défense de la culture*, which was held in 1935 and involved many of these writers, has been commemorated recently in Teroni and Klein's anthology.

7 Paul de Man's *Aesthetic Ideology* (1996) casts doubt on precisely this central role of literary and humanistic study, a fact saluted with much joy by adversaries of de Man.

8 But deconstruction has generated much more than just readings that produce "undecidability." Related to it are, for example, Giorgio Agamben's thinking about "bare life," the wave of trauma studies, the questioning of the nation in the name of a "democracy to come," variants of media studies, animal studies, eco-criticism, etc., and many other theoretical discussions that many people would think both timely and substantive.

9 Further paradoxes flow from the so-called "opening" of the canon. The canon comes to include new writers, but the list is not infinitely extensible, as David Damrosch ("World Literature") pointed out. Ironically, the post-multiculturalism canon is in many regards narrower than the older canon.

2

COMPARATIVE LITERATURE
AS INTERLITERARY THEORY

Interliterary theory has been formulated by the Slovak scholar Dionýz Ďurišin not only as a field distinct from comparative literature, but also as one that will eventually replace it. And yet, braving contradiction, we title this chapter "Comparative literature as interliterary theory." A justification for doing so is in order, which will be provided through a short introduction to this theory, a survey of its main contributions to rethinking comparative literature, and finally an interrogation of some of its tenets with a discussion of future developments.

What is interliterary theory?

Asking what is interliterary theory—or, to use its longer name, the theory of interliterary processes—is like asking what the theory of relativity is: what is one really asking about? Let us begin with the theory of relativity. Answers that take the form of a definition—say "The theory of relativity [either special or general] is … "—will be inadequate, even if provided by Albert Einstein himself: "The special theory of relativity is an adaptation of physical principles to Maxwell–Lorentz electrodynamics" (484). A more useful approach might be to rephrase the question: What does the special theory of relativity do? Originally, it was developed to explain why the speed of light is independent of whether either the source or the observer is considered to be moving, for, as shown by the 1887 Michelson and Morley experiment, the speed of light is the same in all directions.

A *theory*, therefore, is a solution for a problem. What problem does literary theory solve? In the specific case of literary studies, Jonathan Culler has argued that theory—plain *theory* or *critical* theory—"is not an account of the nature of literature or methods for its study (though such matters are part of theory […])" but "a body of thinking and writing whose limits are exceedingly hard to define" (*Literary Theory* 3). For Culler, theory is better defined by its practical effects (not just the solutions it offers for a problem, but the ways it has of reconceiving a problem). His description reads as follows:

> Theory is often a pugnacious critique of common-sense notions, and further, an attempt to show that what we take for granted as "common sense" is in fact an historical construction, a particular theory that has come to seem so natural to us that we don't even see it as a theory. As a critique of common sense and exploration of alternative conceptions, theory involves a questioning of the most basic premises or assumptions of literary study
>
> *(Literary Theory 4)*

Theory, therefore, has many overlapping and sometimes contradictory meanings. In general terms, a theory is a solution for a problem under the form of a speculative, non-obvious, complex explanation. This applies, for instance, to the use of *theory* in "theory of relativity," and there are similar cases in the field of literary studies. As stated by Culler, however, in literary studies (critical) theory may also refer to a "genre," an "unbounded group of writings [...] from the most technical problems of academic philosophy to the changing ways in which people have talked about and thought about the body" (3–4).

In the case of Ďurišin's interliterary theory, *theory* is used in the first sense. Before asking which literary problem Ďurišin aims to solve with his theory, we should stress an implicit—and, from our point of view, wrong—additional meaning of theory that surfaces when he states that "the study of the relationships of a national literature to other literatures, i.e. to the interliterary context, contributes not only to the formulation of the laws of the interliterary process, but also frequently and even primarily to the knowledge of the individual character and specific nature of the national literature" (*Theory* 24). Nothing wrong so far; but the levels get confused when Ďurišin goes on to propose that interliterary theory should replace comparative literature. "We have seen that at the present moment it is necessary to include purposefully within the sphere [of the interliterary theory] what have been so far considered the tasks of literary comparatistics" (149). It seems that Ďurišin's speculative, non-obvious, complex explanation for a problem has led him to replace comparative literature with interliterary theory, which means confusing a discipline (the former) with a theory (the latter). As a matter of fact, Ďurišin is criticizing the traditional "division of labor" in literary studies between the national (national philologies, national literary histories) and the inter- or supranational (comparative literature), for the interliterary process does not stop at either side of these borders. A discipline is much broader a field than a theory. Most disciplines include contradictory theories within themselves. An analogy may be helpful: gravitation is strongly associated with the discipline of physics. Similarly, interliterary theory is strongly associated with the discipline of comparative literature. But interliterary theory is not all of comparative literature, any more than the theory of gravitation equals physics. Indeed, there are schools of thought in physics for which gravitation is an insignificant phenomenon.

That being said, let us come back to our initial question: What does interliterary theory do, that is, what problem does it aim to explain?

Problem

For interliterary theory the problem is posed in the following terms: "there is a contradictory dialectical unity which results in a historical–literary practice through the tension between the history of national literature and the history of world literature" (Ďurišin, *Notions* 14).

Theory as explanation of the problem

The theory which attempts to provide an explanation for this problem is named *interliterary theory* or *theory of interliterary process* because the (inter)literary process makes reference to "the development, the progression and the ways of the literary rise, the growth of literature" (*Notions* 13).

Definition of interliterary theory

Interliterary theory is a speculative, non-obvious, complex explanation of the (inter)literary process between the poles of national literature and world literature through intermediate categories such as "specific interliterary communities, standard interliterary communities, and literary centrisms" (*Notions* 14).

In other (our own) words, the interliterary theory aims to explain how relationships are established between individual works and, as a result of these relationships, how literary groups are created—from smaller to larger—and hence how they determine some dominant directions of (world) literature.

In accordance with our understanding of the interliterary theory (*theory* in the sense of a speculative, non-obvious, complex explanation for a problem) as one theory among others that has contributed to new developments within comparative literature, the title of this chapter needs to be understood as one of the possible ways in which the discipline is inflected.

The interliterary theory as critique of common-sense notions

As was said above: interliterary theory is strongly associated with the discipline of comparative literature. Such a statement requires further qualification. The verbal form "is" needs to be replaced by "should be" in the case that the scholarly community considers (as we do) that this theory may provide insightful contributions to comparative literature. Furthermore, one should not overlook that, though some inflections of comparative literature have a global reach, others remain local. Interliterary theory is an example of the second, locally circulating, kind. It has

local

neither been discussed in any Western textbook nor had much influence in the West; its influence has remained limited to its location of inception (Slovakia, the Czech Republic), with some diffusion to the west (Austria), south (the former Yugoslavia), and east (Russia).

That a theory is a critique of previous common-sense notions is of particular importance in the case of the interliterary theory. In most textbooks on comparative literature one finds a dual history of the discipline, which is made of two consecutive schools, the French and the American. Paul Van Tieghem, with his 1931 textbook *La Littérature comparée*, is credited as the leading figure of the French school, whereas René Wellek, with his 1958 diagnosis of the crisis of comparative literature, and Henry H.H. Remak, who reacted with his 1961 definition of the discipline, are credited as the leading figures of the American school. However pedagogically convenient, such a vision of the history of comparative literature is highly restrictive and grossly misleading. On one hand, the concept of *school* gives the false impression of a cohesive group of scholars who share disciplinary tenets, theories, and methodologies. This is far from being true and, though Claudio Guillén has tried to mitigate the unifying implications of the term *school* by replacing it by *hour* (*The Challenge* 46, 60), the problem still holds. On the other hand, if one takes these national terms too seriously, one will have to wrestle with the fact that many French scholars such as René Étiemble were much more influential in the American academia than in the French; and that Wellek, though he established the Department of Comparative Literature at Yale University and schooled and inspired a generation of comparatists, was a Czech exile who had been trained at Charles University in Prague and participated in the Prague Linguistic Circle. (Indeed Wellek always refused to be considered the leader of the American school.) Most importantly of all, scholars from other parts of the world than France and the US have made substantial contributions to comparative literature; Ďurišin, from Slovakia, is one outstanding example.

In his seminal works—*Slovenská realistická poviedka a N. V. Gogol* (1966; N.V. Gogol and the Slovak Realistic Short Story—his doctoral dissertation) and *Problémy literárnej komparatistiky* (1967; Problems of Literary Comparatism)—Ďurišin reacts against what he identifies as the main tenet of French-style comparative literature, also criticized by Wellek in 1958, namely, the study of influences between literary works. Interestingly, and in contrast to Wellek, Ďurišin's main objection is neither to the "commercial aspect" of influence studies, nor to the methodological obscurity in the analysis of influence within one single literature (as practiced by national literary criticism), or between different literatures (as practiced by comparative literature). What he contests is the conception of influence itself. The classic conception of influence holds that a writer mechanically reproduces an element from a previous work in a passive and one-sided way. For Ďurišin, on the contrary, influence should be reimagined as *reception,* both individually (for a writer creatively rewrites elements from previous works) and systemically (for a writer's attraction to specific works from other literatures reveals something about the systemic status, which is not a value issue, of both the sending and the receiving systems). Ďurišin's arguments on the creative dimension of individual reception paved the way for Hans Robert Jauss's *Rezeptionsästhetik* (Reception studies) in the 1980s. Moreover, his arguments on the systemic conditions of reception were instrumental for Itamar Even-Zohar's polysystem theory, in circulation since the late 1970s.

Such a critique of influence studies as traditionally practiced by comparative literature was possible because Ďurišin built upon the lessons provided, diversely, by Alexander Veselovsky's *Istoricheskaia poetika* (Historical poetics) and the Russian formalists.[1] This might look like a problematic genealogy, for Veselovsky was bitterly criticized by many Russian formalists, Shklovsky in particular. However, one should not overlook the status of comparative literature during the era of late Stalinism, when the discipline—and therefore Veselovsky as its founder in Russia—was accused of being a "bourgeois cosmopolitan direction in literary studies" (cited in Dobrenko 172). It is also in this atmosphere that formalists, such as Boris Eikhenbaum, Viktor Zhirmunsky, Vladimir Propp, and Grigory Gukovsky, among others, were purged by Andrei Zhdanov in 1947–48. Eikhenbaum, for instance, was condemned for comparing Proudhon to Tolstoy and studying the work of Lermontov in the context of European Romanticism (172). A more nuanced approach to the legacy of Veselovsky for formalists is provided by Dragan Kujundžić, who stresses that "Veselovsky represented both an inspiration and the theoretical figure with whom Russian Formalists most vigorously polemicize" (Kujundžić 7).

Something similar may be said of Ďurišin's relationship to Veselovsky's theories. They inspired him to further develop a model of literary evolution by identifying their shortcomings. For Ďurišin, Veselovsky's discussion of how social factors condition the evolution of literature was of key importance, especially in relation to what Veselovsky called *psikhologichesky parallelizm* (psychological parallelism). By this Veselovsky meant that certain schematic verbal formulae are commonly used to represent reality, and hence there exists a similarity of literary motifs worldwide.[2] A comparable explanation was provided in Western Europe in 1929 by André Jolles on the basis of what he called *einfache Formen* (simple forms), including nine varieties (fairy tale, saint's legend, legend, myth, riddle, proverb, case, report, and joke) which he treated as foundational for world literature. But when these minimal units combine into "high" literary works in the sense of Jacob Grimm's *Kunstpoesie* (art literature), then the similarities, argues Veselovsky, cannot be explained by spontaneous generation, but are due to cultural contacts.

> If we may make an analogy: the making of containers is universal among human cultures. But a specific technology involving many factors, for example the salt glaze for pottery, is more likely to have been an invention pioneered in one place and diffused outward from that starting point.

For Ďurišin, however, this view is too restricted in at least two senses. Firstly, it underestimates the role of the artist, for it favors a determinism of the form over the selection and transformation of materials by the artist. Secondly, it cannot explain actual similarities of literary items between cultures that have not been in contact. This latter factor led Ďurišin to develop a complex set of "typological affinities" (literary similarities that cannot be explained by contact) next to the branch of "genetic contacts," which was the main area of comparative folklore and mythology. For his set of typological affinities, Ďurišin mainly drew on Veselovsky's disciple, Viktor M. Zhirmunsky, who chose, ironically, to focus on this kind of similarity after the 1947–48 purge as a way to demonstrate that, when Russian literature is shown to share some peculiarities with other literatures, they are not due to the influence of the latter on the former, but to similarities of social and cultural institutions.

As for the Russian formalists, Ďurišin is interested in how they reacted against some of Veselovsky's tenets and, particularly, in how they challenged the traditional picture of literary evolution as a harmonious process. He finds essential the section of Yuri Tynianov's 1929 *Archaisty i novatory* (*Avant-garde* and Tradition) devoted to the influence of Dostoyevsky (1821–81) on Gogol (1809–52) (remember that Ďurišin wrote his dissertation on the influence of Gogol on the Slovak realistic short story), because Tynianov saw literary continuity as "a struggle, a tension, often between contradictory developmental trends" (Ďurišin, *Sources* 53).

In short, Ďurišin's critique and development of Veselovsky–Zhirmunsky's comparative research and the Formalists' view on literary evolution provided the rationale for his theory of the interliterary process, which aimed to trace literary growth from national literature to world literature. In contrast to the then pervasive influence of the so-called French school of comparative literature, which focused on binary contacts by privileging the source-work, Ďurišin put the emphasis on the individual creative process implied in reception and, equally important, on the specific causes whereby one literary system is attracted to another literary system when importing materials and, conversely, it moves away from other exporting systems (in this line, see Even-Zohar, "The Role of Russian" and Gamsa). This is why Jauss (1125) acknowledges the simultaneity of Ďurišin's research on reception with his own.

Two branches of literary growth

Starting in the late 1960s, Ďurišin's aim was to formulate a general theory of world literature, which in the first instance involved, as seen above, a systematic critique of the so-called French school of comparative literature. In contrast to the dual formula of writers/works "X and Y" or "X in Y" applied by many (French) comparatists, between whom the researcher may certify a *rapport de fait* (factual relationship), Ďurišin argues that literary relations never develop between just two elements, but at several levels simultaneously, such as, for instance, between the source-element, the target-element, and their respective contexts, or between the source- and target-systems and their contexts.[3] The particular reception of Byron in Slovakia during the second third of the nineteenth century, for instance, is the result of the interliterary relations both between English and Slovak literatures and between

Slovak and Russian literatures (including Russian literary figures' particular reception of Byron). These multi-level relationships provide us with information about the systemic situation of Slovak literature at that particular moment (Ďurišin, *Theory of Literary Comparatistics* 114). Furthermore, *rapports de fait* may explain literary similarities between two works of distinct literatures when the writer of the second work has "read" (a word that needs further qualification) a previous work by another writer and incorporated it somehow into his own. But what about similarities between works when the writer of the second work did not know of the other?

"The subject of literary comparatistics," says Ďurišin (seemingly putting aside his proposal about the interliterary theory replacing comparative literature), "consists of the manifold relationships among literary phenomena, against the background of both the national-literary and the interliterary context, while the direction of study arises from the equivalence of these phenomena" (*Theory of Literary Comparatistics* 100). By drawing on seminal work by Zhirmunsky and Irina G. Neupokoeva, and taking into consideration the critique of some inconsistencies by the leading Czech comparatist Frank Wollman, Ďurišin arrives at a binary model of literary relationships, which consists of either genetic contact or typological affinities—the two paths of the interliterary process. Ďurišin's specific contribution includes on one hand, a detailed classification of the similarities, and on the other hand, an identification of sub-kinds according to the media or contexts that explain such similarities. His model is represented in Table 2.1.

Genetic relationships name similarities that are due to a factual contact between two works of distinct literatures. This contact may be either external or internal. External genetic relationships include references to literary works, literary histories, and critical studies, that is to say, what comparative literature traditionally has called *reception* or *Wirkung* (effect, survival), though Ďurišin stresses that for him "reception signifies something different" (*Theory of Literary Comparatistics* 108n2), meaning his understanding of reception as active and creative. For Ďurišin, an example of this kind of contact is provided by the second chapter of Zlatko Klátic's 1965 *Štúrovci a Juhoslovania* (The Followers of Štúr and the Yugoslavs), in which the relationship of the leader of the Slovak national revival, Ľudovít Štúr, with Yugoslavian epic poetry is documented, as well as the reasons why he was attracted to the work of the Serbian poet Branko Radičević. In contrast to the proclivity traditional comparative literature has shown for this kind of research, for Ďurišin it only represents an "empirical and early approach to the analysis of the fruits of interliterary development"

TABLE 2.1 Classification of interliterary relationships

Paths of the interliterary process		
Genetic (contactual) relationships		Typological affinities
External contacts		Socio-typological affinities
Internal contacts	Direct internal contacts	Literary-typological affinities
	Mediated internal contacts	
		Psychological-typological affinities

(*Theory of Literary Comparatistics* 108). Interestingly, Ďurišin also includes "images" (in the sense of national stereotypes) as a kind of external contacts, for they may condition why a particular writer is interested in a certain foreign literature.

As for internal contacts, they name the inclusion of an element (topic, character, style, form, situation, etc.) from a work in another, either "native" or "foreign."[4] Internal contacts are identified "by means of the confrontation of literary phenomena, that is by the analysis and comparison of such literary-historical units" (*Theory of Literary Comparatistics* 118). An example of internal contact is the influence of 1848 *La Dame aux camélias* by Alexandre Dumas, fils, on the 1868–69 *Idiot* by Fyodor Dostoyevsky, as verified by M.S. Altman in his 1963 study "*Dostoevsky i roman A. Duma Dama s kameliani*" (Dostoyevsky and A. Dumas's Novel *The Lady of the Camellias*). Internal contacts may be either direct or mediated. Direct internal contacts take place when the writer reads the work in its original language, whereas mediated internal contacts take place through translation, interartistic adaptation, or any other variety of what Lubomír Doležel would later call "transduction" (see Chapter 6), meaning the text's transmission between media, which always implies a certain degree of transformation.[5] An example of mediated internal contact is the influence of the 1929 novel *Un de Baumugnes* (*Lovers Are Never Losers*), by the French writer Jean Giono, on Slovak novelists such as Margita Figuli and František Švantner, for, as demonstrated by J. Števček, such an influence took place through Dobroslav Chrobák's novel *Kamarát Jašek* (Friend Jašek).

That Ďurišin meant something very different from the traditional understanding of *influence* and *reception* is proved by his classification of the ways in which genetic relationships—either external or internal—may be expressed, as shown in Table 2.2.[6]

From the point of view of reception as an active and creative process whereby the giving element changes the receiving structure and *vice versa*, Ďurišin distinguishes two forms of interliterary reception: either "integrating," when identification of the target-work with the source-element prevails; or "differentiating," when the aim is to stress distinction between the target-work and the source-element. There are six kinds of integrational reception. "Allusion" is a simple evocation of the source-work usually "associated with well-known authoritative figures of world literature" (*Theory of Literary Comparatistics* 171), ranging from direct quotation and paratextual mottoes to paraphrase. "Borrowing" is the inclusion of a topic, image, artistic

TABLE 2.2 Forms of interliterary reception

Genetic relationships		Forms of interliterary reception	
		Integrating forms	Differentiating forms
External contacts	Internal contacts	Allusion	Literary controversy
		Borrowing	Parody
		Imitation	Travesty
		Filiation	
		Plagiarism	
		Adaptation Translation	

device, etc. "Imitation" has a deeper structural role, for the aim is to introduce affinities with the source-work or genre so as to promote the evolution of the literary system in a specific direction. For Ďurišin, the innumerable imitations of Gottfried August Bürger's *Lenore* across Europe are a case in point. "Filiation" indicates borrowing or imitation in which ethnic or other kinds of kinship also play a role, such as happens, Ďurišin says, among Ukrainian, Slovak, and Czech literatures; this points to the constitution of an interliterary community (see below). "Plagiarism" implies that the interest lies almost exclusively in the received phenomenon, which acquires a dominant role in the process of reception. And "adaptation" covers interlingual and intermedial translation.[7] The former, or translation proper, represents for Ďurišin "a highly characteristic and significant form of interliterary reception" (*Theory of Literary Comparatistics* 178), one to which he devoted his attention, though in a restricted way, for the main center for translation studies was located at the University of Nitra under the leadership of Anton Popovič (see Chapter 6).

As for differentiating reception, Ďurišin distinguishes three kinds—literary controversy, parody, and travesty, which he does not define. As his classificatory model is mereological, one has to understand these three categories as strategies of differentiation, from a lower to a higher degree, in relation to the source-work.

The second, main branch of the interliterary process is constituted by typological affinities, which represent a stage closer to world literature, for they embody the general laws of literature as they cannot be explained by contact. According to their degree of intensity and conditionality, Ďurišin distinguishes three categories— socio-typological affinities, literary-typological affinities, and psychological-typological affinities. Socio-typological affinities name similarities that are the result of similar social situations. An example is the growth of "critical realism" as a literary style in twentieth-century European literatures as a result of the rapid growth of capitalism and its imperialist forms (*Theory of Literary Comparatistics* 200). Literary-typological affinities are literary similarities that are not attributable to any kind of external influence. For Ďurišin, such a kind of affinity is best represented by the analysis of genres. And psychological-typological affinities include literary similarities that are due to similar authorial personalities. The order in which Ďurišin presents these three kinds of affinities may come as a surprise, for, if the degree of proximity to literary laws proper is the underlying logic of world literature, the reverse order, from psychological affinities to literary ones, is more evident.

An intercultural interlude

When, in 1958, on the occasion of the Second Conference of the International Comparative Literature Association, Wellek diagnosed that comparative literature was in crisis, three years later—or so the usual story goes—the patient recovered thanks to Henry H.H. Remak's new definition of the discipline, which reads: comparative literature is "the comparison of one literature with another or others, and the comparison of literature with other spheres of human expression" (3).[8] It was a valid solution, at least in the US, for Remak states that his definition is "probably acceptable to most students of comparative literature in this country," meaning the "American school," whereas it "would be subject to considerable argument among an important segment of comparatists which we shall, for brevity's sake, call the 'French school'" (3).

If the 1961 text by Remak is contrasted to the 1958 text by Wellek, one would realize that the former provides a very odd medicine, for Remak's definition does not deal with the central issue stressed by Wellek at all, that is, that comparative literature "has not been able to establish a distinct subject-matter and a specific methodology" ("The Crisis" 162).[9] Does Remak's definition provide any solution for these two issues? Not at all.

Ďurišin, however, did face the first problem presented by Wellek, for inter-literary theory aims to explain, as we have seen above, a process that is continuous and, therefore, does not stop at either side of the national/international. Interest-ingly, Ďurišin's proposals first became "visible" for Western scholars in the early 1980s, when Douwe W. Fokkema ("Comparative Literature and the New Para-digm" 10n20), in a new response to Wellek's crisis, saw the emergence of a "new paradigm" for comparative literature (see Chapter 1), which materialized as a new conception of the object of study, the introduction of new methods, a new vision of the scientific relevance of the study of literature, and a new vision of the social justification of the study of literature, for which Ďurišin's interliterary theory was instrumental. The fact that Ďurišin's works were mentioned only in passing in a footnote by Fokkema may explain, among other reasons, why his contributions still today occupy a minor place in mainstream comparative literature.

Let us come back to Remak's definition and see how his solution consisted in simply enlarging the scope of comparative literature, from the traditional inter-literary axis (the comparison of one literature with another or others) to the "new" interartistic (the comparison of literature and other arts) and interdiscursive (the comparison of literature and other areas of knowledge, such as history, philosophy, social sciences, sciences, religion, etc.) axes. Ironically, and though Remak stated that his definition was "probably acceptable to most students of comparative lit-erature" in the US, new attempts at solving the crisis of comparative literature consisted of further expanding the interliterary axis in American academia through what one may call three consecutive waves—postcolonial studies (see Chapter 3), East/West studies, and world literature (see Chapter 4). These three waves share the aim of overcoming Eurocentrism, a problem that Wellek did not mention, in contrast to the concerns of one of the leading scholars of what Remak calls, for brevity's sake, the "French school," namely, René Étiemble.

Here we want to stress the role played by East/West studies, for they have a direct—though an unnoticed—link to Ďurišin's classification of typological affi-nities. As seen above, Ďurišin conceives literary-typological affinities as including "specific literary phenomena," which "result from the laws of the inner growth for example of literary styles and trends and in the final analysis of the most detailed constituents of the work of art" (*Theory of Literary Comparatistics* 203). Drawing both on this very same tenet and Étiemble's 1960s admonitions to overcome

Eurocentrism by proclaiming that "literature from now on can only mean the totality of all literatures, whether alive or dead, of which there remain written, or even only oral, traces, without further discrimination as to language, politics or religion" ("Do We Have to Revise" 96), East/West Studies emerged as a horizontal axis for the research of affinities shared by Eastern (mainly Chinese and Japanese) and Western literatures. In a way, this meant to return to the binary model of the *rapports de fait*, but applied now to works without historical or genetic relationships.[10] Many scholars who have worked on East/West Studies—such as Étiemble—or are highly interested in the possibilities of the field, found in Zhirmunsky (one of the main influences on Ďurišin) a source of inspiration (see, for instance, Chadwick and Zhirmunsky). Claudio Guillén, for instance, states that "those who have cultivated East/West studies for years, are probably the most daring scholars in the field [of comparative literature], above all from a theoretical point of view" (*The Challenge* 16), and on the pattern of their work formulates his "model C" of supranationality, which makes possible "the dialogue between unity and diversity that stimulates comparatism to focus on the open confrontation of criticism/history with theory" (*The Challenge* 70–71).[11]

The publication in 1990 of *Comparative Poetics. An Intercultural Essay on Theories of Literature*, by Earl Miner, represents a milestone in the history of East/West studies, for the binary comparison of single Eastern and Western works is there abandoned in favor of the comparison of foundational metaliterary reflections from the West and the East, such as Aristotle's *Poetics*, Horace's *Ars poetica*, the "Great Preface" to *Shijing* (Classic of Poetry), and Zeami's *Fūshikaden* (Teachings on Style and the Flower).[12] Drawing on the research by James J.Y. Liu, Miner chooses as objects of comparison what he calls "explicit originative poetics." A poetics is explicit when it is a treatise-like text that addresses the principles of "literature"— as the ones mentioned above. And it is originative when "a critic or critics of insight defines the nature and conditions of literature in terms of the then most esteemed genre" (*Comparative Poetics* 7; see here the connection to Ďurišin's view on literary-typological affinities). By comparing Greek, Latin, Chinese, and Japanese poetics in his 1990 book, Miner concludes that "[w]ith one exception lyric is the foundation genre of the world's explicit poetic systems and is the implicit basis of others" (*Comparative Poetics* 127). The *one* exception is the Western literary system, for its foundational genre is drama. Miner extended this conclusion in 1991 to India, whose foundational genre is lyric as well.

With a single move—the comparison of poetics, and not of literary works— Miner reached large-scale conclusions on how literary systems work worldwide, provided comparative literature with a new comparative lexicon, and faced a key issue for the discipline—cultural relativism. As for the new comparative lexicon, Miner was directly reacting to one of the problems presented by Wellek in 1958, namely, comparison as method. "Perhaps the least studied issue in comparative literature is," says Miner, "what is meant by 'comparative' and, more precisely, what are the principles or canons of comparability" ("Some Theoretical" 135). Miner distinguishes three canons of comparability: alienation, homology, and misreading. By "alienation," Miner understands "a deliberate introduction of something kindred but unconnected historically with the issue or matter at hand" ("Some Theoretical" 139). An example is alienating Western Renaissance sonnet sequences by examining the integration of Japanese royal collections. "Homology" makes reference to the fact that "in different literatures and societies, differing elements may serve the same function and therefore be compared" (137), as happens with the imagery of Chinese drama and the plots of Greek tragedy when it comes to establishing dramatic character. And "misreading" means "interpreting a complex whole by an important subordinate, rather than the dominant, feature" (140). An example is misreading lyrics as narratives, or narratives as lyrics. The 1987 article "Some Theoretical Methodological Topics for Comparative Literature" was expanded in a 1989 French translation. In this version, "alienation" is named *l'épreuve de l'étranger* (the test of the foreign), whereas "misreading" is replaced by *affinités formales* (formal affinities), which consists of taking as object of study a literary phenomenon that is formally identical in more than one culture, such as, for instance, the anthology. This change is relevant, for Miner states that "this third method is the one that I have found most helpful" ("Études comparées" 175).

In short, like Zhirmunsky before him and Guillén after him, Miner finds in "formal affinities" ("literary-typological affinities" in Ďurišin's parlance) the key to literary universals and, hence, a step on the way to what Étiemble calls a *vraiment générale* (really general) literary theory. This is related to the issue of cultural relativism, which, in Fokkema's words, "consists of an attitude of tolerance towards other patterns of culture" ("Cultural Relativism" 240). Cultural relativism has several degrees, and in its most radical one, comparison (of literary theories) is no longer possible, for no theory is either true or false. It is therefore paradoxical that in the history of comparative literature, the debate on the relevance of comparison has focused mainly on the text (Which textual elements guarantee comparability?) rather than on the context (Which production and reception issues guarantee comparability?). In the context of the announcement of the emergence of a new paradigm for comparative literature, Fokkema addresses the issue of which communicative situations guarantee comparability by taking into consideration the following caveat: "Although we wish to respect the ideal of cultural relativism, in practice we are bound to impose our own epistemological considerations upon our object of research. [...] Nevertheless, [...] by focusing on the communication-situation rather than on single texts we are in a better position to respect both the norms of cultural relativism and those of our own epistemology" ("Cultural Relativism" 245).

This is the phenomenon that Mary Garrett has called "methodological paradox," meaning that when one studies an*other* culture, such a study starts within a *location*, most frequently with principles and concepts alien to that culture but familiar for the researcher. There always exists then the danger of imposing external principles and concepts to the culture that is being analyzed. This is why the concept of *literature* has been placed in inverted commas above: a poetics is explicit when it is a treatise-like text that addresses the principles of "literature." In the context of Miner's intercultural poetics, the projection of the modern Western concept of literature and foundational genres on both premodern Western cultures and non-Western cultures has remained undiscussed. Interestingly, such a projection is not exclusive to Western scholars. "In opposition to the 'French' school of influence studies and the 'American' school of parallel studies (to be extremely simplistic)," says James St. André, "the 'Chinese' school proposed its own methodology: the application of Western theory to Chinese texts" (294). But this does not mean, as is the case also with intercultural poetics, a Eurocentric exercise *per se*, for "[t]his methodology, at its best, proved both a new way of reading Chinese texts and a way of examining the claim to universality by Western theory" (294).

Towards world literature

As we have seen, the ultimate goal of the interliterary theory is to provide an explanation of world literature, as stated since the earliest works by Ďurišin in the 1960s. This is a key difference from how comparative literature was practiced up to that moment in the US and Western Europe. One should not overlook this fact when approaching the recent re-emergence of world literature studies in the US (see Chapter 4). "World literature," says Ďurišin, "is the ultimate category of literary research. […] It represents the ultimate category and it is located at the top of our general tenets about the interliterary process" (*Notions* 25). In a way, Ďurišin was coming back to the disciplinary origins of comparative literature, neither in France, nor later in the US, but during the last third of the nineteenth century with an Irish scholar working in New Zealand—a double peripheral condition in the Anglophone world. While chair of Classics and English Literature at University College, Auckland, Hutcheson Macaulay Posnett published in 1886 within the famous "International Scientific Series" of the London publishing house Kegan Paul, Trench & Co. (after some mergers, the current Routledge) a volume titled *Comparative Literature*, in which he conceives of comparison as a method for distinguishing whether "the circle of common speech and thought" is "as narrow as a tribal league," has "many such circles combined into a national group" (78) or, in its maximal version, is "world-literature," whose leading mark "is the severance of literature from defined social groups" (236).

For Ďurišin, the interliterary process starts with national literatures and proceeds from them to world literature through a series of intermediate stages, as shown in Table 2.3.

As Table 2.3 makes visible, the use of the term *interliterary* results in inconsistency, for it can name the general process from national literature to world literature, the intermediate stage between national literatures and world literature, and the process from the intermediate stage to world literature. Moreover, some categories include typological subcategories (this is the case of national literature and interliterary communities), where others include examples (interliterary centrisms) or distinct definitions (world literature). But these are not the only problems.

One of the most controversial aspects of Ďurišin's theory is his understanding of national literatures as the minimal units of the interliterary process. Part of the

TABLE 2.3 The stages of the interliterary process

National literatures	Oral literature of tribal society	
	City-state literature	
	Medieval ethnic literature	
	National literature	
	Modern ethnic literature	
Interliterary stage	Interliterary communities	Specific interliterary community
		Standard interliterary community
	Interliterary centrisms	Central-European centrism
		Northern European centrism
		Southern European centrism
World literature	Additive approach	
	Selective approach	
	Historical-literary approach	

problem lies in applying the concept of "national literature" to five different categories. As the first three categories—oral literature of tribal societies, city-state literature, and medieval ethnic literature—are conceived of as premodern kinds of national literature, and the last category—modern ethnic literature—makes reference to the literature of a community that lives within another community (for instance, Slovak literature in Hungary), the teleological feature of the classification is conspicuous, with the fourth category—national literature—serving as epiphenomemon: "The process of national literature formation has not yet finished, and not only within Europe" (Ďurišin, *Notions* 18). This national teleology is even more prominent when Ďurišin considers national literature to be the main systemic unity: "If the systemic unity of the constituents, manifested by relationships and affinities, represents the national-literary, then what sustains the interliterary will essentially consist of the same particular complex of relationships, expressed, however, by different systemic classification" (*Theory of Literary Comparatistics* 94).

Another controversial aspect of considering national literatures as the minimal units of the interliterary process is linked to their homogenization. If, as Ďurišin argues, the national literary process imprints a sort of unity on the works produced within it, this means that those literary features which have not been assimilated by the national canon cannot proceed to the next stage—the interliterary one—and therefore cannot take part in world literature. In short, world literature according to this theory would be only the outcome of a cumulative and irreversible process, despite Ďurišin's stress on change (the vision of literary continuity as struggle, tension, as seen above).

The nation-state

The nation-state is a very specific kind of polity that is enshrined in European history (the Peace of Westphalia in 1648 and the 1814–15 Congress of Vienna are milestones of this process) and its expansion (today there is no land in the world that is not a nation-state's, not even Antarctica) is inseparable from European imperialism and the consecutive waves of decolonization, from the American Revolution and the decolonization of Spanish America to decolonization after 1945. Paradoxically, decolonization from former European empires was achieved through the agency of the European-style polity *par excellence* (the nation-state) and a conspicuous role in giving those states a new identity was played by its predominant tool for imagining national communities (see Anderson)—national literatures. The word *literature*, meaning *national literature*, is a lexical-ideological loan that expanded through the world in parallel to the nation-state. For instance, the Arabic term *adab* was resemanticized with the Western meaning of literature during the nineteenth century *Nahda* (Cultural Renaissance); Japanese *bungaku* was first used to translate Chinese *wenxue* (itself an ancient phrase meaning roughly "the examination of documents") in 1870, in the context of Westernization promoted by the Meiji Restoration.

National literature: from unit to code

Like grammars for languages, national literatures are systemic self-descriptions, self-organizations that discriminate what is systemic ("native") from what is extra-systemic ("foreign"). They assemble repertoires and works according to a specific plan so that there may exist different plans that compete as to how a set of works should qualify as *national*. In the same way as one does not confuse a grammar with a specific language, one should not confuse a *national literature* with "*X*," nor consider national literatures as minimal units of world literature.[13]

Though dominant worldwide, national literatures are not the only variety of self-description, either temporally (the idea of national literature emerged during the eighteenth and nineteenth centuries) or geographically.

The first intermediate level of the interliterary process is represented by "interliterary communities." As a result of the relevance Ďurišin grants to national literature, he distinguishes two classes of community depending upon their degree of proximity to the national units. A "specific interliterary community" refers to the coexistence of several literary systems whose level of integration is close to that of national literatures.[14] For Ďurišin, the literatures of the former Yugoslavia, the former Soviet Union, and Spain are clear examples of such specific communities in which the proclivity for the "historical-literary unity of national literature" is due to political-administrative factors (*Notions* 22–23). (One wonders to what degree this is still the case. Evident counterexamples exist, where a political frontier does not guarantee cultural integration. Do Arabic-language and Hebrew-language writers in Israel consider themselves part of the same "interliterary community"?) A "standard interliterary community" refers to the coexistence of national literatures whose interaction is the result of several factors, such as ethnicity (Slavic interliterary community), geography (Scandinavian interliterary community), ideology (socialist interliterary community), or religion (Islamic interliterary community), but the outcome of which is not a literary unity as homogeneous as that of a national literature. For interliterary communities, Ďurišin planned a large-scale research study, the results of which are collected in the first five volumes of *Osobitné medziliterárne spoločenstvá* (Specific Interliterary Communities). Published between 1987 and 1993, these volumes represent Ďurišin's alternative to the literary histories sponsored by the Gorki Institute and the AILC/ICLA Coordinating Committee (see Chapter 7), both of which, according to the Slovak scholar, lack what he considers to be a key requirement: "a classification of the initial principles for a systematics of the interliterary process" (*Theory of Interliterary Process* 140). And yet, as happens with the use of "interliterary," neither is the use of "specific" in "specific interliterary community" systematic, for the volumes include chapters that are devoted to literary communities previously characterized as standard.

Literatures in Spain: a specific interliterary community?

Ďurišin has claimed several times that literatures in Spain are a prime example of specific interliterary community. As mentioned above, the main criterion for distinguishing between specific and standard communities is political-administrative, which imposes a higher degree of cohesion. One may wonder in which specific period the network of literatures in Spain started to be so intense as to constitute a specific community. Ďurišin says nothing in this regard, which results in a clear reification of literatures in Spain as contributing to a single national literature achronically. Furthermore, the prominence of the national factor leads Ďurišin to exclude any reference to Portuguese literature, and yet several literatures in Spain (Catalan, Galician, and Spanish) have had a high degree of interaction with Portuguese literature at several moments in history, to the point that there are many bilingual writers (the king Alfonso X the Learned, Jorge de Montemayor/Jorge de Montemor, Gil Vicente, to name but a few) with whom both national literary histories (Spanish and Portuguese) feel uneasy.

In the series devoted to specific communities, there is a single chapter on literatures in Spain. Vsevolod Jevgenijevič Bagno states that there is a *mnohonárodnej literatúry Španielska* (Spanish multinational literature) as constituted by literatures in Spanish, Catalan, Galician, and Basque. It is a Spanish multinational literature with clear-cut borders—those of the nation-state—in relation to which Portuguese literature is a kind of satellite whose link derives from a telluric bond to Galician literature.

From this point of view, the interliterary theory reiterates old ideologemes of Spanish literary history, namely, particularism and exceptionality. "The common literary tradition is a specific question in the Spanish complex. As a matter of fact, it has not existed in the form known in the communities of Eastern and Southern Slavonic literatures" (Bagno 182). For a comparative literary history that takes as one of its theoretical points of departure the interliterary theory and, at the same time, problematizes the constitution of literatures in Spain as specific community, see *A Comparative History of Literatures in the Iberian Peninsula* (Cabo Aseguinolaza, Abuín González and Domínguez).

The second intermediate level is represented by "literary centrisms," which Ďurišin defines either as regional bodies larger than communities, or as communities that play a large-scale integrative role, as may be observed in the "active centrisms within literary life in Africa, Latin America and Asia, for instance" (*Notions* 24). The integration of individual European communities within a higher body (European literature) is a representative example of what Ďurišin would call "European centrism." For his ideas on centrisms, Ďurišin draws on René Étiemble's (*Ouverture(s)*) and Desiderio Navarro's discussions of Eurocentrism, which the Slovak scholar qualifies in the sense that he sees centrism as a consequence of the world literary process itself. Therefore the integration role played by centrisms may be correlated with literary communities that work, in a Wallerstein-like way, as real world-literatures. For the research on centrism, Ďurišin put together new research teams according to the required fields of expertise (Pospíšil and Zelenka for Central-European centrism; Ďurišin and Gnisci for Mediterranean centrism). However, due to Ďurišin's unexpected death in 1997, it is not possible to predict what new directions might have emerged from the study of both centrisms and world literature in this perspective.

Whereas Immanuel Wallerstein's research in economics has played a key role in Franco Moretti's neoformalist approach to genre diffusionism, it has not played an equivalent role in the conceptualization of world literature. Wallerstein—a disciple of Fernand Braudel (see Chapter 7)—is a social scientist who is best known by his "modern world-system theory." His concept of *world-system* draws on Braudel's *économie-monde*. A world-system is larger than nations, but does not have to be global; several world-systems may coexist. Likewise, one may say several world-literatures (in global languages, such as English, Spanish, French, Portuguese, Chinese, Hindustani, etc.) coexist such that they depend more on internal resources (works originally written in the global language) than on translated works.[15] While *world literature* refers to literature in the entire world, *world-literature* is a fragment, the largest fragment within world literature. As such, it has not been taken into consideration by Ďurišin in his interliterary theory.

Still, a clue to such potential new directions may be found in two books. The sixth volume of *Osobitné medziliterárne spoločenstvá*, authored only by Ďurišin, provides us with a terminological and methodological synthesis of the empirical work carried out on interliterary communities in a range of different locations, from Central and Eastern Europe to Africa, Asia, and Latin America. The section on the main forms of interliterariness deserves special mention, for it comprises what we have seen above as forms of interliterary reception, not between single works any longer, but between literary systems in an integrating or differentiating way. We sketch some key examples of phenomena identified by Ďurišin within the materials from the large-scale research on interliterary communities.

Plurifunctionality (*Polyfonctionnalité*)

Though it is a key feature of specific interliterary communities, it applies to the interliterary process in general. It consists of a writer who, within a literary system, plays all the roles of several writers within other systems. This is the case, for instance, with Ján Kalinčiak (1822–71), who for Slovak Romantic literature is the equivalent of Alexander Bestuzhev (1797–1837), Mikhail Zagoskin (1789–1852), Ivan Lazhechnikov (1792–1869), Alexander Pushkin (1799–1837), and Nikolai Gogol (1809–52), all together, for Russian Romantic literature.

Complementariness of oral tradition (*Complémentarité de la tradition orale*)

During certain periods, the oral tradition from a specific nation becomes the shared heritage of a whole interliterary community. This happened with Russian *Byliny* (ballads) and Ukrainian *Dumy* (epic poems) in the Slavic interliterary community.

Delayed incorporation (*Incorporation subséquente*)

It represents a surprising return to previous stages of literary development with the aim of incorporating some of its items within the current literary situation. When *Slovo o polku Igoreve* (The Tale of Igor's Campaign; end of the twelfth century) was discovered in 1795, it created a stir in Russian literary criticism and introduced a new aesthetic trend both in Russian and world literature.

The second book mentioned above is the collective volume *Koncepcie svetovej literatúry v epoche globalizácie* (Concepts of World Literature in the Age of Globalization; Koška and Koprda), which was published posthumously, but planned by Ďurišin himself as a test of his theory on world literature in relation to globalization. It provides good indications of how the theory of interliterary process was being updated by Ďurišin in accordance with new phenomena.

The last stage of the interliterary process is represented by world literature, which for Ďurišin has to determine all our conceptions and terms of literary studies. It is a changing phenomenon, for it changes from one period to another, from one literature to another, and from one reader to another. World literature is defined as the structured system of literary phenomena that are either genetically or typologically related (*Čo je svetová* 200). This definition epitomizes the historical-literary approach to world literature, which aims to overcome two traditional approaches (see Table 2.3): the additive approach, which defines world literature as the mere sum of all literatures in the world; and the selective approach, which defines world literature as a set of canonical masterpieces. *Čo je svetová literatúra* (What Is World Literature?), published in 1992, summarizes three decades of research on the interliterary process from the point of view of world literature (see Chapter 4).

Interliterary theory beyond Ďurišin

We have seen above how misleading is a history of comparative literature polarized in two schools—French and American. Our aim is not to put forward a third school, but rather to contribute to a more multifaceted view of the discipline, which requires surveying modulations of the discipline worldwide. Ďurišin's interliterary theory is of key importance for both such an aim and rethinking future trends. Though the interliterary theory originated with research by Ďurišin, who is its main representative, this does not mean that it is an individual enterprise. We have already mentioned the collective character of the series of case studies in *Osobitné medziliterárne spoločenstvá*, and how specific research projects have been developed by teams, as is the case with the East-Central European and Mediterranean centrisms. Furthermore, Ďurišin acknowledged the centrality of translation studies for inter-literary theory and, though he devoted some studies to translation, he mainly drew on research carried out by Antón Popovič and his team in Nitra.[16]

There are two further ways in which the interliterary theory is a collective product. Firstly, Ďurišin constantly tested the results of his research by having them discussed by colleagues with whom he worked in close collaboration, either at his own institution—the Institute of World Literature in Bratislava—or research centers in Prague and Moscow. A key example of this is the 1985 special issue of *Slavica Slovaca*, in which the main tenets of Ďurišin's interliterary theory are discussed by thirteen scholars. Secondly, after Ďurišin's death in 1997, his theory was amended and expanded by disciples and colleagues who had worked with him, either directly or indirectly. We have already mentioned the case of the posthumous volumes *Il Mediterraneo* and *Koncepcie svetovej literatúry*. An example of the richness and continuous appeal of the interliterary theory is the 2010 collective volume *New Imagined Communities* (Vajdová and Gáfrik), in which Anderson's concept of "imagined community" is coupled with Ďurišin's interliterary community.

Notes

1 For a short but comprehensive overview on Veselovsky, see Boris Maslov's presentation (Veselovsky, "Envisioning" 439–42).
2 The most basic formula of psychological parallelism is explained in the following terms by Veselovsky: "two motifs are contrasted; one makes reference to the other and vice versa, both shed light on each other, but the motif related to human beings prevails" (*Poetica* 170). This example is provided by Veselovsky: "*Pochylyvsja dub na duba, hil'em na*

dolynu / Lipše tebe, ljubcju, ljub'ju, jak maty dytynu" (*Poetica* 171; The branches of the oak lean over the valley due to acorns / I love you best, like a mum loves her son).

3 The dual formula "*X* and *Y*" or "*X* in *Y*" is best exemplified by such studies as those by Joseph Texte about the influence of Goethe and Schiller on French eighteenth-century drama, or by Jules Claretie about the influence of Shakespeare on Molière. Two facts, however, should not be overlooked. Firstly, this formula had a long tradition in German academia, especially within the field of *Stoffgeschichte* (history of circulation of materials), which shows once again how misleading is the opposition between two schools—French and American. Secondly, though Paul Van Tieghem's 1931 *La Littérature comparée* came to represent the textbook *par excellence* of the "French School," even for Ďurišin, Van Tieghem himself stated that a comparative literature restricted to *rapports binaires* (binary relations) was clearly insufficient: "It is not by multiplying the number of this kind of studies or even by adding their results that a great international literary phenomenon would be understood" (170). This is why Van Tieghem advocates that comparative literature has to move forward to the next stage, namely, *littérature générale* (general literature).

4 Ďurišin disrupts the traditional "division of labor" between national philologies and comparative literature, the distinction between "inside" and "outside," in accordance with his conception of the interliterary process as continuous growth.

5 This is why we have said before that "reading" within the framework of influence studies requires qualification, in the sense that what has been read may be a transductional variety of the traditionally privileged "original."

6 "I conceive this comparative concept [influence] as an unfortunate relic of the comparative method of 'influence-seeking' […]. The term 'influence' in its original meaning grants precedence to the giving constituent and suppresses or conceals the original creative activity of the recipient literary phenomenon. In other words it is the result of direct application of causality, where the giving phenomenon as the cause explains the recipient phenomenon as the result" (Ďurišin, *Theory of Literary Comparatistics* 159–60).

7 In a 1985 article, Ďurišin includes adaptation as a sub-kind of imitation, and translation as a sub-kind of the former ("*Aspects ontologiques*" 20).

8 The reading of Remak's 1961 definition as a medicine for the crisis comparative literature was suffering follows from his 1960 article, tellingly titled "Comparative Literature at the Crossroads: Diagnosis, Therapy and Prognosis."

9 By "subject-matter" Wellek makes reference to "foreign trade," interrelations between two literatures in terms of *source* and *influence*, which Wellek on one hand deprecates, for it makes comparative literature "a mere subdiscipline investigating data about the foreign sources and reputations of writers" ("The Crisis" 163) and, on the other hand, he pinpoints that there is no methodological difference between comparing works within a single literature and works of two distinct literatures.

10 Though nineteenth-century comparative literature restricted research on *rapports de fait* to connections within a single cultural or linguistic family (mainly European), East/West studies can also uncover *rapports de fait* between East and West, most readily in the twentieth century. The initial impetus for East/West comparisons, however, came from scholars of the premodern period.

11 Guillén's definition of his "model C" of supranationality reads as follows: "Some *genetically independent* phenomena make up supranational entities in accordance with principles and purposes derived from the *theory of literature*" (*The Challenge* 70).

12 It should be stressed that comparative *poetics*, as practiced by Miner, represents only a portion of what East/West comparison is about. Comparing literary works is a different matter, just as a person's avowed moral philosophy is not identical to that person's daily behavior.

13 Despite the relevance of identifying what entity is described by national literatures, this is not an issue generally discussed in comparative literature. For an identification of "*X*" with *literary life*, see Domínguez, "Literary Emergence."

14 It is worth reading Ďurišin's conception of specific interliterary communities in relation to Jakobson's idea of *Sprachbund* ("Über die phonologischen").

15 A standard definition of "global language" encompasses two factors: number of speakers and world distribution. "A language achieves a genuinely global status," David Crystal says, "when it develops a special role that is recognized in every country. […] To achieve such a status, a language has to be taken up by other countries around the world. They must decide to give it a special place within their communities, even though they may have few (or no) mother-tongue speakers" (3–4). In the case of the languages mentioned above, English, Spanish, French, and Portuguese currently qualify as global languages, whereas Chinese (Mandarin) and Hindustani represent enormously big language-fragments with important diasporas. Arabic occupies an intermediate place. For a typology of literary units that avoids the label of "world-literature," see Beecroft and Chapter 4.

16 Anglophone academia has gathered the studies carried out by the Cabinet of Literary Communication and Experimental Methodology in Nitra led by Popovič under the label of the "Nitra School" (Możejko). This is in sharp contrast with Ďurišin's interliterary theory, which, except for Fokkema's short note, has not attracted the attention of Anglophone academia. An important reason for this may lie in the fact that Ďurišin, in contrast to Popovič's work in Canada, was not allowed to go to Western countries (Guillén invited him to lecture at Harvard University, but in vain). His participation in AILC/ICLA conferences was restricted to those occasions in which the conferences were held in near countries, such as Austria and Hungary.

3

COMPARATIVE LITERATURE AND DECOLONIALITY

A review of textbooks of comparative literature shows that the inclusion of post/colonial issues is quite recent in the history of the discipline if one takes into account that the field of postcolonial studies came into widespread consideration after the publication of Edward Said's 1978 *Orientalism*. Susan Bassnett's 1993 *Comparative Literature: A Critical Introduction* was the first textbook to address the "post-colonial world" on the grounds that the emerging field of postcolonial studies has similar aims to those of comparative literature. Thus, by drawing on the opening statements of Bill Ashcroft, Gareth Griffiths, and Helen Tiffin's 1989 *The Empire Writes Back* to the effect that "the term 'post-colonial' [...] is most appropriate [...] for the new cross-cultural criticism which has emerged in recent years and for the discourse through which it is constituted" (2), Bassnett wonders "What is this but comparative literature under another name?" (10). One has to conclude, therefore, that "cross-cultural criticism" is the catchword of both fields, and yet Ashcroft, Griffiths, and Tiffin explicitly state that their "book is concerned with writing by those peoples formerly colonized by Britain" (1)—writing in English, a key issue on which Bassnett says nothing. Furthermore, postcolonial studies is not an exclusive alternative name for comparative literature. "We should look upon translation studies," Bassnett goes on to say, "as the principal discipline from now on, with comparative literature as a valued but subsidiary subject area" (161). Such statements were obviously designed to support a central argument of the textbook, namely, "Today, comparative literature in one sense is dead" (47). However provocative Bassnett's stance, her inclusion of postcolonial studies in a textbook devoted to comparative literature was in accordance with the signs of the times. In 1993 Charles Bernheimer too in the third report on the state of the discipline for the American Comparative Literature Association (see Chapter 1) stressed that "[c]omparative literature should be actively engaged in the study of the canon formation and in reconceiving the canon," an aim for which postcolonial theory was considered instrumental (Bernheimer Report 44).

It is tempting—and surely quite right— to say not only that postcolonial studies transformed comparative literature, but that the latter aimed to change postcolonial studies as well. After ten years of cross-fertilization, and in contrast to the above-quoted definition of postcolonial studies by Ashcroft, Griffiths, and Tiffin, Waïl S. Hassan and Rebecca Saunders have called for "comparative approaches to postcolonial studies," which would allow "postcolonial studies to move beyond monolingualism and narrow textualism" (19). This is the foundation of what Hassan and Saunders have termed "the project of comparative (post)colonialisms." And yet, though postcolonial studies has embraced a broader discursive grounding, it remains predominantly monolingual (in English). This explains, in part, why this chapter is titled "Comparative literature and decoloniality," and not "Comparative literature and postcolonial studies."

The reader may have noticed that "decoloniality" is an odd word that cannot be found in an English dictionary. As a noun, the closest common word in English is "decolonization," which means the "withdrawal from its former colonies of a colonial power" (*Oxford English Dictionary*). One has to assume, on one hand, that "decoloniality" has a different meaning from "decolonization"—otherwise, it would be a superfluous term—and, on the other hand, that it is paired with "coloniality," which in its turn should differ from colonization. Despite these differences, the chronological information provided by the *OED* is extremely relevant. "Colonization" was first used in 1770 by Edmund Burke when arguing in the British Parliament against unrestrained royal power in relation to the growth of Britain by conquest. Decolonization was first used in 1938 by the German economist Moritz Julius Bonn as a result of the breakdown of the imperial order due to the European "Civil War" (1914–45). It was in the aftermath of the decolonization process that, in 1952, Erich Auerbach qualified Goethe's concept of *Weltliteratur* at the paradoxical interface of an increasing number of new nation-states (former colonies)—and hence an increasing number of national literatures (see Chapter 4)—and a standardization, a "process of leveling" that "proceeds with a greater rapidity than ever before" (127).

De/coloniality has been coined by Latin American scholars—from sociologists and philosophers to anthropologists, semioticians, and literary critics—within the project of a critical understanding of modernity. In 1991, the Peruvian sociologist Aníbal Quijano published an article titled "Colonialidad y modernidad-racionalidad," in which the distinction between *colonización* (colonization) and *colonialidad* (coloniality) was first made as it was later used by members of the "Grupo Modernidad/Colonialidad" (Group Modernity/Coloniality).[1] According to Quijano, whereas colonialism may be over as a political order after the post-1945 decolonizations, coloniality is still active as the most widespread method of domination across our world. For Quijano, coloniality names "the relationship between the European—also called 'Western'—culture and the others," which is a relationship of "colonial domination" (169). It is, therefore, a colonization of the imaginary of the colonized from within. Such colonization was achieved mainly through the repression of the modes of knowledge and meaning by imposing the colonizers' patterns of expression and beliefs (169). It is a three-stage process. First, the repression we have just mentioned, which results in the impossibility for the colonized to produce culture. Second, colonizers impose a mystified image of their patterns of knowledge and meaning, which are set apart from the colonized. And third, these patterns are later taught, in a partial and selective way, to some colonized in order to co-opt them onto some of the colonizers' power institutions. This three-stage process results in the transformation of European culture into a universal cultural model, a seductive one, for it makes possible the access to power (169).

One may wonder what the differences between post/colonialism and de/coloniality are when an influential definition of the former stresses that it is "the prefix 'post' [that] complicates matters because it implies an 'aftermath' in two senses—temporal, as in coming after, and ideological, as in supplanting. It is the second implication which critics of the term have found contestable: if the inequities of colonial rule have not been erased, it is perhaps premature to proclaim the demise of colonialism" (Loomba 7). According to the leading decolonial thinker Walter D. Mignolo, the difference lies in that while the "de-colonial shift [...] is a project of de-linking," "post-colonial criticism and theory is a project of scholarly transformation within the academy" ("Delinking" 452).[2] In the concept of "delinking" Mignolo brings together Samir Amin's concept of *desconnection* (delinking), which remains rooted at the level of economics and politics, and Quijano's concept of *desprendimiento* (delinking; included in the above-quoted essay), which introduces the epistemic level. "Delinking" means to change the "hegemonic ideas of what knowledge and understanding are and, consequently, what economy and politics, ethics and philosophy, technology and the organization of society are and should be" ("Delinking" 459). Such a project requires, according to Mignolo, to break with Western epistemology as ruled by the theo-logical and the ego-logical politics of knowledge and understanding ("Delinking" 459).[3] To this, a double-sided chronological difference should be added, for, while postcolonial studies has focused on the past three centuries, de/coloniality traces its origins back to "the Christian and Castilian colonization of the Americas" (Mignolo and Tlostanova 111), which resulted in four radical changes: (1) massive appropriation of land and massive exploitation of labor, (2) establishment of Christian institutions to control authority, (3) control of gender and sexuality, and (4) control of knowledge and subjectivity. This means that de/coloniality not only precedes, but more importantly made possible, post/colonialism. "[I]n order to imagine Orientalism in the eighteenth century you have to have Occidentalism as a point of reference. And Occidentalism, in its specific relation to Orientalism, is a sixteenth-century invention," namely, "the European invention of the West Indies after the 'discoveries'" (Mignolo, *Darker Side of Western Modernity* 56). The above-mentioned four changes are at the base of the "colonial wound."

The colonial wound

Mignolo defines the *herida colonial* (colonial wound) as "the fact that regions and people around the world have been classified as underdeveloped economically and mentally" ("Epistemic Disobedience" 3). Within this framework, the composite Europe-Modernity appears as both the economic and epistemic ultimate destiny of humanity through the successive stages of Christianization (sixteenth–seventeenth centuries), civilization (eighteenth–nineteenth centuries), modernization (twentieth century), and democratization (mid-twentieth and twenty-first centuries).

The control of knowledge in the colonies implied, simultaneously, the denial of knowledges and subjectivities in "native" languages. The main aim of Mignolo's *The Darker Side of the Renaissance*—a 1995 book in which "de/coloniality" is not yet elaborated as a key concept—is to show the cultural colonization of the Americas in relation to, for instance, writing (the alphabet versus graphic inscriptions), the materiality of the book (the European codex versus the *amoxtli* and *quipu*), and discursive genres (history versus *toltecáyotl*).[4]

In contrast to the poststructural dependence (Michel Foucault, Jacques Lacan, and Jacques Derrida) of postcolonial theorists (Edward Said, Gayatri Spivak, and Homi Bhabha), decolonial theorists start from other sources, from Felipe Guamán Poma de Ayala, Mahatma Gandhi, and José Carlos Mariátegui to Aimé Cesaire, Frantz Fanon, Rigoberta Menchú, and Gloria Anzaldúa, among others.

For Mignolo, the Quechua nobleman Poma de Ayala embodies "the fractured perspective of a subaltern Amerindian" (*Darker Side of the Renaissance* 246). His 1612–15 *El primer nueva corónica y buen gobierno* (The First New Chronicle and Good Government) is seminal for the decolonial shift inasmuch as Poma de Ayala provides a harsh critique of Spanish colonial rule and opposes pre-Inca and Inca knowledge to European knowledge.

FIGURE 3.1 Felipe Guamán Poma de Ayala (in the middle) as an ethnographer interrogates the "natives" about their histories and legends (*El primer nueva corónica y buen gobierno*)

Where should comparison be located?

Interestingly, while the concept of decoloniality emerges progressively in Mignolo's writings, references to comparatism fade away, though more slowly than references to comparative literature. Are these phenomena unrelated?

In his 1991 article "Canon and Corpus," comparative literature is still a discipline that may be applied to "literatures" in colonial situations, provided that two caveats are taken into consideration and two questions posed. As for the caveats, Mignolo pinpoints that, on one hand, comparative literature is a European invention rooted in the comparatism that emerged during the expansion of the Portuguese and Spanish empires, when the transition from three major languages of scholarship (Greek, Latin, and Hebrew) to Western national languages and national literatures, as a result of the configuration of nation-states, took place. On the other hand, in contrast to the specific location of comparative literature (an invention of Western Europe), comparative processes are universally shared by human beings (219). As for the two questions, a transfiguration of comparative literature requires, according to Mignolo, one to wonder first, "What could a comparatist compare?" and second, "Who is comparing what and from where?"

Do not these questions have other disciplinary overtones? As a matter of fact, these questions are identical to the ones posed by anthropology in relation to its disciplinary tenets. Consider, for instance, the seminal works of James Clifford around issues such as anthropologist/"native"-informant, the ethics of comparing human groups, the poetics of the "scientific" ethnographic report, border-crossing, and travel. A neglected issue in the history of comparative literature in early nineteenth-century France is precisely how comparative literature found an academic niche of its own by simultaneously distancing itself from anthropology and using some of its methods and techniques. On one hand, comparative literature built a space of its own by restricting its corpus to "modern literatures" or, as Joseph Texte put it, literatures *depuis la Renaissance* (after the Renaissance), for it is in the late fifteenth/early sixteenth century that single literatures become distinctive, in contrast to the dominant anonymity and oral transmission of medieval literatures (notice the chronological coincidence with the emergence of what Mignolo calls Occidentalism). On the other hand, the opposition national/foreign literature and the concentration of comparative literature on the latter replicate the labor division of anthropology, whereby the anthropologist analyzes *other* human communities.[5]

Comparative literature as fieldwork

A case in point of the forgotten early history of comparative literature is the 1848 book *La Grèce, Rome et Dante. Études littéraires d'après nature*, by Jean-Jacques Ampère, whose other publications' key role in the foundation of comparative literature is broadly acknowledged (see Chapter 1). In contrast to his disciplinary discussions (the subfields of literary studies, including comparative literary history) and comparative research (the unfinished *Histoire de la littérature au Moyen Âge*), the above-mentioned book has not attracted the attention of comparatists. And yet, in it Ampère argues in favor of what he considers a new kind of literary criticism—the *critique en voyage* (traveling criticism)—within comparative literature. The *critique en voyage* consists of "comparing art with the reality that has inspired it and explain[ing] art through that reality" (i).

La Grèce, Rome et Dante is Ampère's narrative of his first journey to the "Orient" (Asian Turkey) in 1841 together with the writer Prosper Mérimée, the archeologist Jehan de Witte, and the Egyptologist Charles Lenormant. It is a typical orientalist narrative in which Ampère maps the West/East divide, discusses the Eastern influences on Homer, and calls the attention of French critics to Dante's work for the first time, always by focusing on the role played by landscape and how it contributes to understanding literary works.

If the Sorbonne opened its doors to comparative literature in 1832 by inviting Ampère to lecture, something similar happened with anthropology, whose disciplinary foundation is marked by the creation of the Société Ethnologique in Paris in 1839. Interestingly, with the *critique en voyage* Ampère replicated in literary studies the rite of passage of traditional anthropology—fieldwork. As the anthropologist, the comparatist travels to *other* literatures (quite literally in the case of the comparatist-*en voyage*), observes them (as the anthropologist observes *other* human communities), selects some informants (the landscape in Ampère's proposal), and writes a "scientific" report that is mainly addressed to the source-audience.

Notice, on one hand, how this variety of comparative literature is part and parcel of the Orientalist project and, on the other hand, how travel and border-crossing (a *leitmotiv* in the history of comparative literature) has recently re-emerged in anthropology as a disputable issue in relation to, for instance, "domestic fieldwork." Not to mention that the chiasmus is incomplete if one does not include in this picture that, while traditional anthropology has been restricted to the so-called "pre-literate societies," traditional comparative literature has been restricted to alphabetic writing of "modern societies."

The link Mignolo establishes between comparative literature as a European invention, comparatism during the Spanish and Portuguese expansion, and Occidentalism as the condition for Orientalism is also telling from the point of view of the history of comparatism. Note that we are talking now not of the history of comparative literature, but of the history of comparatism as a mental operation. According to Guy Jucquois (*Généalogie*), comparatism in Western thought had three main stages of development, which coincided respectively with the Sophists of ancient Greece, the Renaissance, and the nineteenth century. While traditionally the disciplinary origins of comparative literature have been traced back to the early nineteenth century as an offspring of the third stage of comparatism (the dominant evolutionism of this period was instrumental for the Orientalist enterprise), decolonial thinkers in general and Mignolo in particular pinpoint the relevance of the second stage in the constitution of the future discipline, for it was then that "the concept of literature had been forged and consolidated under the experience of alphabetic writing" ("Canon and Corpus" 223–24). If comparative literature aims to face the rich spectacle of literary plurality across the world, its bewilderment is preceded by comparative ethnology, which since the early sixteenth century aimed to face the rich spectacle of human cultural differences according to the positions which "the various human societies had reached on an historical time-scale" (Padgen 4).

Though decolonial thinkers do not draw on historians of comparatism, they arrive at identical conclusions. For Jucquois, for instance, "comparatism is simultaneously an epistemology, a methodology, and an ethics," for "it epistemologically presupposes a methodological distancing from phenomena under study and a personal ethical implication" ("Le Comparatisme" 18). Some pages later, Jucquois states that "comparatism consists of carrying out simultaneously the study of both the observed object and the observing subject and proceeding through the interrelationships between them in order to make explicit the links of object, subject and the sociocultural and historical context" (39). Isn't this statement identical to Mignolo's two questions regarding comparative literature?—"What could a comparatist compare?" and "Who is comparing what and from where?" A third dimension to Mignolo's two dimensions of "delinking" may be added now, this time by drawing on historians of comparatism. Delinking also means *décentration* (decentration)—a movement beyond the ego-logy—for "diversity is constituting and constitutive of human life, both individual and collective" ("Le Comparatisme" 29).

Some lessons from comparative philosophy

A comparative literature that addresses literatures in colonial situations requires, according to Mignolo ("Canon and Corpus" 238), a "diatopical hermeneutics" as a result of the asymmetry of power relations. The concept of diatopical hermeneutics is taken from Raimundo Panikkar (also known as Raimon Panikkar and Raymond Pannikar), a Spanish specialist in comparative religion and advocate of interreligious dialogue. In recognition of the relevance for comparative literature of Panikkar's reflection on comparative philosophy—where the concept of diatopical hermeneutics is embedded—it will be reviewed here at some length.[6]

Let us come back to the main tenet of de/colonial studies. While imperialism/colonialism may be over, de/coloniality unveils the hidden side of "modernity" through the domination relation between European culture and other cultures. For Panikkar, comparatism was and still is instrumental for such a power relation (remember the role of comparative ethnography since the sixteenth century) because comparative studies "belong to the thrust toward universalization characteristic of western culture" (116). When political control is no longer possible, the West un/consciously achieves such a control by building global and homogeneous pictures of the world—the literary world included—that rest on comparisons. The traditional ideas of "classic" and "universal/world literature" are a case in point, with the lion's share reserved for some five or six "major" European literatures, a literary "hall of fame" to which other literatures see their access denied. The fact that comparative literature emerged as a distinctive discipline during the imperial age, therefore, is not unrelated to de/coloniality.

Interestingly, Panikkar traces the origins of comparative philosophy back to comparative philology (117), and yet the links between the latter and comparative literature remain generally unnoticed, though both disciplines work with something so fundamentally human as language. Be that as it may, Panikkar distinguishes four varieties of comparative philosophy as it has been practiced so far. First, "transcendental philosophy," which puts on a universal scale the different self-understandings of the diverse philosophies (122). Second, "formal" or "structural philosophy," which consists of a formalized analysis of the common patterns in the diverse philosophical systems (124). Third, "linguistic philosophy," which equates each philosophy with the language in which it expresses itself (125). And fourth, "phenomenological philosophy," which consists of comparing the way a particular philosophical problem is dealt with by more than one philosophical school (126).

Interesting

Similarities between comparative philosophy and comparative literature?

Though there are obvious overlaps, there exist some similarities between both disciplines as traditionally practiced. Transcendental philosophy may be equated with a Eurocentric comparative literature that sees modern US–European literatures as literary art at its best, in relation to which other literatures will never be coeval. Structural philosophy may be equated with a comparative literature that classifies literary similarities across the world as either genetic contacts or typological affinities. As linguistic philosophy focuses on how a language determines the way a philosophical problem is phrased, this variety may be equated with the growing importance of translation for comparative literature (see Chapter 6). And phenomenological philosophy may be equated with either the traditional binary analysis of *rapports de fait* or East/West studies (see Chapter 2).

For Panikkar, none of these varieties of comparative philosophy is self-conscious about a key problem, namely, any project of comparative philosophy starts from a concrete philosophical position. This is why Panikkar advocates a "dialogical" or "imparative philosophy" (V.L. *imparare*, 'to speak overtly,' 'to negotiate'), which consists of "a philosophical stance that opens itself up to other philosophies and tries to understand them from the initial perspective—though it changes in the process. […] It should further cultivate an attitude of learning from all of them" (127). Comparative philosophy *qua* imparative philosophy is, therefore, ready to learn "from whatever philosophical corner of the world, but without claiming to compare philosophies from an objective, neutral, and transcendent vantage point" (127). Such a comparative practice is rooted in what Panikkar calls "diatopical hermeneutics" (the concept to which Mignolo calls attention), a method of interpretation that is required when the distance to overcome does not exist either within one single culture (morphological hermeneutics) or across times (diachronic hermeneutics), but "between two (or more) cultures, which have independently developed in different spaces (*topoi*) their own methods of philosophizing and ways of reaching intelligibility along with their proper categories" (Panikkar 130).

Now we can come back to comparative literature and see how productive this reflection on comparative philosophy is. It is indeed paradoxical that when postcolonial studies and decolonial studies interrogate the tenets of comparative literature, none of these fields takes into consideration the self-interrogation that has generated from within comparative literature, namely, East/West studies (see Chapter 2). Though it is also quite true that scholars of East/West studies do not generally enter into conversation with post-/de-/colonial scholars, at least in this area of disciplinary reflection, either. The diatopical hermeneutics that Mignolo sees as so crucial for undertaking a comparison of literatures in colonial situations has been discussed by scholars of East/West studies in terms, for instance, of what Mary Garrett has called "methodological paradox" (see Chapter 2), meaning that the researcher cannot avoid _her/his_ location. And Panikkar's five varieties of comparative philosophy have striking similarities with Cao Shunqing and Zhi Yu's typology of approaches to intercultural dialogue through the comparison of literary theories worldwide: (1) different discourses but common topics, (2) different discourses but common language situation, (3) dialogue between discourses through translation, and (4) interlocked categories and survival of different discourses. Cao and Zhi's fourth variety has identical aims to Panikkar's imparative philosophy, that is, to overcome monological (literary) theories by way of "multiple discourses of the contemporary literary theory" that "survive at the same time [...]. This is a radiant state in which different cultural discourses have their own say" (102). To this picture, one may add Desiderio Navarro's discussion of Eurocentrism (see Chapter 2), Roberto Fernández Retamar's arguments against the possibility of understanding Latin American literature when read from European standards, and Mao LuMing's application of the linguistic distinction etic/emic to intercultural research, among other possibilities.[7]

An imparative comparative literature remains, however, more in a programmatic-oriented stage than in an analytic-oriented one. An important contribution in the direction of an imparative comparative literature is due to Lu Xing, who considers highly debatable Charles Taylor's approach to intercultural understanding—"language of perspicuous contrast."[8] This approach aims to cherish the values of non-Western cultures and integrate them with the Western ones thanks to a "perspicuous contrast" that makes visible opposing meanings between cultures. Taylor argues that his approach is based upon Hans-Georg Gadamer's idea of *Horizontverschmelzung* (fusion of horizons), and it will reduce the tendency to deal with other cultures as incorrigible and hence avoid prejudices on cultural superiority.[9] Though Lu agrees with these aims, he stresses that this approach may perpetuate the perception of cultural differences as absolute. "A language of perspicuous contrast tends to present mutually exclusive worldviews between two cultures. Consequently, the perception of difference is heightened, creating barriers and intensifying stereotypes associated with cultures" (91). In contrast to Taylor's language of perspicuous contrast, Lu advocates a "language of ambiguous similarity," which is based on the principle that the human invention of language is both culturally specific and universally similar, and hence our world perceptions are simultaneously diverse and similar (91). Through the search for a language of ambiguous similarity, one verifies that cultures are not incongruous, mutually excluding, and that categories are not opposing binaries. A common ground for communication is established, the attitude of incorrigibility is tempered, and intercultural interests are promoted (91–92). Lu performs his search for such a language by comparing rhetorical traditions, as can be seen sketchily in the following passage.

> the meanings of *ming*, *shuo*, and *bian* may be more closely related to *logos*, the word used by Greek sophists to mean forms of argumentation, discussion, questions and answers, and speeches. The concepts of *yan* and *bian* may resemble more closely the Greek notion of *rhêtorikê* which included formal speech discourse and persuasion for a political purpose. Further, *rhêtorikê* and *ming bian* share more ambiguous similarities. Both *rhêtorikê* and *ming bian* refer to speech and argumentation. More specifically, *rhêtorikê* means creating change through persuasion; *ming bian* is associated with the ability to change attitudes and beliefs. *Rhêtorikê* involves the faculty of inquiry and is the counterpart of dialectics. Likewise, *ming bian* contains a process of making distinctions and categorizations. *Rhêtorikê* refers to persuasive discourse used in political and judicial situations. Similarly, *ming bian* aims at achieving social order and justice. Clearly the ancient Chinese and Greeks shared certain similar rhetorical notions and conceptualizations, including: perceptions on the role of speech in changing attitudes and behaviors; as modes of epistemological and intellectual inquiry; and ideas regarding the impact of language and moral, political, and social issues. These similarities exist within different linguistic systems, which, when viewed superficially, appear to have little in common. By juxtaposing their similarities, more commonalities between the two rhetorical systems are to be recognized.
>
> Regarding the relationship between *rhêtorikê* and *ming bian*, it must be noted that the two are not identical. The meaning of each word emerged from within its social, philosophical, and linguistic context.
>
> *(Lu 92–93)*

Another important contribution in the direction of an imparative comparative literature—at least as procedure—is Cao Shunqing's 2013 *The Variation Theory of Comparative Literature*. In this case, Cao starts by making his *etic location* visible. In contrast to the "French school" and "American school" of comparative literature,

Cao Shunqing
third-phase theory
Comparative literature and decoloniality **51**

Cao advocates a "third-phase theory," namely, "a novel and scientific mode of the Chinese school," a "theoretical innovation and systematization of the Chinese school by relying on our *own* methods" (*Variation Theory* 43; emphasis added). From this etic beginning, his proposal moves forward emically by developing a "cross-civilizational study on the heterogeneity between Chinese and Western culture" (43), which results in both the foreignization of Chinese literary theories and the Sinification of Western literary theories.

Some questions for an imparative comparative literature

As mentioned above, an imparative comparative literature remains so far more in a programmatic-oriented stage than in an analytic-oriented one. This situation is not unrelated to another phenomenon, the also already mentioned progressive loss of importance of comparative literature within decolonial studies. While comparatism *qua* method played a key role, for instance, in Mignolo's 1995 *The Darker Side of the Renaissance*, it plays no role at all in his 2000 and 2011 books *Local Histories/Global Designs* and *The Darker Side of Western Modernity*. This diagnosis may be applied to the research by other members of the Grupo Modernidad/Colonialidad.

It may be useful to recall now in which directions decolonial studies initially pointed for comparative literature. By drawing on Mignolo's publications in which comparative literature was still at the center of the decolonial argument ("Canon and Corpus" and "Los límites"), three areas become relevant: oral literature, non-Western artifacts, and emergent literatures. Before surveying them, it should be stressed that Mignolo restricts these three areas to the case of Latin America from a quite specific point of view, namely, "the lack of comparative literature tradition in Latin America," where Brazil would be an exception ("Canon and Corpus" 222, 239n5). Such a statement requires further qualification (see below).

1. Oral literature. "As a result of some specific colonial situations, as the ones in Mesoamerica and the Andes," says Mignolo, "it is possible to challenge at the same time both the concept of literature and the concept of discursive practice as based upon alphabetic writing" ("Los límites" 15). One of the possibilities referred to here is oral literature. We have already stated that comparative literature found a disciplinary niche precisely by excluding from its corpus oral literature as packaged under the general label of "premodern *literature*." This exclusion was based on the assumption that oral literature does not exist in the West in modern times (it is here—not in "*oral* literature," a concept that Pio Zirimu replaces by "orature"—that the real oxymoron lies for Western categories, for orality is at odds with modernity) or, if it exists, it is negligible. Since the foundation of comparative literature, the labor distribution between modern written literatures (*depuis la Renaissance*) for comparative literature and premodern oral literatures for anthropology, ethnography, mythology, and folklore studies still operates, and therefore the challenge for comparative literature as posed by decolonial studies is most relevant.

A mutation within the study of orality, however, should be taken into consideration, namely, the emergence of oral studies as a distinctive field that aims, on one hand, to provide a comprehensive view of what is generally—and paradoxically, for its change-resistant overtones—called "oral tradition," and on the other hand, to show its liveliness also in modern and contemporary times (as for the latter issue, see for instance Foley, *Oral Tradition and the Internet*). One may say that, due to its broader focus in relation to the above-mentioned disciplines and fields, oral studies has constituted itself as the disciplinary equivalent of comparative literature for oral literature, which is defined by Jane Nandwa and Austin Bukenya as "those utterances, whether spoken, recited or sung, whose composition and performance exhibit to an appreciable degree the artistic character of accurate observation, vivid imagination and ingenious expression" (1). And though comparatism has been instrumental for both oral studies and its disciplinary predecessors, it remains restricted to oral compositions to a large extent. Consequently, not only is oral literature a challenge for comparative literature in the terms posited by Mignolo, but written literature is also a challenge for oral studies. It is in this line that the leading scholar on the subject of comparative oral traditions, John Miles Foley, has argued that the "great divide model" of orality versus literacy obscures more than it explains. Furthermore, though oral literature dwarfs written literature in amount, among other issues, the access role written literature plays with regard to a large number of oral compositions is undeniable, not to mention the lengthy "interface period," that is, the coexistence of both media. One may expect, therefore, a fruitful reintegration of oral literature within comparative literature, a "true comparative literature" as Lee Haring calls it, for "comparative literature, which bases itself upon both the plurality of the objects of study and the analogical method, is especially relevant in the field" of oral literature (Le Blanc 116).[10]

2. Non-Western artifacts. Similarly, Mignolo's above-quoted passage poses another challenge to comparative literature inasmuch as the Western notion of literature also needs "to be revisited from the point of view of speech and writing" ("Canon and Corpus" 224). The cases of *amoxtli* and *quipus* have been mentioned above. It is an uncharted field for comparative literature, a situation that may be due to the very terms in which the issue has been defined. "[I]t is not about comparing writers and literary works, but about comparing semiotic practices in several cultures, as well as the ways in which such practices are conceived" (Mignolo, "Los límites" 15). This absence in comparative literature may pinpoint its presence in another field, for instance media studies, its bent towards the post/modern and the popular notwithstanding. Such a distinction, however, replicates the traditional opposition content/form, and Mignolo's argument may be used, therefore, as an opportunity for reintegrating both within comparative literature.

3. Emergent literatures. Mignolo claims that the need to rethink the field of comparative literature is also posited by "emergent literatures" ("Canon and Corpus" 221–22). For this concept, Mignolo draws on Wlad Godzich, who, according to the former, differentiates between "emerging" and "emergent" literatures. The concept of emerging literatures is embedded in an evolutionary view of literature, whereby they would not be "fully developed" as yet. Emergent literatures, in their turn, challenge the actual configuration of comparative literature and resist being

treated as emerging. Such a conceptual distinction is highly debatable, as proved by three facts: (1) both concepts have been used interchangeably by scholars; (2) the geography of emerging/emergent literatures is restricted to a single location (broadly speaking, Jameson's "Third-World Literature"); and (3) Godzich does not provide a clear definition of emergent literatures, except for stating that they "represent a different conception of field and of object than that represented by the often used expression 'emerging literatures'" (35), whatever this different conception might be. The second fact—the geographical—is especially relevant here, for a review of scholarship on emergent/emerging literatures (Galli Mastrodonato; Guillén, "Emerging Literatures"; Grassin; for a different approach, see Domínguez) shows that European languages are their means of expression in new nation-states after the 1945 decolonization, especially former British and French colonies. In short, the geography of emergent/emerging literatures is the one of postcolonial studies.

★

In contrast to the usual discussion of postcolonial studies from a comparative perspective since the 1990s, we have decided to explore the intersections between comparative literature and decolonial studies. This does not imply a denial of postcolonial studies' relevance. On the contrary, postcolonial studies is embedded in decolonial studies according to Mignolo's argument that de/coloniality not only precedes but, more importantly, made possible post-/colonialism. Besides, a move from postcolonialism to decoloniality challenges the former's dominant monolingualism (in English), which has been instrumental for later constructions, such as "global English fiction" and world literature (in translation into English). But replacing one monolingualism (postcolonial English) by another monolingualism (decolonial Spanish) is a naïve exercise that we do not want to repeat.[11] It is undeniable, however, that Amerindian languages—suffice to mention here only the languages at the root of Mignolo's argumentation, i.e. Anahuac, Nahuatl and Quechua—have not as yet entered into the "field" (in Godzich-Mignolo's sense) of comparative literature. Consequently, we take decolonial arguments on the subalternization of languages as a critical standpoint for the project of an "enlarged" imparative comparative literature, a project that is more radical than the one advocated by postcolonial studies (still rooted in the formula "Europe and the rest") in the line of Gayatri Spivak's relationship between comparative literature and area studies. This radicality is about neither the number and location of languages, nor the endangered diversity of languages in academia—though they are crucial issues too—but about a self-reflective questioning of comparative literature *qua* discipline, which includes the two issues just mentioned (the number and location of languages of discursive practices under comparison, and the increasing monolingualism of global academia), as well as the decolonization of knowledge. It is the project that Dipesh Chakrabarty has called "provincializing Europe" and Armando Gnisci *decolonizzazione europea* (European decolonization), which, from our point of view, cannot overlook, as has been the case, the fact that the subalternization of languages has taken place not only outside Europe, but also *inside* Europe. But an imparative comparative literature will not stop at deconstructing and overcoming Eurocentrism, but will address all kinds of ethnocentrisms all over the world, as well as non-European imperialisms.

An imparative comparative literature that draws on decolonial studies should also be self-reflective about some of the latter's tenets, such as, to name but a few, the geographical (the Americas) and chronological (late fifteenth- and sixteenth-century) restrictions of coloniality, its monolingualism, and the denial of comparative studies of literature in Latin America.[12] In contrast to the progressive loss of importance of comparative literature within decolonial studies, our survey aims to show some exciting perspectives for future cross-fertilizing developments. A sign of the vitality of such developments may be found in recent research in comparative literature that draws from decolonial studies. Suffice to mention Revathi Krishnaswamy's concept of "world literary knowledges," whose aim is "to open up the canon of literary theory and criticism to alternative ways of conceptualizing and analyzing literary production" (408).

Notes

1 Grupo Colonialidad/Modernidad is associated with the work of chiefly Walter D. Mignolo, Aníbal Quijano, and Enrique Dussel. Other scholars associated with the group include Santiago Castro-Gómez, Fernando Coronil, Eduardo Restrepo, Edgardo Lander, Nelson Maldonado, Zulma Palermo, and Catherine Walsh, among others (Escobar 203n3).

2 The restriction of postcolonialism to an analytic project, in contrast to the de/colonial broader scope as being both analytic and programmatic, is highly debatable.

3 Theo-logy is "the historical and dominant frame of knowledge in the modern/colonial world from the sixteenth to the first half of the eighteenth century" ("Delinking" 459–60), that is, God as the guarantor of knowledge, while Ego-logy places "Man and Reason in God's stead, and centralized the Ego" (*The Darker Side of Western Modernity* 15).

4 *Amoxtli* is an Anahuac and Nahuatl word that names an object that Franciscan missionaries "read" as book. *Toltecáyotl* is a Nahuatl word for the artifact that preserves the cultural tradition of a community. For the decolonial logic, neither can *amoxtli* be replaced by "book," nor *toltecáyotl* by "History," for Western epistemology would resist books being named *amoxtli* or deny epistemic value to *toltecáyotl*.

5 *Chaires de littérature étrangère* (chairs of foreign literature) was an early name for comparative literature (see Espagne). Tellingly, as the anthropologist, the comparatist needs to be acquainted with the culture in which the target-literature has been produced and have some degree of proficiency in its language, with translation representing a problematic issue for the disciplinary identity until very recently, as posed by the question: Is the comparatist allowed to work with translations? These "negative effects" are not alien to either anthropology (a case in point is the controversial mediation of Elizabeth Burgos in Rigoberta Menchú's testimony) or postcolonial studies as encrypted in the question "Can the subaltern speak?"

6 The history of comparatism as a mental operation and the diverse moments in which a comparative discipline may emerge leads to the distinction of three levels (see Preface): (1) predisciplinary: comparison as mental operation, (2) disciplinary: a discipline in which the comparative method prevails, and (3) transdisciplinary: communication among comparative disciplines. Interestingly, the oft-repeated mention of the disciplinary crisis of comparative literature since René Wellek's 1958 lecture (see Chapter 1) has taken into consideration neither the predisciplinary nor the transdisciplinary perspective. When reading Panikkar's discussions on comparative philosophy, the reader will see how much these discussions may contribute to comparative literature.

7 The distinction etic/emic has to do with the issue of objectivity in research. First elaborated within linguistics ("emic" derives from phonemic and "etic" from phonetic), it
was later applied to anthropology for describing viewpoints during fieldwork. According
to Conrad Phillip Kottak, "[i]n the field, ethnographers typically combine two research
strategies, the emic (native-oriented) and the etic (scientist-oriented)" (53). Mao argues
that after an inevitable first stage in which research is based upon etic tools (concepts
alien to the culture under study), it has afterward to proceed to an emic stage, though
concepts of the target-culture will always be filtered by the etic approach. It should also
be noticed that neither de/colonial studies nor comparative literature have integrated
results from comparative rhetoric (for an introductory reading, see Kennedy).

8 "[T]he adequate language in which we can understand another society is not our language
of understanding, or theirs, but rather what one could call a language of perspicuous
contrast. This would be a language in which we could formulate both their way of life
and ours as alternative possibilities in relation to some human constants at work in both.
It would be a language in which the possible human variations would be so formulated
that both our form of life and theirs could be perspicuously described as alternative such
variations" (Taylor 125).

9 "Every finite present has its limitations. We define the concept of 'situation' by saying
that it represents a standpoint that limits the possibility of vision. Hence essential to the
concept of situation is the concept of *horizon*. The horizon is the range of vision that
includes everything that can be seen from a particular vantage point" and "the horizon
of the present is continually in the process of being formed because we are continually
having to test all our prejudices. An important part of this testing occurs in encountering
the past and in understanding the tradition from which we come. [...] understanding is
always the fusion of these horizons supposedly existing by themselves" (Gadamer 313, 317).

10 Interestingly, Haring's claim about a "true comparative literature" has less to do with the
reintegration of oral literature than with what he calls the theoretical base of comparative
literature—"common sense anthropology" (37).

11 The reader may have noticed that we have exclusively mentioned "Spanish" as decolonial
monolingualism, whereas decolonial thinkers trace the origin of coloniality back to the
late fifteenth- and sixteenth-century Spanish and Portuguese expansion and, hence, the
role of Portuguese as a new hegemonic language of modernity should also be acknowledged. Paradoxically, decolonial thinkers deal with Portuguese expansion only collaterally,
which may be due to the fact that they focus on the Americas (actually, the Spanish-
speaking Americas)—a highly debatable restriction—while Portuguese expansion included
the Indian Ocean and Southeast Asia as a result of the duopoly endorsed by the 1494
Treaty of Tordesillas. Moreover, Portuguese(-speaking) scholars have not been involved
in decolonial studies, though decolonial thinkers claim the influence of the Portuguese
sociologist Boaventura de Sousa Santos.

12 The appropriation of postcolonial theories by medieval studies is indicative of a colonization
process that decolonial studies does not address either, namely, the colonization of pre-
modernity by modernity (for a helpful overview, see Lampert-Weissig). Mignolo's statement about the lack of comparative literature in Latin America, except in Brazil, without
further proofs seems to be due more to lack of information than to an actual lack of
comparative literature. His allusion, for instance, to a "long and solid tradition" ("Canon
and Corpus" 239n5) in Brazil, as represented by Tânia Franco Carvalhal and Afrânio
Coutinho, notwithstanding the relevance of their contributions, overlooks seminal discussions by Latin Americanists who, though wishing to apply the comparative method to
literatures in Latin America, feel uneasy about the Eurocentric tenets of the discipline. A
case in point is Pedro Henríquez Ureña's 1945 *Literary Currents in Hispanic America*.

4

WORLD LITERATURE AS A COMPARATIVE PRACTICE

One day in January 1827, the aged poet Goethe told his friend Eckermann that he had been reading a Chinese novel. "That must be very strange indeed," said Eckermann. "Not as strange as people might think," said Goethe; "the characters think, act and feel as we do, and one feels oneself almost to be one of them, except that everything is clearer, more chaste, and more moral among them […] I see ever more clearly," continued Goethe, "that poetry is a common possession of all humanity […] National literature is no longer of much account; the age of world literature is upon us, and everyone must work to hasten its arrival" (Goethe 327–29).

Retelling this famous episode can be for us an opportunity to ask, "What is world literature?" But not in the sense of seeking a definition; rather of asking, "What happens to bring about the appearance of the phrase, 'world literature'?" We can begin by enumerating the conditions. A German poet born in 1749 is reading a Chinese novel, so translators must have been at work and publishers (in England, as it happens) must have seen some profit in publishing it. In that novel he recognizes a society much like his own, or one even more refined (he muses that the Chinese have thousands more of such novels, "and already had them when our ancestors were living in the woods"), so the translators' work must have been successful in transmitting, or forging, ways of "thinking, acting and feeling" shared by the Chinese novelists and their German reader. This feeling of familiarity causes the German reader to feel his own "national literature" as a limitation on his sensibility, and to call for an "age of world literature," so there must have been already some notion of a "world," of a frame of reference that is complete and all-inclusive, and in which "literature" must henceforth be made to thrive.

Variations on world literature

For some 185 years now, "world literature" has been the name for a way of thinking about comparative literature that has issued, variously, in a conception of the worldwide field of cultural exchange, a horizon for literary evaluation, a canon for purposes of reading and teaching, a pedagogical program, and a field of research. Differing causes have pushed the development of these variations on the theme, so that it would be a stretch to take them collectively as having the same reference or implications; and, as often happens in comparative literature, where "world literature" is concerned, our announced ambitions and our actual scope are two different things. "World literature" is *always* (as Goethe said in 1827) about to arrive; it is an object of desire, a future completeness, a standard of unattainable achievement. Whatever the purposes behind its articulation at a given time, the concept of "world literature" has served repeatedly to define linkages between literary study and whatever is supposed to lie outside the literary field—its "world," in a formal and logical sense. The effect of demanding recognition for "world literature" is to say: "See what our previous ideas about literature have made it easy for us to ignore, and go beyond these limits."

World literature implies a definition of the world. (On the historicity of the concept of "literature," see Hoesel-Uhlig; on the plurality of "worlds," see Hayot.) Goethe used the phrase as a counter to *national* literature, which, especially in early nineteenth-century Germany, had been formulated as a declaration of cultural independence from the then current models of neo-classicism (mainly French adaptations from the Greeks and Romans). Thus a purportedly *universal* set of genres, styles, and standards had already been displaced by *national* particularity, and would soon, in Goethe's eager imagining, give way to *world* literature, not a space of sameness but an exchange among different traditions. *Exchange*

Exchange was the aspect of Goethe's remark that stayed in the minds of Marx and Engels, who wrote in 1848 that

> The bourgeoisie has through its exploitation of the world market given a cosmopolitan character to production and consumption in every country. […] The intellectual creations of individual nations become common property. National one-sidedness and narrow-mindedness become more and more impossible, and from the numerous national and local literatures, there arises a world literature.
>
> *(Marx and Engels 12–13)*

Observe how, although they call it by the same name, Goethe and Marx/Engels characterize the process differently. Goethe had been prompted by a Chinese novel to recognize "a common possession of humanity" in fiction-writing and the thoughts and feelings it records; thereupon he urged his fellow readers and writers to venture out onto that wider stage and participate in the making of a world literature. The authors of the *Communist Manifesto* see the rise of "a world literature" as conditioned on the imposition of sameness across the world by "the bourgeoisie […] through its exploitation of the world market." What Goethe thinks he discovers as a fact of universal human nature, Marx/Engels insist the bourgeoisie have made; and where Goethe anticipates a confluence of differences, Marx/Engels see all "national and local" differences as having been made obsolete.

Both are right, but on condition that we separate out the ambiguous meanings. A capacity to create works of verbal art is, indeed, common to all humanity, though not equally realized in every human being or equally fostered by every human society. Before we can recognize the "literature" of another human group *as a literature*, however, someone has to perform the translation, the mediation, or the analogizing that refashions a piece of mere behavior into literature.

> An Iroquois work, even if it were full of absurdities, would be an invaluable treasure; it would offer a unique specimen of the workings of the human mind, when placed in circumstances which we have never experienced, and influenced by manners and religious opinions entirely contrary to our own. We should be sometimes astonished and instructed by the contrariety of ideas thus produced [...] We should there learn not only to own, but to feel the power of prejudice.
>
> *(Edward Gibbon, "An Essay on the Study of Literature" [1761],*
> *cited in Reiss 136–37)*

For thousands of years, fairy tales have been told all over the world, but only in the past few hundred years have they been considered as belonging to the same overall type of object as epic poems, lyrics, or dramas. When an ancient civilization is dug up and its clay tablets decoded, scholars must determine what in the archive is history, law, accounting, prayer, and so forth, and what is literature. If a previously unknown human group comes into contact with another civilization, some part of their songs and tales may become "literature" through being translated, anthologized, appreciated. Since the Dada movement of the early twentieth century, nonsense syllables, lottery tickets, and handbills have been eligible for interpretation as literature, if only they were copied into a text that was to be received as an artistic performance. In all these acts of appropriation and categorization, a middleman is essential: the translator, critic, or anthologist who performs the act of assigning the text to the sphere of verbal art.

Goethe, in his gesture of recognizing and welcoming the foreign (Chinese) novelist as a fellow contributor to world literature, forgot the translator, the publisher, and the many other agencies that smoothed the road from Beijing to Weimar: economic, philosophical, political, technical agencies. Marx/Engels, in their assertion that a new world had been born from the world-spanning, homogenizing activities of capitalism, took the objects of exchange to be mere incidentals in the story of how the networks of exchange were built. The "national one-sidedness and narrow-mindedness" Marx/Engels see as doomed relics are the very goods Goethe supposed writers and nations should bring to the feast of world literature.

If the benefit of enlarging literature to the scale of the world was, for Goethe, to increase the variety of literary goods on offer, Marx and Engels, like many economists since, saw in the removal of impediments to trade a step towards unification: the virtues of scale will reward those who deal in the articles most readily valued and exchanged in the largest possible market. Regarding this distinction, Goethe can be seen as obliquely confirming Marx/Engels' point. For the work in which he could recognize the delicate sentiments of the Chinese was a vernacular novel, a type of work that raised fewer difficulties for the translator than, say, Chinese formal verse; it had also the advantage of corresponding to a familiar genre on the European side, the courtship romance. Compared with many types of East Asian writing, the Chinese novel was more than halfway along the road to acceptability to a reader such as Goethe. (It would be nearly another century before Chinese and Japanese poetry could be translated and presented in such a way that Westerners could see the point of it.) A genre or a work that had no echo on the reader's side would be as good as lost for world literature—though such a genre or work potentially could hold the highest possible literary value for a differently situated observer such as the imaginative Edward Gibbon. Thus, in our account of world literature, relying only on the premonitory discussions of Goethe and Marx/Engels, we can see the necessity for carefully differentiated and contextualized understandings of:

the species-wide faculty of artistic creation, balanced against the modes of perception
   and blindness specific to the place and time of the receiver;
the sympathetic insight transcending eras and cultures, balanced against the mediation
   of translators and reciprocal literary history;
the individuality of works and cultures, balanced against the marketplace of
   communication.

In no case of a work's promotion to the status of "world literature" can we simply say it is a matter of one factor, to the exclusion of its counterpart.

A conversation among equals?

For an unwittingly Marxian interpretation of Goethe's concept after seventy years of its worldwide circulation, consider how the Danish critic Georg Brandes responded to a German newspaper's inquiry into world literature in 1899.

> A few writers out of many thousands, a few works from hundreds of thousands, are part of world literature. Everyone has the names of such writers and works on the tip of the tongue: the *Divine Comedy* belongs not to Italy alone, nor *Don Quixote* to Spain. [... But] it is incontestable that writers of different countries and languages occupy enormously different positions where their chances of obtaining worldwide fame, or even a moderate degree of recognition, are concerned. The most favorably situated are the French writers, although the French language occupies only the fifth rank in terms of extension. When a writer has succeeded in France, he is known throughout the world. English and Germans, who can count on an immense public if they are successful, take second place. It is only writers from these three nations who can hope to be read in the original by the most educated people of all nations [...] But whoever writes in Finnish, Hungarian, Swedish, Danish, Dutch, Greek or

the like is obviously poorly placed in the universal struggle for fame. In this competition he lacks the major weapon, a language—which is, for a writer, almost everything.

(62–63)

If Goethe's imagination of world literature made it a conversation among equals, each tradition bringing its own personality to the table, by the time of Brandes the designation "a work of world literature" is conferred only in the ultimate elimination round of the "universal struggle for fame." Both the rule of play and the unit of account have changed: it is now a competition for recognition, or for market share, and the winners and losers are authors. The arena, however, is not one and the same for all. Those writers who use a small number of favored languages are at a crushing advantage. The "cosmopolitan character of production and consumption" (as Marx/Engels would say) on the "world market" is such that French, English, or German exerts an irreversible dominance. Language, formerly the organic tissue connecting the writer with a public and a literary heritage, is now in all but a few cases a liability, a symptom of "national narrowness and one-sidedness." The transition from "national literatures" to the "world literature" is just as jarring as Marx/Engels said it would be.

More than 100 years later, the effects of scale have consolidated the literary market. France still has a special position in the arbitrage of taste (see Casanova), but in many areas of writing, other languages have been displaced by English, the one language in which it is essential to publish. Practices of world literary recognition such as the annual Nobel Prize confirm the author, and secondarily the nation, as the units to which fame is conferred or from which it is withheld. And as in Brandes's time, cosmic justice does not appear to lead the process. Brandes illustrates the dynamic of world fame with two Danish examples: Hans Christian Andersen, whose "fairy tales [have] made their way everywhere through their general comprehensibility" though among his countrymen he was "inconsequential as a thinker and never had an intellectual influence"; and Kierkegaard, "the greatest religious thinker of the Scandinavian North [...] No one knows him" (65). A difficult writer in a small language, Kierkegaard seemed to Brandes in 1899 a hopeless case. Time, translation and the rise of existential philosophy have since redressed the balance somewhat, and Kierkegaard now has his place on the world stage—but he will never be as familiar a household word as Andersen.

Brandes contrasts world fame with quality—his estimate of quality, of course; but the critic who first gave Ibsen, Nietzsche, Dostoyevsky, and Kierkegaard a worldwide audience deserves a hearing. World literature is a sorting of the canon of great works over a long time and through many changes of taste. We are accustomed to speak as if the present fame of the shallow writer were a social phenomenon and the future fame of the currently obscure one were the result of an intrinsic literary judgment. Knowing what we like, detaching ourselves from the madding crowd—these are habitual gestures among literary intellectuals. The sociology of world literature proposed by Pascale Casanova (a former student of Pierre Bourdieu) draws no such distinction between acclaim and value. She sees the literary world as a hierarchy of universes, with the top level of prestige also claiming the widest area. This might indicate a static picture of dominance by the few. But since literature is always avid for novelty, and since competition among authors, genres, and styles is perpetual, writers from the margins can break through to the center, if only their way of attaining it can be justified in the (mercifully shifting) terms of the central judges' aesthetic. Particularly informative are the cases of William Faulkner and South American fiction, both examples of regional writing raised to universal importance through Parisian interpretation and promotion. Casanova's focus on publishing is valuable as a counterbalance to the tendency to assume that literary reputations are made or broken in the classroom.

Casanova reconceives world literature as a set of institutions and processes that determine the outcome of writers' bids for fame. David Damrosch's formulation, "World literature is writing that gains in translation" (*What Is World Literature?* 291), likewise puts more stress on the circulation of works than on their content. A truly sociological theory of literature would, in order to confirm its disciplinary purity, have to handle the books as mere black boxes through which some kind of social action (the real focus of the research) is performed. (Compare Collins for an account of philosophy as a worldwide, networked endeavor.) Without going quite so far, the authors who consider world literature primarily as a matter of circulation are apt to view the works' content as secondary to, yet allegorical of, and derivable from, their place in social processes. Fredric Jameson, in a much-cited essay animated by "the old question of a properly world literature" (67), contends that Third World fictions are always allegorical of the postcolonial nation-building effort. Franco Moretti, searching for laws of world literature, finds that "in cultures that belong to the periphery of the literary system [...] the modern novel first arises not as an autonomous development but as a compromise between a western formal influence (usually French or English) and local materials" ("Conjectures" 58). The peripheral novel, that is, mirrors in its structure the process of its construction; it has no subject other than its relation to the world literary market. In such accounts of worldwide literary circulation, the outside and the inside of literature are mutually convertible; the metadata (to borrow from the vocabulary of the US National Security Agency) and the data amount to the same thing. "The one-and-unequal literary system is not just an external network here, it doesn't remain *outside* the text: it's embedded well into its form" ("Conjectures" 66).

The school and the library

In two locations, however, gaps emerge between the patterns of circulation and the things circulated. One is the classroom; the other is the library. In the classroom, we see that although the canon of world literature is always expanding, the number of hours devoted to it in a semester or an academic career do not have the same flexibility. For every work that comes in, something must go out. As a paradoxical result of the geographical broadening of world literature, the number of authors taught overall shrinks, and so does the amount of context—of world—that can be provided (Damrosch, "World Literature"). World literature, intended to enlarge the canon, creates a "hypercanon," an unusually small number of books on which an unusually heavy burden of representation is placed: one novel by Rushdie will stand for all of South Asia, one novel by Achebe will represent Africa, and so forth, in the North American university curriculum.

Globalization raises a few writers to unforeseen heights. And yet the library, as Moretti observes, regorges with unread books. We claim to study "the novel," but most of us are deeply acquainted with no more than a handful of novels in the most easily accessible languages. The historical and geographical vastness of actually published fiction baffles us. Moretti proposes dealing with this enormous archive by dividing the labor of reading. The critic or theorist of world literature will no longer read literary works. A multitude of readers skilled in the local languages and forms of the various literatures will read the thousands of novels and write summaries, plot data points, file reports. The theorist, combining the hundreds of reports (already a significant feat of reading), will be in a position to work out the laws of world literature, "without a single direct textual reading" ("Conjectures" 57). Moretti is unconcerned by the possibility that any of these local experts might be wrong about the primary texts, and thus infect the higher-level discussion with error (61); the concord of the multitude will serve as proof that the analyses are globally correct.

What seems here a protocol for research is actually a social experiment designed to mirror one understanding of how world literature works. World literature, in this model, is a process of diffusion whereby cultural forms are exported from a center to various marginal areas and thence re-exported to the center, having acquired new connotations in the course of their sojourn. In what terms are the locally knowledgeable reporters, the close readers, to report on the works of fiction? Are not terms (even the most abstract: period, genre, form, sequence, narrator, autodiegesis, *fabula*, *sjuzhet* ...) loaded with implications? But if the test for the accuracy of the local reportage is the degree to which it mirrors the overall picture, it seems that there is no role for exceptions to play, except that of indices of "national one-sidedness" or obstacles to circulation.

"World Literature" is one of those concepts that, without examples, is inane; but once it has begun to be understood through examples, it runs the risk of becoming hostage to this or that prestigious example. So the only way to make progress in understanding the phenomenon to which the phrase refers is to keep on adding concepts, letting them cancel out or reinforce the influence that they may severally have on the general concept. Choosing the core example of a program of research or teaching in "world literature" may be the most significant intervention the researcher makes. But that example must be followed with others, the more challenging and resistant the better.

The usual example around which "world literature" is theorized, the modern novel, conforms to the expected pattern: originating in Europe, it is carried to Africa, to Asia, to the Middle East, by colonial bureaucracies or by indigenous intellectual reformers. But this is to define "novel" in a curiously tautologous way. Not that the long prose fictions of China (to turn back to Goethe's example) or Japan are necessarily members of precisely the same set as European novels post-1750; that would be to make nonsense of cultural specificity; but the very existence of these fictions compels us to rethink our inherited definitions, to make room in our cosmology for these new planets, just as the nineteenth-century Chinese and Japanese intellectuals were compelled to entertain the thought that the peoples of Europe and the Americas had, independently, come up with texts that read very much like a *xiaoshuo* or a *shôsetsu*.

Another reason to question the privilege of the diffusion of the European novel as the type-case is the fact that this pattern of diffusion is often said to correlate with, or be explained by, the "world-systems" economic history of Immanuel Wallerstein (see Chapter 2). The "world-system" is the gradually achieved weaving of all human societies into one capitalistic network, a process begun in the late Middle Ages with the capitalization of agriculture, and only now reaching completion. If the "world" in "world literature" is Wallerstein's world, it will tend to track processes of European empire-building—certainly an important chapter in the history of the world, but not the whole of it. Sheldon Pollock's history of Sanskrit and neo-Sanskrit literature, propagating its way across Southeast Asia, includes European empires only as a footnote and a methodological obstacle. Janet Abu-Lughod's reconstruction of a medieval world-system has not one hegemonic "core" but a "relative balance of multiple centers" and "many zones of subsistence untouched by the cores" (371–72). Both these descriptions are consciously designed to counter the seemingly irresistible argument of the formation of the single "world market." And indeed accounts of "world literature" can be drawn from such histories as Pollock's and Abu-Lughod's: complex, explanatorily powerful, and descriptively persuasive accounts that make for different understandings of what "literature" is and does. There are many histories of the world, just as there have been many networks of literary creation and influence. The issue is how to adopt a point of view without allowing it to obliterate other points of view.

Acculturation, transculturation, globalization

The Europe-derived empires of the modern period differed from earlier empires (Egyptian, Babylonian, Persian, Chinese, Roman, Mayan, Mongol, Ottoman, Manchu, and so forth) in their efforts to present their colonization as a "civilizing mission" to be achieved through education. A new professional specialization arose, that of the district officers or middle managers who positioned themselves between the "natives" and the metropolitan authorities: they resolved disputes, carried out infrastructure projects, organized public services, collected taxes, suppressed rebellions, and sent reports on local conditions back to their superiors. (One such mediator, Sir Edward Jones, stumbled on the kinship of the languages of Europe and India, a discovery that founded nineteenth-century comparative linguistics.) The frequent strategy of seeking cooperation with local élites resulted in the formation of a class of "natives" who possessed authority, and owed loyalty both to their home civilizations and to that of the colonizers. The "*évolués*," as the French called this class of educated colonial subjects, were in a complex position, all the more so in that many of them moved into resistance once decolonization became a foreseeable outcome. Such people were living as interpreters, comfortably or uncomfortably, between two cultures.

Simultaneously with the European expansion into the Americas, Asia, and Africa, a new discipline arose, first suggested by writers such as Bartolomé de las Casas, Michel de Montaigne, Denis Diderot, and the Abbé de Raynal. From the observation of different ways of life (many of them in the process of extinction) and a skepticism about the correctness of European ways, these writers adumbrated a method that would become institutionalized as cultural anthropology (Tylor). One of the questions that anthropologists debated was whether "acculturation," the full adoption of a culture other than that into which one had been born, was possible or desirable (Herskovits; Malinowski). Finding that "acculturation," "diffusion," "assimilation," and similar terms always biased cultural exchange in a unipolar direction—making one culture the giver and the other culture the recipient—the Cuban ethnographer, musicologist, and historian Fernando Ortiz proposed a new term, "transculturation," as better expressing

> the different phases of the process of transition from one culture to another because this does not consist merely in acquiring another culture, which is what the English word *acculturation* really implies, but in the process also necessarily involves the loss or uprooting of a previous culture, which could be defined as a deculturation. In addition it carries the idea of the consequent creation of new cultural phenomena
>
> (Ortiz 102–03)

Ortiz explained numberless phenomena of Cuban life, from cigar smoking to musical melody, as consequences of transculturation; and by now the same could be done for practically every population in the world, as interchanges and interdependence leave no nation or culture untouched (for an overview of the effects of globalization since 1945, see Iriye 681–814).

As Ortiz insisted, it is the production of new practices, concepts, values, and identities, which could not have been foreseen by members of the predecessor cultures, that distinguishes transculturation. The concept is worth keeping in mind as a corrective to the facile categorizing of works, authors, languages, and practices as belonging to this or that culture. A longer historical view will show any culture as having emerged from a transcultural process, as do, for that matter, works and genres of literature. Comparatists are better situated than members of other literary disciplines to trace these lines of mixed descent (see Pratt). In a historical and culturally alert view, world literature certainly cannot be confused with an average or minimum of cultural specificity, or with a cultural production aimed at a uniform "world market."

The content of world literature?

Can the "literary world-system" be framed in terms other than those offered by Goethe, Marx, Brandes, and their more recent epigones? If not the novel and if not European expansion, what might be the content of "world literature"? Accounts centered on different kinds of literary object will yield different chronologies, different geographies, different means of diffusion. Take the fable with talking animals: by virtue of its multicultural spread and typological influence, it has at least as good a right as the novel to be chosen as the foundation of world literature. A geography of beast-fable literature might center on ancient India and spread to Iceland on one side and Borneo on the other, enveloping Europe as a mere afterthought. As philologists and poets have known for centuries, Aesop's fables are adaptations from the *Panchatantra*, as are core texts in Persian and Arabic literatures; retranslations and readaptations over the centuries have resulted in a tangled skein of literary history, but with a recognizable leading thread.

Poetry, it is often said, resists translation. But the forms of poetry are notoriously contagious, especially when allied to music. A history of poetic end-rhyme might begin in ancient China, where the bronze inscriptions and dynastic hymns of the Zhou turned increasingly, over the period 1200–400 BCE, to rhyming lines of equal length arranged in four-line stanzas. A form of densely allusive poetry with recurrent verses and rhymes, the *pantun,* seems to have been carried centuries ago from the Malay archipelago to Madagascar, where it is known as *hain-teny*. It was taken up in nineteenth-century European poetry (as *pantoum*) from philological descriptions. In such transactions, it is unlikely that much of the content migrates with the form; but perhaps the form generates an appropriate content in each new place and language to which it comes. Often, too, new poetic forms are generated out of the contact between languages (Mair and Mei).

To take animal fable or poetic form as the core of a world literary history, however, would mean discarding the units of account by which we are used to evaluating literary notoriety: the author, the work, the nation. As in linguistics, as in folklore or comparative mythology, our attention would have to be drawn to a replicating bundle of features always on the move and ceaselessly changing. The text at hand, in these disciplines, is only an index. Close reading does not exaggerate the text's uniqueness, but seeks to reveal the importance of a detail by noting its recurrence, survival, or regular patterns of change.

Brandes, in answering the question about world literature, thought "in the first place of the works of discoverers and inventors in the natural sciences. The writings of Pasteur, Darwin, Bunsen or Helmholtz certainly belong to world literature; they apply directly to the human race and enrich humanity as a whole" (62). These examples may seem off-topic; of the four, probably only Darwin is much read in the original today, though the discoveries of each now belong to common knowledge. But rather than leaning on some 200 years' idiomatic precedent and restricting "literature" to the field of *belles-lettres*, we could learn from the history of scientific diffusion. Indeed, if circulation is the test, the works of natural scientists, when evaluated for the speed with which they travel and make themselves at home in the remotest cultures and languages, are, as Brandes pointed out, the most successful kind of world literature. This kind of writing has, moreover, most completely bent to the requirements of the one world market for attention: standardized in format, nearly anonymous, usually written in the one dominant language, scientific papers offer little in the way of local color. (For observations on the anonymity of scientific authorship as contrasted with the individuality of literary authorship, see Foucault; but these distinctions are by no means necessary or permanent.) A technological discovery is not important because of its author, or because of its range of diffusion, but because of the effects it has. Witness

> those three [inventions] which were unknown to the ancients, and of which the origin, though recent, is obscure and inglorious; namely, printing, gunpowder, and the magnet. For these three have changed the whole face and state of things throughout the world; the first in literature, the second in warfare, the third in navigation; whence have followed innumerable changes, insomuch that no empire, no sect, no star seems to have exerted greater power and influence in human affairs than these mechanical discoveries.
>
> *(Bacon 300)*

What if we thought of a literary work as a discovery—even as a "mechanical [or scientific] discovery"? If considered as elements of the same world literature that contains Pasteur, Darwin, and Edison, poems, plays, and fictions would begin to look like something other than objects of aesthetic appreciation. A literary invention would be recognizable as such by its capacity to stand as a model for future writing (here the Moretti model of imported form and local content could be given more specific shape, and Moretti's chronicle of the invention of the detective story put to wider use). They could be proofs-of-concept in the exploration of new ways of being human. In either case, they would now be seen as useful precedents for reiteration—a formula that would apply as well to the poetic forms transiting across borders of language and custom. If folklore and mythology give us a vision of world literature as an atlas of migrating themes, and the history of poetic devices gives us a vision of world literature as a bestiary of migrating forms, the migration of one of these internationally received models would combine both pathways. Kenneth Burke had a sense of works of art answering social and cognitive needs. It is perhaps he who can help us think about a world marketplace of literature not simply as a forum where tokens are exchanged, but as a place where needs are met, often from unforeseen suppliers.

> A work like *Madame Bovary* [...] is the strategic naming of a situation. It singles out a pattern of experience that is sufficiently representative of our social structure, that recurs sufficiently often *mutatis mutandis*, for people to "need a word for it" and to adopt an attitude towards it. Each work of art is the addition of a word to an informal dictionary.
>
> *(Burke 259)*

To see these "words" and their "situations" migrate to and from the farthest limits of their diffusion in space and time requires a special sharpening of the comparatist's optic. The history of literature should be a history not only of authors, works, and movements, but of the discovery and adaptive use by readers of such "equipment for living."

from reader's perspective

5

COMPARING THEMES AND IMAGES

"Literature is by essence thematic," according to George Steiner. By this he means that any work contains a wealth of allusions to previous literature, a "shorthand" for evoking similar situations or experiences; and he takes the opportunity to lament the loss of cultural literacy and scold postmodern fiction for offering "a series of variations without a theme" ("Roncesvaux" 299–300). Steiner's implied distinction between literature and what is less than literature cannot, however, be made on the basis of thematic reference, for popular culture is just as loaded with reference as the most refined poetry. Pixar's *Wall-E* (2008) contains quotations of and homages to Kubrick's *2001* (1968), in particular a quotation of the latter's soundtrack's quotation of Richard Strauss's *Also sprach Zarathustra* (1896), a tone-poem written in reference to Friedrich Nietzsche's 1892 book of parables using the ancient prophet Zoroaster as an ironic borrowed identity. Most moviegoers recognize at least part of this network of allusion as they watch *Wall-E*, though not everyone's perception reaches as far back as Zoroaster. At other times, a cultural strategy seeks to keep the references hidden. The immense fame of Elvis Presley is built on the work of black blues artists, many of whom died penniless. Under segregation, Presley and his quotations could be received where the unacknowledged originators could not. Thus, in a mixture of adoption and denial, "race music" became "all-American rock and roll."

Identifying the theme is our primary rapport with a work of literature. We ask: "What's that book about?" We say that Flaubert's *Sentimental Education* is about the adventures of a naïve, self-centered young man in a chaotic time—and that Tutuola's *The Palm-Wine Drinkard* is about the same thing. (Of course it is never *exactly* the same thing—but close enough for purposes of comparison.) Though formalist and rhetorical analyses of literature have always advanced the claim that content is irrelevant to literary composition, that the *how* is essential and the *what* merely incidental, thematics springs incessantly back to life. Still, theme is rarely what makes a work of literature memorable as literature: in other words, the recognition and disavowal of theme follows the lines of the distinction of "literariness" from ordinary language.

Misunderstanding themes

In any case, even the simplest piece of writing has thematic strands: argument, imagery, style, situation. Thematic units—whether known as topic, myth, *leitmotiv*, symbol, image, mirage, or device—account for the coherence of a work and link it to other works. Recognition of such units is indispensable to any reading. It is when we try to build a more ambitious argument about their occurrence and function that they matter for comparative reading.

The critic I.A. Richards, while teaching English literature at Tsinghua University in Beijing in the 1920s, assigned his class Thomas Hardy's novel *Tess of the d'Urbervilles*. The novel is famous. Tess is born in a poor farming family, but her beauty catches the attention of a local landowner who seduces her and then moves on to other quarry. She marries another man who, horrified when she tells him the truth about her earlier relationship, refuses to live with her as man and wife; he goes to Brazil to start over again, leaving Tess behind. She becomes the mistress of the man who originally caused her trouble, but pushed beyond endurance by her husband's departure, she stabs the man, and is tried and found guilty of murder. It is a long novel, so it took Richards and his class months to get through to the end of the story. And when they did, in Richards's words:

> I had read aloud as clearly and slowly and eloquently as I could all the key passages. I had worked very hard, and at last I came to the last paragraph which I read aloud too. I came to the raising of the black flag to show that Tess has been hanged: "Upon the cornice of the tower a tall staff was fixed. Their eyes were riveted on it. A few minutes after the hour had struck, something moved slowly up the staff and extended itself upon the breeze. It was a black flag." At that moment my class burst into spontaneous applause, the only applause that marked the whole passage of the course. I couldn't get out the next sentence. I couldn't break through the applause. I thought, here is a chance, so I issued sheets of paper instantly and got them to say what they liked about what they had just been applauding. There it was, the great majority all agreeing together, in step. You see in their protocols what it was. Tess had been an unfilial daughter in the very beginning of the book. She hadn't treated her father with proper respect, and they had been waiting all through a very long book to see her get her due, and at the very end, that great artist, that wonderful man, Thomas Hardy, had seen that she got it: to be hanged to death—just what she deserved.
>
> (I.A. Richards, "The Future of Reading," cited in Ming 281)

How could the students have failed to catch Hardy's evident sympathy for the heroine, his piling up of adverse circumstances to make her crime understandable if not permissible? If one considers this moment in a long-ago classroom from the point of view of an English fiction specialist, the Chinese students had got it all wrong; the leading themes in their interpretation of the novel were, if anything, opposed to the themes of the novel as Hardy seems to have conceived it. But if one considers it from the point of view of the comparatist, the students' "misunderstanding" expresses a powerful cultural bias, through an interaction with the foreign work. Their encounter with Thomas Hardy, we can say, was *about* the wishes, fears, obsessions, and repressions of two different publics.

It was not just a matter of failing to get the point of a single novel; it had to do, rather, with what the students thought was the reason for writing a literary work in the first place. Meaning is contextual.[1] The object "literature" itself exists in a context. When a work written with the understanding that stories told in a tragic mode are most valuable encounters an audience whose understanding is strongly influenced by stories told in a didactic mode, the meaning of the outcome of a story like that of Tess changes: rather than the victim of her circumstances, she becomes an example of what happens to bad people.

And to take a further step, contexts are not self-evident. No one in Richards's classroom had expressed the theory that novels are supposed to convey a straightforward moral teaching; that theory was implicit, therefore inaudible, though it directed the students' reading in the most absolute way. It came out only through the response to a novel from a different tradition. And even though Chinese audiences are trained to look for a harmony between the outcomes of stories and their didactic intent, the very existence of this expectation makes it likely that, at some time, someone in China will have written against the tradition, deliberately parodying or subverting the didactic convention. If such a work exists, it will be effective because it defies its context.[2]

Parody and subversion are useful examples for undermining one assumption of old-fashioned historical comparison, that influence is a matter of debt and of "foreign trade in literature." Under that assumption, the influential work is superior to the works produced under its influence. But consider David Henry Hwang's *M. Butterfly* (1988). Though it quotes and plays on Puccini's opera *Madama Butterfly* (1904) from beginning to end, it is a violent rejection of everything the earlier work had asserted as true about men, women, the East, the West, money, power, colonialism, and so forth. To treat *M. Butterfly* as a work "under the influence" of *Madama Butterfly* would be to miss the point entirely.

National images

When people from different cultures—or, for that matter, from different villages—are in contact, they are apt to construct generalizations or "images" of the foreign personality. The French comparatist Marius-François Guyard proposed the study of such "images" (or, occasionally, "mirages") as a central task for comparative literature (Guyard 110–19). It is certainly an area where the literary criticism of stale topoi can make a social difference. Joep Leerssen has proposed to study the widespread, perhaps universal, structure of the constellations of meaning that form around the "national character" of neighboring, exotic and rival peoples.

> Amongst other Nations of the World the English are observed to have gained much, and improved themselves infinitely by voyaging both by Land and Sea, and of those four Worthies who compassed about the Terrestrial Globe, I find the major part of them were English […]
>
> One thing I would dissuade [the traveler] from [… is] the excessive commendation and magnifying of his own country […]
>
> Having passed the Pyrenees he shall palpably discern […] the suddenest and strangest difference 'twixt the Genius and Garb of two People, though distant but by a very small separation, as betwixt any other upon the surface of the Earth […] they differ not only Accidentally and Outwardly in their Clothing and Carriage, in their Diet, in their Speeches and Customs; but even Essentially in the very faculties of the Soul, and operations thereof, and in every thing else … the one is Active and Mercuriall, the other is Speculative and Saturnine; the one Quick and Airy, the other Slow and Heavy; the one Discursive and Sociable, the other Reserved and Thoughtful; the one addicts himself for the most part to the study of the Law and Canons, the other to Positive and School Divinity; […] the one apprehends and forgets quickly, the other doth both slowly, with a judgment more abstruse and better fixed […] It is a kind of sickness for a Frenchman to keep a Secret long, and all the drugs of Egypt cannot get it out of a Spaniard. […]
>
> Go to their Garb and Clothing, the one wears long hair, the other short; the one goes thin and open clad, the other close and warm […] the one goes gay without, the other underneath; the one wears his cloak long, the other short […] the Frenchman buttoneth always downward, the Spaniard upward; […] the one shuffleth the Cards better, the other plays his game more cunningly […]
>
> *(Howell 15, 19, 30–33)*

> Since Matteo Ricci entered China, the number of Europeans here has not ceased to grow. A certain Alfonso Vagnoni, living in Nanjing, did nothing but stir up the populace with the religion of the Lord of Heaven […]. They hold nighttime meetings and disperse at dawn. Their religion is no different from the [Daoist] sects of the White Lotus and Non-Action.
>
> The people who come from Italy are particularly clever, accomplished scholars. Their only intent is to spread their religion; they do not seek salary or advantage. In their books are many things that we have never encountered before, and so, for a time, those desirous of strange and new things gave them their approval.
>
> *(Zhang Tingyu 929–30)*

Though there are some points of national character, and a manner, that more or less run through all the different inhabitants of this nation [Spain], as a certain appearance of gravity, and steady equanimity of behavior, even when they are more facetious; though a sameness of taste, amusements, and passions, prevail; yet there are obviously distinct races of people. [...]

This Galicia is again a different kind of country from the last, and though a continuation of the same range of mountains, these are of a different shape, soil, and composition, and inhabited by a distinct race of people. [...]

These Gallegos seem mostly poor and ragged, are rather a small or short race of people, and have a strong resemblance to the peasantry of some of the French provinces. I fancy they are rendered short and thick by the custom of carrying burdens on their heads, particularly the women, who bear very heavy loads in that manner, and often carry the men across the rivers on their heads in a basket.

(Jardine 53–54, 55)

From such examples one sees that the country of the author is always the normal country, where things are done correctly; other nations are excessive and perverse. In the end, such comparisons—no doubt the reason behind the phrase "invidious comparisons"—send us back to the comparer; we do not take them as reliable information about the nations described.

From similarity to difference

One genre within comparative literature looks for recurrent themes or images in works from a variety of traditions. Thus the theme of a journey to the afterlife might be a common thread for linking works from any number of periods and cultures. Birds in world literature, the lover's lament, the number three—many are the topics that might lead to a catalogue, far from uninteresting, of instances. Viewed from the standpoint of similarity, the examples in the catalogue would all amount to the same thing. But viewed from the standpoint of difference, it is likely that no two examples would reveal precisely the same set of meanings, the same implications, the same function in the work where they occur; and since literature is a form of expressive behavior, scholarship owes its readers some account of the meaning of the objects it studies.

At times, it was an important aim of comparative literature to reveal the similarities among works, authors, movements, periods, and cultures. This mattered when chauvinism forbade a more cosmopolitan view of literary creation (as happened in the Soviet Union of the 1950s, when anyone who wrote about Pushkin's borrowings from Schiller or Washington Irving was sure to attract angry criticism). It matters still when a national tradition overshadows news of works from abroad (always a danger for speakers of the internationally dominant language, at the present moment English). But part of the mission of comparative literature is to create a *milieu* favorable to its cosmopolitan ambitions. Once the existence of parallels and analogies in world literature is generally admitted, the question can be raised as to how and why the similarities exist. Are they to be explained as borrowings from one and the same tradition (as E.R. Curtius showed for many of the themes and images of medieval Europe, derived from Latin writers)? Do they reflect an unchanging core of human nature (as some psychological theories suggest, with their "family romance" and their "archetypes")? Or are human beings repeatedly faced with the same problems, and thus come up again and again with similar solutions?

Some ethnographic collections are organized by geographical area—Africa in one hall, the Pacific Northwest in another, and so on. This arrangement, familiar from the Smithsonian or the Field Museum, allows the visitor to apprehend a culture as a whole through a selection of objects. But some collections, notably the Pitt-Rivers Museum in Oxford, England, are organized by task. In one area the visitor can examine dozens of types of small boats from different cultures. In another, dozens of scythes, spinning-wheels, or shoes. The needs, we see, are more or less the same, but they are satisfied using different materials, employing different tools and techniques, under different conditions of use.

Comparative literature can profitably alternate between the culturally totalizing and the functional modes in considering how to put works of verbal art in meaningful relations to one another. A Latin hymn by Prudentius reflects a great deal about the context (religious, cultural, stylistic, rhetorical, linguistic, and so forth) of its times; but if put next to a Siberian shaman-chant, their common function will become prominent.

One character in George Eliot's *Middlemarch* spends his life drafting a "Key to All Mythologies"—and is thought ridiculous for it. Few themes or images prove to have the same meanings when found in different times, places, or languages. War, love, death, journeys—just to name a few putative universals—never scan exactly the same. Beyond the establishing of basic possibilities of translation, the intercultural reader should feel that the rewards are in discovering what is different and individual about a work, not in confirming what it shares with all other works. Even where the words are, to all intents and purposes, the same, the meaning emerges from their grasp on a situation.

An example may make this point clearer. One of China's (and the world's) great novels, a vast family chronicle often thought to be a disguised autobiography, includes in its opening the following passage:

> Having made an utter failure of my life, I found myself one day, in the midst of my poverty and wretchedness, thinking about the female companions of my youth. As I went over them one by one, examining and comparing them in my mind's eye, it suddenly came over me that those slips of girls—which is all they were then—were in every way, both morally and intellectually, superior to the "grave and mustachioed signior" I am now supposed to have become. The realization brought with it an overpowering sense of shame and remorse, and for a while I was plunged in the deepest despair. There and then I resolved to make a record of all the recollections of those days I could muster—those golden days when I dressed in silk and ate delicately, when we still nestled in the protecting shadow of the Ancestors and Heaven still

smiled upon us. I resolved to tell the world how, in defiance of all my family's attempts to bring me up properly and all the warnings and advice of my friends, I had brought myself to this present wretched state, in which, having frittered away half a lifetime, I find myself without a single skill with which I could earn a decent living. I resolved that, however unsightly my own shortcomings might be, I must not, for the sake of keeping them hid, allow those wonderful girls to pass into oblivion without a memorial [...] I might lack learning and literary aptitude, but what was to prevent me from using invented speeches and rustic language to enliven the telling of a story? In this way the memorial to my beloved girls could at one and the same time serve as a source of harmless entertainment and as a warning to those who were in the same predicament as myself but who were still in need of awakening.

(Cao and Gao, The Story of the Stone *1: 20–21)*

The English-speaking reader has no trouble following the general argument. But what precisely, in the middle of the last imperial dynasty of China, a middle-aged man might have meant by using the word "failure" can only be discovered by further investigation into the examination system with its tricks, traps, and consequences; and this model of a career path implies, by tacit antithesis, the histories of those who dropped out or gave up and eventually became heroes of a Chinese counterculture— such canonical figures as Qu Yuan and Tao Yuanming; and these distinguished "failures" then evoke the similarly unusual careers of intellectual women in the late empire, who wrote and published despite their having no hope of advancement through the male-only examination system; all of which builds a gallery of types, images, and models through which the novel's principal character, for all his indivi-duality, will pass as a comparative case study. The reader who lacks this contextual information can certainly understand, follow, and sympathize, but the reader who knows more sees more. And if the reader is attempting to draw this Chinese novel into a global comparison-set that might include, say, works by Augustine, Rousseau, Proust, and Beckett, the information specific to imperial China may at first seem to be a clutter of irrelevant detail, but in the long run will underwrite a more intelligent and subtle reading of all the works in the set.

If meaning is contextual, a thoughtful comparison will not be about things or texts, but about the relation of things to their contexts that makes their meaning possible. Even when we seem to be comparing A to B, we are really trying to work out the relation of object A to its context, A′, *in relation to* the relation of object B to its context, B′. To compare Chinese landscape poetry with British landscape poetry risks dullness; but to ask what Chinese landscape poetry does or has done at different moments of that culture, and to compare the results of that query with what British landscape poetry does or has done, results in a complex group of internally linked meanings from which robust accounts of function and value, not to omit beauty, can emerge. Under such conditions as these, Richards's experience in the classroom could never be accounted a failure.

Yet many programs of research in our area still seek to establish invariant, universal laws. Nineteenth-century theories of rhythm traced our pleasure in poetry to physiological constants; sociological theories of literature tried to situate every work in the evolution of its society as part of an overall deterministic plan for the human race's movement through a set of stages; today, neuroscience holds out the temptation of an explanation of literature through brain function (Bortolussi and Dixon; Cooke and Turner; Crane; Hogan; Spolsky; Wolf; Zunshine). For such approaches as these, showing how two things are similar is a step on the path of progress. Science necessarily generalizes and trims away detail on the way to framing laws of nature. The ambitious comparatist, however, should be wary of filtering out the specific, idiomatic features of a text in order to make it fit within a determined schema.

Pursuing similarity, but using similarity as a starting point for discovering what is different, orients a comparative project toward close reading and yet includes, via similarity, the necessary move away from mere description toward explanation. If I have discovered a similarity, I now have the task of explaining why this similarity matters, what causes it, what its effects are, and what we might learn from it for future observations. Likewise, an analogy does not reduce one thing to another—as would happen if our ultimate question were "Is this the same as that?"—but asks rather, "What can this tell us about that?" The form of this second question makes a space for polyglottism, multidisciplinarity, scholarly collaboration—the very dimensions into which more and more of the comparative enterprise is likely to shift.

Thematics as thematization

Thematic approaches to literature generally have to withstand a charge that they are simplistic and superficial. If literature consists of a "form" enveloping a "content" (as people often say, schematically), then to pull out the "content" means breaking the form, and that means abandoning the integrity of the artwork. But at least since Aristotle, people have known that a beautiful work of art can be made that represents things ugly or disgusting in themselves—just as a beautiful person, poorly represented, makes for an ugly picture. The dissatisfaction with thematic reading is a concern for the aspects of the work that cannot be inventoried among its "content."

But in response it must be said that the contents of a work of art (even of a newspaper story) represent a choice from a much larger set of potential contents. A theme is something that an author (or a collective tradition) has chosen to thematize, that is, to put at the center of attention. When John Donne, ever the witty seducer, bemoans his imminent departure for the front in these words:

> Long voyages are long consumptions,
> And ships are carts for executions.
> Yea, they are deaths; is it not all one to fly
> Into another world, as 'tis to die?
> Thine arms imprison me, and mine arms thee;

Thy heart my ransom is; take mine for me.
Other men war that they their rest may gain,
But we will rest that we may fight again.
Those wars the ignorant, these the experienced love,
There we are always under, here above.
There Engines far off breed a just true fear,
Near thrusts, pikes, stabs, yea, bullets hurt not here [...]

("Elegy: Love's War," Donne 126–27)

we see his decision to thread together military and sexual languages as a play on our attention: he distracts himself and us from the war to which he is summoned by making it the analog of the sexual exercises he would prefer to conduct, and makes the sexual plot all the more vivid, the more details he can pilfer from the vocabulary of fighting: the reader has to pause and imagine what the bedroom equivalents of "near thrusts, pikes, stabs, yea, bullets" must be. The choice to treat love and war as converging, rather than mutually exclusive, themes creates the poem's drama, wit, and individuality.

Not that the combination of love and war was unprecedented; indeed, it is part of European literature since Homer. Donne simply works out an area of the theme that Virgil or Petrarch had left incomplete. Curtius's history of medieval literature as a series of expansions and variations on classical themes (into which this example from Donne could well have been integrated) seeks out such opportunities to show twenty centuries of European literature as a fundamental unity, with a particular and recurrent fondness for the theme of Nature, whether shown as goddess, as potential and fruitfulness, or as the ideal landscape. Curtius's reader sees this insistent choice as Curtius's thematization of the desire for wholeness that animates the whole book. This critical theme gives it, when compared with other masterpieces of mid-twentieth-century scholarship, an archaic and absurdly innocent tone.

Thematic material, then, is not simply the "stuff" of which literature is made, as clay is the stuff of which pottery is made, but commands attention, shapes the imagined world into a world made of *these* possibilities, implies structure and consequence. Just as a house made of brick will take a different shape and weather differently from a house made of wood, so too a poem built around the "love and war" topos will go in different directions from a poem following the Platonic identification of beauty and truth. By choosing to have so large a part of his history revolve around images of Nature, Curtius excluded a possible history that might have given the leading role to images of artifice, or of chaos, or of conflict.

Moreover, for modern people at least, theme is not simply a matter of inventorying—of what is "in" the text, of what it "has" in common with other texts. In a famous self-analytic moment, Freud found himself unable to remember the name of a painter of the Italian Renaissance, because the painter's name echoed words that had painful associations for him (Freud 5–11). By blocking out words having any resemblance to the dangerous terms, Freud's unconscious was able to keep the peace. But forgetting, just like slips of the tongue, sooner or later becomes obvious and distracting, and brings the suppressed themes back into consciousness. The "athematization" (if we may call it so) of the taboo ideas led to their commanding an even greater part of the mind than they might have done if they had been allowed to be acknowledged, to become thematic.

In a similar way, Edward Said focuses attention on something that previous readers of Jane Austen's *Mansfield Park* had treated as unimportant, the "incidental" and "passing" references to Sir Thomas Bertram's ownership of an estate in Antigua. Austen is often treated as a chronicler of drawing rooms and a tightly enclosed society, suitable for charming Hollywood treatments, and her hints of the style in which Sir Thomas manages his slave plantation are discreet; but their very faintness, under Said's gaze, ensures that they will reveal the degree to which the plantation system is taken for granted by every well-to-do English person: "no matter how isolated and insulated the English place (e.g., Mansfield Park), it requires overseas sustenance" (*Culture* 89). After this rereading, it is fair to say, no one can enumerate the themes of *Mansfield Park* in quite the same way as before. *Mansfield Park* is now about slavery and absentee ownership, along with its more conventionally recognized themes.

Thematization, then, is an operation on meanings dormant in language, in society, in culture, performed by authors and also by readers. The alert reader detects patterns of association or exclusion that give the themes of a work their active role in generating new meanings. With this aim, thematic reading cannot be put aside as mere positivistic *Stoffgeschichte*.

Notes

1 An utterance "becomes only intelligible when it is placed within its *context of situation* [...] the conception of context must be substantially widened [...] In fact it must burst the bonds of mere linguistics and be carried over into the analysis of the general conditions under which a language is spoken" (Bronislaw Malinowski, cited in Ogden and Richards 306; italics in original).

2 Examples of such subversive works include Li Yu (attr.), *Rou pu tuan* (1657; *The Carnal Prayer Mat*) and Cao Xueqin, *Honglou meng* (*ca.* 1750; *The Story of the Stone*).

6

COMPARATIVE LITERATURE AND TRANSLATION

If comparative literature is an account of the "foreign trade of literatures" (Wellek, "The Crisis" 163), translation is one thing it cannot do without. For by "foreign trade" we mean especially borrowings and exports to and from other languages. Does a Spaniard think of Borges or Cortázar as *foreign* writers? I suppose not, nor do English-language readers require a translator's help in appreciating the work of most Australian or American writers. *Most*, but not all, for within a single widely diffused language like English or Spanish there is a central zone of easy accessibility, and many regional, historical, professional, class, or ethnic dialects. By force of habit and exposure, Chaucer's English is easier for most readers today than his contemporary the Pearl Poet's, and a film set in Scotland or Mississippi may add subtitles for the benefit of its viewers who are accustomed to a standard variety of English. The necessity of such translation *within* a single language alerts us to the fact that the boundaries of any language are not clean lines, but gray zones. "As there are no precise boundaries between languages, [there can be] no [precise] subdivisions among the dialects of these languages [...] From the moment that there are only open dialects, formed by adding together the waves [of linguistic variation] in which they participate, there are no closed languages" (Saussure, *Cours de linguistique* 462; our translation).

Nonetheless, comparative literature has always understood itself to be concerned primarily with the relations among literatures of *different* languages. Its founding principle is that literary traditions are different, just as languages are, and the act of comparison comes to bridge their differences, as the act of translation bridges the differences among languages. Contributing to this self-definition of comparison as cultural translation were the political conditions of the period of the discipline's formation, the early nineteenth century, when a "literature" was supposed to be the shared possession of the speakers of a single language and thus, at least in aspiration, the cultural heritage of a single nation. (The careers of the romantic poets of subordinated nations—Mickiewicz in Poland, Petöfi in Hungary—confirm the rule. They consolidated a cultural heritage for their new national audiences.) Since most university-educated Europeans in the nineteenth century had a mastery of two or three languages (usually their own, plus Latin, and then French, German, or English), writers could be expected to find their international influences on their own, without the help of scholars. For example, in some of his late poems, Shelley imitates Dante in form and matter; Pushkin rewrites a poem by Horace; Baudelaire translates Poe, De Quincey, and Emerson. Today, with the growth of translated literature, Coetzee may write a novel about Dostoyevsky, Octavio Paz may dedicate poems to Wang Wei, and Haruki Murakami's novels can assume a detailed knowledge of Mozart's *Magic Flute* and Kerouac's *On the Road*. This is the ordinary cosmopolitanism of literature, whether vehicled by translation or through acquaintance with the original languages.

The (in)visibility of translation

Many of the most influential works in any tradition are translations, not "native" compositions. English literature cannot be imagined without the King James Bible (1611), the *Arabian Nights* (translated in 1706, 1859, 1885, etc.), *Don Quixote* (translated by Shelton, 1612; Smollett, 1755, etc.), the *Grimm Brothers' Fairy Tales* (1823), or the *Rubáiyát of Omar Khayyam* (translated by Edward Fitzgerald, 1859, 1868), to mention just a few of the works that are taken for granted as part of the linguistic and cultural background of everyone who uses English. Translations enrich and enlarge every culture.

We usually forget translators' names. If the goal of translating is to efface itself, to let the work being translated appear as if for the first time in the language of the translation, by forgetting them we do the translators honor and acknowledge their success, but at the cost of losing the actual history of the circulation of works and ideas. Lawrence Venuti has attempted to reverse this habit of "the translator's invisibility." Translators are not invisible by nature, but we expect them to create for us the illusion that we are in direct contact with the author: who would not prefer Lev Tolstoy's company to Constance Garnett's? If Constance Garnett makes herself too visible, we blame her translation as unidiomatic, stilted, laden with errors and paraphrases, and the like. But the truth of the matter is that, in reading a translation of Tolstoy, we are always reading someone's report on what Tolstoy said, formulated in the terms and with the preoccupations of the translator's own times: Victorian Britain in Constance Garnett's case, the US of our day in that of the translating duo Richard Pevear and Larissa Volokhonsky. Thus, despite dreams of a "definitive" translation, translations have to be redone every generation or two.

Why should the work of translators not be honored as poetic craft and brought to the front of the stage, rather than kept behind the curtain? Venuti suggests that translations should "foreignize" the language in which they are written, rather than "nativizing" the thoughts and expressions of the foreign author. Rather than "moving the writer closer to the reader," translators should "move the reader closer to the writer," as Venuti puts it, reusing a formulation of the German theologian and translator Friedrich Schleiermacher (*The Translator's Invisibility* 49).

Making translation visible has a cost. The reader can now no longer overlook the fact that he or she is reading a mediated, second-hand text, and may be led to question the accuracy of the rendition or the competence of the translator—or to do so more impatiently than does the reader of a smooth translation, where the persuasive authority of the writing sweeps such doubts aside. A virtue in critical terms (for who, on the critical front, can resist the call to make visible the mechanisms of production?) may be a drawback in terms of popular reception or aesthetic enjoyment. Novelists seeking entry into the English-speaking literary world (as it is set up at present, at least) would be justified in worrying if their translators chose to "foreignize" their works, for that is a sure way to drive away conventional readers. Poets, whose readers are perhaps readier to confront strange uses of language, may be less automatically suspicious of the choice to foreground the labor of translation. Where there are prejudices to counter, a smooth translation may be fairer (in an ethical sense) to the author than one that treats the target language too roughly and suggests that the original was itself barbaric. Compare:

> King speak: Sage! Not far thousand mile and come; also will have use gain me realm, hey?
>
> *(Whitney 331)*

> The king said, "Venerable sir, since you have not counted it far to come here, a distance over a thousand *li*, may I presume that you are provided with [counsels] to profit my kingdom?"
>
> *(Legge 124)*

Given the sentiments current in the English-speaking world about China and the Chinese in the later nineteenth century, Whitney's attempt to show, "as nearly as we can represent it" (331), the monosyllabic character of the Chinese language reads as dehumanizing, and Legge's, by contrast, as a "nativization" of the foreigner into the polite company of scholars and humanists. "Nativizing" versus "foreignizing" is not a one-dimensional issue. It always involves a context of reception.

Transduction

As the previous paragraphs with their frequent mention of trade-offs must have suggested, translation is a matter of weighing possibilities, alternatives, and consequences. Our concern in comparative literature is not particularly with the accuracy of translations, but with what they do on arrival, how a work (or even the rumor of a work) excites readers and writers in the target language. The effective history of, say, *Gargantua and Pantagruel*—the imitations it spawns, the literary behavior it licenses—is not dependent on perfect translations. Its after-effects are a kind of translation in themselves, or better yet a "transduction" (Doležel, "Literary Transduction" 167–68).

Transduction gives the best measure of a work's influence. A work with a long-enough history (say, the Homeric epics) can stimulate many epochs of "reprocessing," all differing from one another. One could say that those different modes of later reception were potentially contained in the ancient epics, but that would be no more than a half-truth: the potential had to be activated by times, languages, cultures, and ways of thinking that Homer's contemporaries could never have imagined.

Translating is always an act of comparative literary judgment. To choose a word, a sentence pattern, a tone, a genre, and so forth is to offer an analogy between two fields of culture and meaning. Like any analogy, it is bound to fail in some respects. But the worth of an analogy is what it succeeds in suggesting.

An example

Moby Dick has been translated into French at least four times in the past seventy years. The earliest version (1939), by the novelist Jean Giono and two collaborators, is known for being the freest, and also often the briefest. Numerous critics have blamed Giono for taking liberties with the text, a complaint that, moreover, has served to justify the production of further translations (notably by Armel Guerne [1954] and Philippe Jaworski [2006]). Readers impatient with Melville's style may find Giono's version an improvement over the original. But a look at the novel's famous opening line ("Call me Ishmael."), where Giono is already diverging from the English sentence structure, shows that what is at stake is not literalness.

"Je m'appelle Ishmaël. Mettons." (Melville/Giono 1939: 1)
To retranslate: "My name's Ishmaël. Let's say." (Or: "For example"; "Why not?")

With this small linguistic gesture, Giono claims a place for Melville's novel alongside existing narratives in the French tradition of the *"récit,"* a genre that foregrounds the authorial voice and raises the question of fictionality. The *"Mettons"* puts Melville in the company of *récit*-writers such as Gide, Paulhan, Céline, Blanchot, and Giono himself. This is unlikely, transfiguring company for the nineteenth-century American author. Keeping consistency with this generic decision may have directed Giono's other choices in rendering or altering Melville's text. And these decisions make sense in the implied presence of other choices. One could imagine a translation that would seek to emulate the style and tone of Melville's contemporary Jules Verne. The result would have accommodated some obvious features of *Moby Dick* (the adventure tale, the fascination with technology, the Promethean main character) but would have left out many others. Most importantly, no doubt, for Giono, a translation in the Verne manner would have had little appeal in the literary world of 1939. *Moby Dick* would have been dead on arrival. But would a translation in the Verne style have been more "faithful" than one in the style of Céline?

This is not really a question. Translators and publics do not really have the option of faithfulness, only choices among more or less suitable "manners." Translations are pastiches. The translator's task is to make a home for the work in the new language, and there are many kinds of home to choose among.

A broad rethinking of the field of translation studies has been made possible by the work of Itamar Even-Zohar and Gideon Toury on the "literary polysystem" as a composite of works, modes, and potentials active at a given moment in a given language's literary field. We now are able to see a translated work as validated not only by its relation to the original it represents, but also by reference to norms of the "target" language and culture into which it enters. Ever since the word "intertextuality" became common currency in the 1970s, critics have been accustomed to saying that language is always citational—but this thesis tends to be articulated broadly (see Derrida "Signature événement contexte") rather than followed out in detail. Translation affords an opportunity to test this assertion in particular contexts. More recently, machine translation has taken advantage of vast collections of digitized material to establish correlations between sequences in different languages at scales greater than the individual word. Combining these three points of view—a target orientation, citationality, and large-scale plural correlations—with specific examples should lead to a better understanding of translation, at once formally more precise and culturally more suggestive.

When describing a text as a composite, a patchwork put together from bits of other texts, we often reach for such similes as the mosaic; but to represent the double perspective put forth here, we would have to add that every piece of the mosaic retains a vestigial string connecting it to its previous home in a slab of stone. Imagine, then, that by tugging on the strings we could cause the mosaic pieces to pivot between their two contexts. However technically improbable, that would be what a comparative reading of translated writing would seek to do. The words in the target language are chosen in order to activate some potential that the translator recognizes in the source language and wishes to reactivate in the new readership. Like an actor or a performer of a musical composition, the translator voices the source text, choosing one interpretation over others. Thus Giono's rendering of "Call me Ishmaël" emphasizes the narrator's command over the facts of the story, which could be entirely made-up or arbitrary, and the narrator's awareness that this is so; Guerne's rendering, "*Appelons-moi Ismahel*," suggests that the narrator and his hearers are in some way jointly responsible for the way the story develops, an implication that lacks a meaningful relation to the genre rules that Giono invokes. Yet another rendition (say, "*On m'appelle Ishmaël*") might emphasize the tragic abandonment associated with the name "Ishmaël," and lead the novel in a different direction. The choice of a single word can direct a work's "transduction."

By choosing, the translator makes determinate aspects of the text that had remained indeterminate in the original. Another example: when translating from a language such as Chinese, where singular and plural are rarely marked, into an

Indo-European language, the translator must decide if the objects named are one or many. Conversely, Indo-European languages often leave vague aspects that need to be specified in Chinese (such as which of two brothers or sisters is the elder). By contrast, American English of the mid-nineteenth century and 1930s French exhibit countless parallels in syntax, lexicon, and fields of cultural reference, even when it comes to whaling slang: that is to say, the specifications are by and large made in advance. Translating between languages that have less history in common, or that are farther apart in some other dimension of meaning, leaves more areas of indeterminacy to be filled in, possibly arbitrarily, by the translator. These indeterminacies make it hard to judge such a translation by its accuracy (sometimes there may be no mark to miss), but likewise leave the standard of appropriateness open to individual whim. If genius is (as Kant said) creativity unbounded by rules, some situations leave translators little choice but to rely on genius.

Untranslatable?

Drawing attention to the "target" side of translation—to the effect a translation has upon arrival—may seem to risk abandoning the translator's responsibility to offer a faithful and accurate version of the source. (For further exploration of the ethical connotations of "faithfulness" and related norms, see Bermann and Wood.) It may seem to promise a game in which the translator can never lose. Or to put it less positively, if translation works by citation of pre-existing texts and contexts chosen from the target environment, it appears that, in the last analysis, "nativizing" translations are the only kind—even that the "foreignizing" translations are just "nativizing" translations in thin disguise (disguised, that is, in one of the recognized codes for exoticism current in the language of arrival). But is it impossible for translations to fail? Can translations fail, not in detail and locally (as when one gets a word or an implication wrong), but globally, when two languages are deeply incommensurable? Is it not possible that two languages may be so different that no sustained translation from one into the other will accurately represent the content to be translated? Are not some things generally held to be untranslatable? And if so, should not comparative literature, as the theory of literary translatability, declare itself incapable of following the objects of its interest when they cross into such a terrain?

The word "untranslatable" is used to mean different things, sometimes with tacit implications. When someone says that a word of a certain language "cannot be translated" into English, one can always ask why, and get in return a description of the nuances, the specifics, the implications that the word carries in its own language. The description is, then, a translation, or at least a paraphrase, so translation was in some degree possible (cf. Davidson, "A Nice Derangement"; "On the Very Idea"); what was impossible is, perhaps, translation of the foreign word into a single equivalent English word. Likewise, if a pun, a book title, a line of verse, or the like is said to be untranslatable, it too can be explained, only not rendered in a form quantitatively analogous to the original's. It is worth remembering that in translating we are not always constrained, as opera singers are, to get across the meaning with exactly the same notes. The requirement that translations be equivalent in outer form puts exceptional demands on translators, some of whom, much of the time, are able to fulfill them. But for the theory of translation, the demand of formal equivalence is insufficiently motivated. Where incommensurability might seem to pose the greatest danger—that is, in translating between languages with little shared history and few precedent translations—indeterminacy is also greatest, making it almost certain that the person who uncovers an incommensurability will be the person taking the first steps to solve it. Translating the word for "ale" as "wine" might be a mistake in some circumstances (minding a bar, for example), but might be appropriate in others where it is desirable to signal something like the upper-crust connotations of "wine" (see Liu, *The Art* 59). Rendering it as "alcoholic liquor otherwise unspecified" preserves a slice of indeterminacy large enough to at least save the translation from incorrectness, though it would utterly lack the vivid reference of the original. When we hear talk of incommensurability, it is usually a matter analogous to "wine" being replaced by "ale" and the customer feeling cheated. But as Davidson would point out, the fact that there is enough concord on the difference between the two is a precondition for the problem of reference being straightened out: disagreement, not incommensurability ("A Nice Derangement").

At least in the US, the difference between comparative literature and world literature comes down to translation. Scholars of comparative literature pride themselves on reading works in their original languages, for reasons both of critical probity (one can't just take a translator's word at face value) and of the need to distinguish their enterprise from that of World Literature in English Translation. But the insistence on language mastery yields to calculations of what is feasible or advisable. Early in the history of the field, the standard of language attainment could be upheld because the great majority of scholars (in the US at any rate) were comparing works written in the major, familiar, European languages. The rare comparatist with an interest in Japanese, Chinese, Arabic, Sanskrit, or the like would have acquired the European languages as well. Multiculturalism, when it came in the 1980s, encouraged the criticism that the language requirements of comparative literature were both geographically provincial and intellectually élitist. In response, leading figures in the field recommended that works in non-European languages, read in translation, could be made part of the comparatist's stock-in-trade ("Bernheimer Report" 44). This solution allowed élitism to be hidden away, that is, reinscribed in the syllabus: there were languages worth knowing, and there were languages worth knowing about. A more thorough response to the lopsided development of topics of comparative research in different linguistic and cultural areas would insist on the value of primary texts, in whatever language, and particularly those texts written in remoter, older, more difficult, or institutionally fossilized forms of a language, for it is these that pose the greatest challenges to translation. Their challenges to cultural appropriation are even greater. A novel by Banana Yoshimoto needs no strenuous mediation for North American readers—it has already appropriated itself. A Vedic hymn that has given rise to a dozen discrepant understandings over the centuries will take the reader farther off the beaten path.

World Literature has often asserted—*pour les besoins de la cause*—the availability, which is to say the translatability, of all literature for the properly situated observer. Those for whom creation in foreign languages is not just a document of World Literature in the waiting may insist on the irreplaceable poetry of the original and its loss in translation. "Severed from place, thrown into the maw of the global culture industry or survey course, and subject to pedagogical transmission by instructors with low levels of cultural literacy and nonexistent knowledge of a translated work's original language, local or native literature relinquishes its self-defining properties once it is exported and trafficked like an artifact" (Apter 326). What resists being "severed," "exported," and "trafficked," what must be protected from "the entrepreneurial, bulimic drive to anthologize and curricularize the world's cultural resources" (3), is the intrinsic, the idiomatically Untranslatable. What word in any language but Russian can take the place of *pravda* (33–34)? Where but in Walter Benjamin can we seek the meaning of the *Jetztzeit* (66)? "There is a quality of militant semiotic intransigence attached to the Untranslatable," says Apter (34), a quality that should result in "a politics of literature critical of global literary management within corporate education" (16). One might, however, with no less justification, make translation the analog of cosmopolitan openness, or nomadic flight, as against tyrannical autarkies. Arguments that might furnish a basis, in EU trade negotiations, for protecting the *"appellation contrôlée"* of champagne or Pont l'Évêque have also been used to assert the uniqueness of this or that country's culture and political system, sealing them off from outsiders' concern. American, Japanese, German, Chinese, Russian (etc.) exceptionalisms all have a dubious past.

For Apter, the value of universal translation is commercial, and that of non-translatability the contrary of commerce: home, identity, the sacred. "The difficulty remains concerning how to take sacral untranslatability at its word without secularist condescension" (14). But the very accounts (sometimes philologically questionable) offered on behalf of the Untranslatable to demonstrate how the keywords of a particular language and time remain indissolubly rooted in the situation of their emergence are, in English, French, or whatever medium paraphrases, citations, and translations. To call something Untranslatable is all very well, but the moment one has begun to explain why it is so, one has begun to move it over into the translation zone. An acceptance of the inevitability of translation would have allowed for a more precise characterization of the so-called Untranslatables. For these are not simply terms intrinsic to a particular language; they get their name as a result of multiple attempted, but not perfectly successful, acts of translation, acts that leave a remainder that is itself available to description (Cassin). There is nothing sacral about them, if by that term we mean whole and immune to the workings of substitution.

Perhaps the fiction of the Untranslatable should not be taken as referring to what *cannot* be translated, but masks a distinction between what *has not been* translated (yet or successfully) and what *is not being* translated, a difference at least open to empirical study. When foreign words appear in a text, they make it macaronic: a mixture, a multiple. The act being performed by the macaronic writer is not one of translation, but of transcription, inscription, or imposition, little different from inventing a new word. "Paris rawly waking […] In Rodot's Yvonne and Madeleine newmake their tumbled beauties, shattering with gold teeth chaussons of pastry, their mouths yellowed with the pus of flan breton" (Joyce 42). The words "chausson" and "flan breton" are indissociable, it seems, from the Parisian experiences Stephen Dedalus is recalling, and they appear here in French as synecdoches of France. Citing them here is, precisely, not a translation, but a bypassing of translation. It is not that no equivalent could ever be found for the two terms (the dictionary proffers "popover" and "custard"), but Stephen prefers not to.

Non-translation, the extreme of "foreignization," does more violence to the target language than even rough translation. In some literary traditions, the greatest influences are wielded by a non-native work that retains its original language, as witness the classical-Arabic *Quran* in Persian, Turkish, Urdu, and Malay cultures. Medieval European literature can hardly be discussed without its Latin models (Curtius). Diglossia, as this condition is called, assumes knowledge of at least two languages whose relationship, as mediated by social action and context, may never allow them to be found in the same utterance. Diglossia puts certain realms of language outside—usually above—ordinary speech. If diglossia is stratifying, its counterpart, macaronic, installs a carnival, mixing sacred and profane (Bakhtin). Sometimes, as in Rabelais, the macaronic diglossia works to make the inferior language (French) a sarcastic commentary on the superior one (Latin):

> Et [Pantagruel] trouva la librairie de sainct Victor fort magnifique, mesmement d'aulcuns livres qu'il y trouva, comme Bigua salutis, Bragueta iuris, Pantoufla decretorum, Malogranatum viciorum, Le Peloton de theologie […] Le moustardier de penitence, Les Houseaulx, alias les bottes de patience, Formicarium artium.
>
> *(Rabelais, Œuvres 195–96)*

> In his abode there [Pantagruel] found the library of St. Victor a very stately and magnific one, especially in some books which were there, of which followeth the Repertory and Catalogue. Et primo, The for Godsake of Salvation. The Codpiece of the Law. The Slipshoe of the Decretals. The Pomegranate of Vice. The Clew-bottom of Theology […] The Mustard-pot of Penance. The Gamashes, alias the Boots of Patience. Formicarium artium.
>
> *(Rabelais, Gargantua 200–01)*

Here vernacular and Latin, vulgar and erudite, are mashed together joyously. Yet the poetic effect of their combination depends on the two registers being kept distinct, in the reader's mind if not on the page.

Macaronic writing accelerates the process of mixing at work in all languages over time. The French and Latin that noble houses, law courts, churches, and universities used in medieval England sank into the vocabulary of the common language; Chinese adopted words from neighbors, conquerors, and Buddhist missionaries;

contemporary Japanese is extraordinarily hospitable to words from elsewhere. Diglossia maintained over time turns into macaronics, into creolity (Bernabé, Chamoiseau, and Confiant). Indeed, we are writing these pages in a kind of macaronic—in an English that has been enriched by borrowings, echoes, calques, misunderstandings from abroad. To think for too long about macaronics and creoles causes one to doubt that *languages*, those poles between which translation is supposed to occur, exist. Perhaps between any two languages there is a zone of mutual borrowing, a zone where translation is superfluous or always erroneous. Perhaps "pure" Arabic, Chinese, and the like exist somewhere, but as regions notably poor in semiotic exchange. We must, if this view of the macaronic has any basis, be willing to discard our mental maps of languages occupying, without differentiation, a bounded territory. Languages are, rather, always overlaid, locked in struggles for dominance, fragmenting, occasionally brought to musical and political harmony.

The existence of translations should never be an excuse for maintaining monolingualism. On the map of comparative literature, monolingualism is a blank. Through attention to multilingualism, code-mixing, and creolity, comparatists can make translation something other than a connector between two blank zones.

7
COMPARATIVE LITERARY HISTORY

At the nineteenth-century French origins of comparative literature as a discipline, some of its practitioners advocated calling it the "comparative history of literatures." Jean-Jacques Ampère, for instance, in his speech at the Athénée de Marseille (12 March 1830), argued that "literary science" (*la science littéraire*) is made up of two branches, namely, "literary philosophy" (*philosophie de la littérature*)—what we call today "literary theory"—and "history of literature" (*histoire de la littérature*) (*De l'histoire* 7). As for the latter's methodology, Ampère distinguishes two methods—comparison and filiation. Comparison is "a method for highlighting the key features of literary works with the help of parallels and contrasts." Filiation, in its turn, is a "closer bond" (*un rapport plus intime*) whereby literary works "are linked to one another due to the fact of their production: works produce other works down through the centuries" (*De l'histoire* 30, 31). Once these methods are applied, literary history stops being both "a catalogue of publications and a collection of anecdotes" (14) and a classification of writers and works according to their position in time (33), to turn into *comparative* history (*histoire comparative*; 8).

Broadly speaking, one may say that Ampère's description of literary history covers what we call today "comparative literature," whereas "comparative literary history" is a distinctive field within the former. What is comparative literary history, then? In *La Littérature comparée* (1931), Paul Van Tieghem stated that the distinctiveness of comparative literary history—which he calls "international literary history" (*l'histoire littéraire internationale*)—lies in its content and organization. As for content, international literary history challenges national canons inasmuch as writers considered "secondary" in their national traditions may play a key role within the international scene.[1] As for organization, international literary history should adopt a "rational order" (*un ordre rationnel*), which may stem from either long periods (*grandes périodes*) or literary areas that in a specific sequence of time contribute to the development of a topic, style, genre, movement, etc. (205–07). Alas, for Van Tieghem (200), international literary history is a field within "general literature" (*littérature générale*), and not within comparative literature.[2]

More recently, Claudio Guillén has argued that "historiology" is a research field proper of comparative literature, for "[t]he fundamental components of literary historiography, the large entities—periods, currents, schools, movements—that provide the structures, make it understandable, and order its temporal evolution, are rarely restricted to single nations" (*The Challenge* 288). Though Guillén does not provide a concise definition of comparative literary history, the following passage—attesting to a typically systems-oriented taste—is illustrative. Comparative literary history aims at following "[t]he temporal itinerary of literature [... as] a complex and selective process of growth. Literary systems evolve in a very special way, characterized by the continuity of certain components, the disappearance of others, the awakening of forgotten possibilities, the swift irruption of innovations, the tardy effect of others" (294). Clearly inspired by Guillén, Franca Sinopoli (1) gives this clear definition. "By 'comparative literary history' one commonly understands a literary history which has as its own object of study the network of interactions among several literatures."

Taking both definitions as a departure point, let us explore comparative literary history by turning to two domains. Firstly, and in a rather general way, we will approach comparative history. Interestingly, the links between comparative history and comparative literary history—though they share one and the same method— have not been established, with the result that there is little awareness of what one can learn from the other. The reason for this may lie in the fact that all-embracing approaches to comparative history—such as those of Karl Marx, Max Weber, Oswald Spengler, Arnold Toynbee, and the like—are no longer taken as seriously as they once were. Yet more nuanced forms of comparative history have become popular in recent years. Secondly, and in a more detailed way, we will examine the products of one active laboratory of comparative literary history, namely, the ICLA/ AILC's Coordinating Committee for Comparative Literary History in European Languages. Some final remarks will follow.

What can we learn from comparative history?

Many recent books include the phrase "comparative history" in their title, such as Ben-Ami Scharfstein's 1998 *A Comparative History of World Philosophy: From the Upanishads to Kant*; Laird W. Bergard's 2007 *The Comparative Histories of Slavery in Brazil, Cuba, and the United States*; and Wim Klooster's 2009 *Revolutions in the Atlantic World. A Comparative History*, to name but a few. Interestingly, none of these books provides an explanation of what "comparative history" means, as if the phrase were self-evident. The titles make clear, though, that a *comparative* history, on one hand, covers an area larger than the nation (more than one country, the Atlantic, the world) and, on the other hand, may be restricted to a single discipline or theme (philosophy, slavery, revolution), at the risk of evoking a (surely misplaced) sense of vagueness. Among the books mentioned, Scharfstein performs a comparative-historical analysis within a discipline—philosophy—whereas Bergard and Klooster perform a comparative-historical analysis to write a history of an object (revolutions, slavery). In the latter case, what we are reading is a comparative history as a specific variety of (general) history. Is literature to be treated as discipline or object by its version of "comparative history"? We shall first draw lessons for comparative literary history from the object-related version.

"History cannot be a science," said the French sociologist Émile Durkheim in 1898, "unless it provides explanations, and it cannot provide explanations unless it makes comparisons" (ii). A supporter of Durkheim's arguments, the classicist Gustave Glotz, gave a speech titled "Réflexions sur le but et la méthode de l'histoire" (Reflections on the Aim and Method of History) on the occasion of the inauguration of the chair of Greek history at the Sorbonne in 1907. In this speech, Glotz argued that history might experience extraordinary advances similar to those in other sciences only if the comparative method were applied, provided the method was used with caution. His speech was extremely influential for historians such as Henri Pirenne and Marc Bloch, the latter being the co-founder of the Annales School.

Though a longer genealogy of comparative history may be traced (see Hannick 301–21), for the purposes of this section, Bloch and his 1928 seminal essay "Pour une histoire comparée des sociétés européennes" (A Contribution towards a Comparative History of European Societies) will suffice as a starting point. Bloch—who was influenced by work in comparative linguistics—distinguished two ways historians might use comparison. But before dealing with them, it is worth reading Bloch's definition of comparison, for, as should be clear by now, it is uncommon to have a precise and unambiguous definition.

What does it mean to compare in general history?

To choose from one or several social situations, two or more phenomena which appear at first sight to offer certain analogies between them; then to trace their line of evolution, to note the likenesses and the differences, and as far as possible explain them. Thus two conditions are necessary to make a comparison, historically speaking, possible: there must be a certain similarity between the facts observed—an obvious point—and a certain dissimilarity between the situations in which they have arisen.

(Bloch 45)

As for the uses of comparison, on one hand, one may compare societies that are far removed from one another in time and/or space, as was often done in the nineteenth century (for example, in Giuseppe Ferrari's chronological pairing of Chinese and European societies, or Bachofen's reconstruction of a primordial matriarchy). This use of comparison, which Bloch sees as characteristic of (general) linguistics, leads the scholar to discover the "fundamental unity of the human mind" (47). On the other hand, as advocated by Bloch himself following Glotz's caveat, one may compare contemporaneous societies that are geographical neighbors and have constantly influenced each other. This kind of comparison is characteristic of historical linguistics and, though more restricted, leads to less hypothetical, more precise conclusions (47).

Bloch provides us with some examples of how comparison—in the restricted, Glotz-like sense—may be applied. Let us see one such example. Concerning fourteenth- and fifteenth-century French general/provincial assemblies (*états généraux/provinciaux*), Bloch sees that many studies have aimed at identifying the institution from which they evolved. This goal has been pursued by way of local investigations into the origins of these assemblies in Artois, Bretagne, or even the whole of France. As it is a general phenomenon with a European scope (the German *Stände*, the Italian *Parliamenti*, the Spanish *Cortes*), Bloch concludes that their origins may be traced only by applying the comparative method. "For a general phenomenon," argues Bloch, "can only be produced by equally general causes" and hence comparison alone "will be able to select from the tangle of conceivable causes those which exercised a general effect—the only real ones" (56).

The comparative research carried out by Bloch—especially his 1924 book *Les Rois thaumaturges,* a comparative study of ideas about the supernatural powers of kings in medieval England and France—was highly influential and led to a renewed interest in comparative history after the 1950s. However, its status as a sub-discipline of history is still contested, for some scholars argue there is no single method of comparison. In many cases, it is considered a genre rather than a method of history-writing, one that, at best, uses analogies, so that no previous methodological discussion is required. Furthermore, the constantly increasing demand for specialization in academia seems at odds with the wider perspective provided by comparative disciplines, including comparative history. But for the sake of clarity, let us retain this definition of comparative history.

Definition of comparative history

1. An orientation toward the study of the past, based on the use of analogies between two or more societies or periods.
2. A sub-discipline of historiography characterized by the systematic comparison of carefully defined ideas or institutions in different societies.
3. A specific method of historical explanation in which developments in one social situation are explained by comparing them to developments in other social situations.

(Ritter 55)

As stated in the introduction to this chapter, the links between comparative history and comparative literary history have not been explored, despite the fact that the former has transcended the typical objects of general history—such as economy, social structures, commerce—and reached so-called "intellectual history," of which *Les Rois thaumaturges* is again a case in point. And yet, both sub-disciplines may learn from each other.

Some lessons of comparative history

1. Comparison as method may be applied to several kinds of objects, from *états généraux/provinciaux* and the use of gold coins to landholding systems and kings with supernatural powers.

    1.1. Typically, these objects transcend the boundaries of any single social system.
    1.2. Comparison is not equal to the juxtaposition of the objects of study.
    1.3. A history can be *comparative* even though it deals with a single object, provided that comparison is used in formulating problems and explanations are comparatively tested.

       1.3.1. When applied to, at least, two different objects, there are no *a priori* rules to determine how different/similar these objects should be.

2. In contrast to nineteenth-century comparative history ("comparison in the grand manner"), contemporary comparative history in the wake of Bloch privileges comparisons of synchronic societies in contact over societies that are remote—spatially and/or temporally—from each other.

    2.1. It is implicitly stated that temporal and spatial proximity assures similarity.

3. Though initially interested in stressing similarities, comparative history progressively has oriented towards what makes distinctive an object of study.
4. Comparison as method is one thing; comparison as perspective is another. Comparison as perspective challenges ethnocentric biases.
5. Though the comparative method may be applied for distinct purposes and in different contexts, a single logic underlines these various uses—the logic of hypothesis testing.
6. Comparison may be applied only once a previous stage has been passed through, namely, the stage of painstakingly collecting evidence about minor, local facts. Comparative history cannot proceed without these previous studies with a local focus. On the other hand, the evidence by itself cannot compel general conclusions.

Experimenting with comparative literary history

In 1964, during the Fourth Conference of the Association Internationale de Littérature Comparée/International Comparative Literature Association (AILC/ICLA),

Jacques Voisine proposed the association should sponsor a *histoire comparée* with an international scope.[3] An *ad hoc* committee was created—the Coordinating Committee for the Comparative History of Literatures in European Languages—and Voisine was elected its first president. Nine years later, the first comparative literary history under the aegis of the AILC/ICLA was published, Ulrich Weisstein's *Expressionism as an International Literary Phenomenon*. Five decades after its creation, as of today the series comprises twenty-six volumes, ranging from the Renaissance to postmodern times. Due to its number of volumes, geographical scope, and timespan, the research carried out by the Committee is unparalleled when it comes to surveying what comparative literary history is.

Working papers that either set out the guidelines of the general research carried out by the Committee, or provide information on—at that time—ongoing projects, provide precious insights into comparative literary history as a field of pragmatic investigation. For the sake of simplicity, we will focus on five such papers.

The second president of the Committee, Henry H.H. Remak, was responsible for the "General Preface" of many volumes in the Comparative History of Literatures in European Languages. The "two fundamental premises" of the project are, according to Remak ("General Preface" 5), on one hand, "that the writing of literary histories confined to specific nations, peoples or languages must be complemented by the writing of literary history that coordinates related or comparable phenomena from an international point of view," and on the other hand, "that it is not possible for individual scholars to write such comprehensive histories." Three years later, and very much in the same line, the third president of the Committee, Jean Weisgerber, contributed to a collective book on literary theory with a chapter in which he described the tenets of comparative literary history by drawing on the Committee's already published volumes devoted to four fields: expressionism, symbolism, verse genres between 1760 and 1820, and the *avant-gardes* (a topic for which Weisgerber was the main editor). Firstly, Weisgerber justifies restricting the project to European languages on the grounds of the team's field of specialization, though he rejects any accusation of Eurocentrism, for the survey includes "works written in these languages by Africans and Asians" (353). Secondly, he describes the key features of the project: comparative literary histories complement rather than replace national literary histories, are carried out by teams of international scholars with an interdisciplinary training, and are eclectic in their use of literary tools. Finally, Weisgerber asserts that periods form the main axis of the project, although some areas are becoming prominent for certain comparative literary histories, such as sub-Saharan Africa, Latin America, and the Caribbean. Twenty years later, the seventh president of the Committee, Margaret Higonnet, endorsed Remak's guidelines, to which she added, in a new version of the "General Preface" to the series, the change that initiated in 1986 a "second structural orientation of the series" which explores "the significance of regional determinants, leading to subseries on Africa, the Caribbean, East Central Europe, Iberia, and Scandinavia" (x).

Two further documents, written at the same time as a comparative literary history was being developed, are instrumental for assigning new referents to comparison in the projects of the Committee—comparison as to the movement between past and present, and comparison as applied to geographic areas, though most histories are still period-oriented.[4] The first paper is by Mario J. Valdés, the second by Marcel Cornis-Pope and John Neubauer.

Mario J. Valdés and Djelal Kadir co-edited *Literary Cultures of Latin America: A Comparative History*. This history was not overseen by the Committee, and yet we mention it here because Valdés was the Committee's fourth president. Furthermore, the selection of a geographical area as historiographical object in the Committee's histories owes much to various works by Valdés, in which he reflects on the applications of Fernand Braudel's methodology to the literary sphere.

For Valdés, comparative literary history is "a collaborative interdisciplinary study of the production and reception of literatures in specific social and cultural contexts [… it] examines literature as a process of cultural communication within one language area or among a number of them without attempting to minimize cultural diversity" ("Rethinking" 75). Besides the emphasis on comparative literary history—"a relatively recent development in literary studies" (75)—as interdisciplinary teamwork, this short quotation makes reference to two important changes in relation to the ongoing projects of the Committee, namely, the focus on language rather than on (national) literature, and the understanding of literature as a kind of cultural communication. As for the latter, Valdés sees the social contextualization of literature as one of the main outcomes of applying the "Braudelian model" to literary history. "In comparative literary history," says Valdés, "literary works are recast as historical events within a dynamic cultural context. This undertaking, of necessity, reexamines and redefines fundamental historiographic blind spots such as cultural space, institutional promotion or suppression of literature and the politics of participation in the literary/historical event and also questions the basic assumption of historical narrative: the narrative time frame and narrative authority" ("From Geography" 202).

The French historian Fernand Braudel was the second-generation leader of the above-mentioned Annales School. In contrast to Bloch's understanding of comparison as a goal in itself, for Braudel, comparison is exclusively a heuristic tool, one that can convey the multiplicity and richness of the historical experience (Gemelli 124). *La Méditerranée et le monde méditerranéen à l'époque de Philippe II* was his first (1949) and most influential book. In order to understand why Valdés speaks of a "Braudelian model" of comparative literary history, let us concentrate upon two features of Braudel's first book. Firstly, how does Braudel define his object of study? "The Mediterranean is not even a *single* sea, it is a complex of seas," says Braudel and, hence, "[n]o simple biography beginning with date of birth can be written of this sea; no simple narrative of how things happened would be appropriate to its history" (*The Mediterranean* 17; "Preface to the First Edition"). Such a statement, in the case of Valdés, should obviously be put in relation to the way Latin America is conceived of: "the referent of Latin America, as weak and diffuse as it is, cannot in itself constitute the basis for a comprehensive study of the literary production of the area as a distinct world category" ("From Geography" 203). Secondly, each of the three volumes of *La Méditerranée* has a distinct level of inquiry:

the environment, where change is almost imperceptible; long-term social, eco-nomic, and cultural history, where change can be rapid; and events, the time of the *courte durée*. Similarly, Valdés and Kadir organize their history of literature in Latin America into three volumes, which reflect Braudel's three levels—configurations of literary cultures, institutional modes, and cultural modalities, and subject to history. Furthermore, in contrast to the usual understanding of comparison in literary studies as a method that relates objects in different languages, Valdés's use of "comparative" in "comparative literary history" draws on Braudel's relations of times. This is what Valdés calls "the challenge of a history of literary production and reception" ("Rethinking" 76), meaning that "[t]here is no question that the significance of past actions must first be understood in terms of their agent's own values and aes-thetic perspectives and not in terms of our very different ones. But on the other hand, to ignore the meanings of our own redescriptions of the events would be to play the fool" (80). This is the tenet that Braudel, in the preface to his massive history of the pre-industrial modern world, phrased as "[c]omparative both through time [...] of the long term and the dialectic of past/present" (*The Structures* 25). Next to this dimension of comparison, Braudel also considered making his history "comparative through as wide a space as possible, since I wanted my study to cover the whole world if such a thing could be done" (25). This desideratum may be linked to the spatial turn of the Committee's comparative literary histories.

Marcel Cornis-Pope and John Neubauer, on their turn, see as their first challenge that of defining the region—East-Central Europe, which is much more diffuse than Latin America. "What we may call the 'future-directedness' of the term may be an asset rather than a liability. It implies that East-Central Europe is no geographical or political given but rather an invention whose reality must be constructed out of linguistic, religious and ethnic elements that were differently grouped in the past and may, indeed, be grouped by others in the future differently from the way we propose it" (*Towards a History* 18-19).

Next they ask whether a comparative literary history represents any kind of progress in relation to national literary histories. For Cornis-Pope and Neubauer, it is a paradigm change, a perspectival change rather than progress or a "better" option. Like a national history, a comparative one is no less instrumental when it comes to imagining a—in this case—transnational area, and hence participates in the region's *invention* (19). In the case of East-Central Europe, their comparative literary history "will make sense if it furthers, however little, the communication between the peoples" of the region (22). In the remainder of their position paper, Cornis-Pope and Neubauer survey specific literary topographies, some of which are discussed below.

Some relevant contributions of the AILC/ICLA Committee's comparative literary histories

As said before, most of the Committee's histories are time-oriented, whereas the set now seen as "regional subseries" has dealt—and still deals—with sub-Saharan

Africa, the Caribbean, Latin America (with its specific status), East-Central Europe, the Iberian peninsula, and Scandinavia.

Though dominant, the focus on time has many inflections, from timespans (1400–1600 for the Renaissance, 1680–1760 for Modernity) and genres and techniques during a specific period (romantic drama, romantic irony, romantic poetry) to movements and schools associated with specific eras (symbolism, *avant-gardes*, modernism, postmodernism). Whereas from its inception the project has aimed, according to the "General Prefaces" by the Committee's presidents, at focusing on "related or comparable phenomena from an *international* point of view" (emphasis added), the first comparative histories show an understanding of "international" as *the addition of national sets*. Thus, for instance, after a general chapter in which the object of study is approached from an international perspective (let us say expressionism or symbolism), several chapters follow that address the issue within national borders, such as expressionism in Hungary or Poland, and symbolism in Belgium or Finland. This shows how strong still was the link with nineteenth- and early twentieth-century comparative literary histories, except for the fact that the minimal unit is not national literatures as before, but national movements, styles, etc. Conversely, these first histories by the Committee have a distinctive feature that has become less common later, namely, attention paid to artistic phenomena other than the literary.

Time-oriented histories by the Committee are extremely valuable contributions to the development of comparative literary history in themselves. They contribute to reassessing the concept of "literary period" and challenge the projection of local timespans into the international field. And yet they have not created a lexicon of their own which would take shape in new directions for the comparative method beyond the links among several literatures. This does not mean, of course, that space-oriented histories represent a better option. Let us recall how Albert S. Gérard (1: 23) justified his geo-literary object—sub-Saharan Africa.

> the purpose of the HALEL [History of African Literature in European Languages] project was to deal with creative writing in European Languages produced south of the Sahara. This corpus, however, is typically what mathematicians call a fuzzy set. Although it is geographically well defined, there is neither compelling objective evidence nor unquestioned agreement as to which works and which authors constitute "African literature."

A geographical category—sub-Saharan Africa—is offered as sufficient criterion for delimiting a literary corpus, even if the resulting corpus is nothing but a "fuzzy set." But fundamental questions go unanswered, such as: what are the bases for the geographical category in question, especially when racial and religious factors play a role in its identification? Africa in this context is converted into the scene of a possible clash of civilizations: "it has not seemed possible at the present stage to integrate Mediterranean Africa in our consideration: for the time being, it seems best to regard it as part of the Muslim world, which is not to overlook the historical fact that Islam has also made and is still making deep inroads into Sub-Saharan

Africa" (Gérard 1: 22). The mere fact that it was not deemed necessary to delve deeper into this geo-categorization (Mediterranean Africa/sub-Saharan Africa) is highly indicative of the subconscious workings of meta-geography. In this case, these workings lead to a geo-literary equivalence in which the identification of African literature with the creative output of sub-Saharan Africa is dependent upon the elimination of the geo-cultural component of the Mediterranean.

This notwithstanding, space-oriented histories have proved to be more amenable to rupture with nineteenth-century comparative histories, even spatial ones (such as Jean Charles L. Simonde de Sismondi's *La Littérature du midi de l'Europe*), and more prone to experimentation, as a result of which they have spawned a rich lexicon of their own. Some of these contributions will be sketchily sampled now.

Maps

Comparative literature in particular, and literary studies in general, show little relation to any basic spatial instrument used by other humanistic disciplines (history, geography, sociology, ethnography, anthropology, linguistics) or by the social sciences, such as cartography. This indifference seems even more glaring when one considers how many primary comparatist notions reveal an evident spatial character: European literature, Commonwealth literature, national literature, world literature, or emerging literatures, among many others. What about space-oriented, comparative literary histories?

Literary Cultures of Latin America: A Comparative History includes an enormous number of maps, most of them devised as tools for locating military interventions, languages, population density, urban centers, and so forth. An exception, in the sense of providing *literary* maps, is the Appendix by Hervé Théry, "The Main Locations of Latin American Literature." The aim of Théry's maps is to substantiate the concept of "cultural center," which other contributors to the history define as "magnetic poles of attraction of a symbolic-cultural order, exercised by a two-way movement—centrifugal and centripetal—in the interior region of a given country's region, but centered around an axis-city" (Coutinho and Peralta 310).

Of Théry's five maps, let us concentrate on Map 4, which shows the birthplaces of writers who died in the relevant "cultural centers" (175).

The map shows an archipelago of cultural centers that coincide with the Latin American urban network, here the top-level cities—Buenos Aires, Rio de Janeiro, Mexico, etc. As can be seen, the places of death are fewer than the places of birth, which is a result of a general rural-to-urban migration pattern, but also of the fact that writers need to move to specific cities to succeed in their literary careers. Moreover, the greatest literary capital city of Latin America is shown to be Buenos Aires, for it has the largest and most diverse recruiting area, whereas Havana and Rio de Janeiro are magnetic poles exclusively for writers born in the Caribbean and Brazil, respectively. Second to Buenos Aires as literary capital city of Latin America comes Paris and therefore (confirming and reshaping a conclusion of Pascale Casanova) "Europe is part of the cultural field of Latin America" (Théry 170). This is

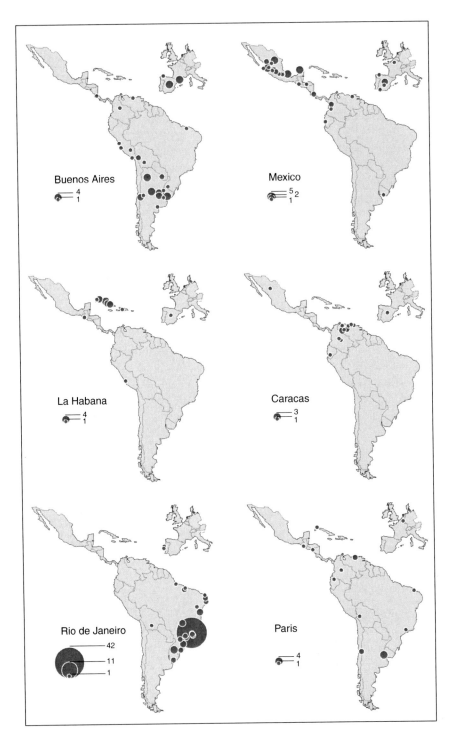

FIGURE 7.1 Map 4 © Hervé Théry, 1996

a good example of the fact that political geography and literary geography are not always identical. Literature has its own workings and, in its geography, distant places in the order of the real may be contiguous in the order of the symbolic.

Silences, which in maps are blanks, may be as eloquent as sounds. Patagonia and Amazonia are the blanks *par excellence* of Latin America in terms of cultural centers. No surprise there, for their population density is very low. And yet, "[t]heir place in Latin American literature and their imaginary geographies create a beautiful paradox. The blank areas of the map can sometimes be as interesting as the areas of major activity" (Théry 170). One might compare the Wild West and its place in the North American imaginary.

Nodes

Cornis-Pope and Neubauer's above-quoted position paper argues that the structuring concept of their comparative history is that of the *node*, which "acquires different meanings in the different parts, corresponding to different conceptions of comparative literature" (*Towards a History* 35). There are temporal, topographical, institutional, and figural nodes. In general terms, a node is a hub within a network.

Part 1 of Volume 1 of *History of the Literary Cultures of East-Central Europe* is organized around "nodes of political time," that is to say, temporal nodes which, starting from 1989, go backwards to 1776/1789. These nodes sometimes may be single years, such as 1989 (the fall of the Berlin Wall); other times they are a cluster of years, such as 1867/1878/1881, which mark political compromises with a single or refractive effect: on one hand, 1867 for the Compromise that gave rise to the Austro-Hungarian Monarchy and 1878 for the Austrian occupation of Bosnia–Herzegovina, events which were crucial for people in the orbit of Austrian power, and on the other hand, 1881, which was important for the Balkans (the Austro-German–Russian alliance). "Nodes of time are points (or 'crossroads') at which various strands come together without forming the heart or essence of an organic unit," say Cornis-Pope and Neubauer. And they add, "Indeed, the political dates we chose tend to be moments of *dis*juncture [...]. Nodes are then simply historical moments (with a certain 'thickness') that occasion short and incomplete transnational narratives that differ from the national perspectives on the events" ("Literary Nodes" 34).

As for the experimental conditions of temporal nodes, the authors voice skepticism towards traditional literary periods and their teleological character. A similar strategy was adopted by Denis Hollier in his often-imitated *A New History of French Literature* (1989), which is built upon 175 essays keyed to specific years between 1778 and 1989. Cornis-Pope and Neubauer's temporal nodes differ from Hollier's, however, in at least two key features. On one hand, they are not years relevant for a single national literature, but a seminal attempt at an inter-periodology, as practiced by Hans Ulrich Gumbrecht in his *In 1926*. On the other hand, the sequence of year clusters follows an "inverted" order, which echoes the Braudelian tenet on comparison as a means of understanding of the dialectic of past/present as seen from the present: 1989, 1956/1968, 1948, 1945, 1918, 1867/1878/1881, 1848, 1776/1789.

Figural nodes are dealt with in Volume 4, from national poets and female identity to outlaws, trauma, and mediation. "[W]e do not regard figures as static but as subjects that enter, grow, decline, and vanish from the literary realm through canonization, suppression, and medial transformation" (Cornis-Pope and Neubauer, "General Introduction" 8). One figural node of the type "outlaw" is Juraj Jánošík, a famous Carpathian highwayman who "was never more than a regional hero in Poland, [...] entered Czech culture merely between the mid-nineteenth and mid-twentieth centuries as a symbol of Czech–Slovak affinities, [... and] rose to become a powerful national hero in Slovak culture" (Raßloff 442). This properly transnational *post mortem* career is a guide to the working of regional intellectual and literary history.

Marginocentric cities

The "marginocentric city" is another concept owed to the creative talent of the editors of the comparative literary history of East-Central Europe. These are "multiethnic nodal cities [...] that at favorable historical conjunctions have rewritten the national cultural paradigm from the margin, ascribing to it a dialogic dimension, both internally (in dialogue with other ethnic traditions) and externally (in dialogue with larger geocultural paradigms). It is their very marginality, [...] as well as their multiethnic composition that has allowed these cities to look simultaneously to both East and West, establishing a fertile nexus between cultural traditions" (Cornis-Pope and Neubauer, *Towards a History* 26). Some of the marginocentric cities that are studied in Volume 2 are Vilnius/Wilno/Vilna, Czernowitz/Cernăuţi/Chernivtsi/Czerniowce, and Prague/Praha/Prag.

Bratislava/Pressburg/Poszony/Posonium

Let us consider a marginocentric city—Bratislava—that was not included in Cornis-Pope and Neubauer's history. Their technical definition of "marginocentric" is beautifully illustrated by a quotation from Claudio Magris's *Danube*, which draws on the narrator's experience of contemplating the 1745 book in four languages, *Taxa Pharmaceutica Posoniensis*, by Ján Justus Torkos.

> The Central Europeans are ignorant of the science of forgetting, of filing away events. This manual of pharmacy in four languages, with its adjective "Posoniensis," reminds me of how at school, my friends and I used to discuss the city's name, which ones we liked best: Bratislava, the Slovak name, Pressburg, the German one, or Poszony, the Hungarian name derived from Posonium, the ancient Roman outpost on the Danube. The fascination of those three names bestowed a special glamour on a composite, multinational history, and someone's preference for one or the other was, in a childish way, a basic stance taken towards the *Weltgeist*. That is to say, we

had to choose between the instinctive celebration of great, powerful cultures such as the German, the ones that make history, or our romantic admiration for the exploits of rebellious, chivalrous and adventurous peoples such as the Magyars, or else our fellow-feeling for what is more subdued and hidden, for the small peoples such as the Slovaks, who remain for a long time a patient, unregarded substratum, a humble, fertile soil waiting centuries for the moment of its flowering. (Magris 220)

In accordance with Cornis-Pope and Neubauer's concept of marginocentric city, Magris makes visible to the reader how a pharmacology manual published in four languages (Latin, Slovak, Hungarian, and German) in mid-eighteenth-century Bratislava can pinpoint a "hidden" story (hidden at least for national literary history), the story of a multicultural and plurilingual city, a hub which encloses a network within itself. Thus, whereas a national history of "Slovak" literature might highlight the relevance of Adam František Kollár as a pro-Slovak activist, a comparative literary history that approaches Bratislava/Pressburg/Poszony/Posonium as marginocentric hub may remind us that his book *De originibus et usu perpetuo potestatis legislatoriae* (1764, On the Origin and Constant Use of Legislative Power) was burnt publicly in the city's squares. And yet the motivation for the tax reform advocated in the book was not to secure more money for Maria Theresa, but to stem the migratory outflow of the nobility's serfs, a fight that was endorsed by the above-mentioned quasi-Robin Hood figure Jánošík. Conversely, the marginal position of Bratislava within the Habsburg dominions made Joseph II's attempts at Germanizing it less effective.

Having surveyed the AILC/ICLA Coordinating Committee's official statements on its tasks, position papers, and some of the more experimental contributions, we may draw some conclusions on the state of comparative literary history. Though the Committee's volumes do not cover the field of comparative literary history in its entirety, it is undeniable that it represents the most important contribution so far.

1. According to the Coordinating Committee's mission statement, its comparative work concerns European languages, either in Europe or in other regions of the world.

    1.1. A comparative history such as the one devoted to sub-Saharan Africa disregards any literary works in languages other than European.

2. In contrast to individual comparative general histories, such as those by Bloch and Braudel, teamwork is considered a *sine qua non* condition for comparative literary history.

3. Whereas comparative general history relies on data provided by local history, comparative literary history is posited as a complement to national literary histories.
4. The temporal axis is still dominant as transversal comparison across literatures.

   4.1. Literary periods thus become the equivalent of the objects studied by comparative general history.
   4.2. Due to the focus on European literatures, traditional literary periods, such as Enlightenment, Romanticism, Modernism, to name but a few, retain their prominence.

      4.2.1. Some histories explore the specific modulations of these periods for some literatures. This may (unintentionally) lead to the idea that the latter somehow depart from the "major literatures," which would represent the rule.

   4.3. Some histories adopt more abstract labels, such as year-numbers.

5. Space has emerged as a new focus of comparative literary history, though it is not identified with national literary areas as it was during the nineteenth century, when comparison was implicitly made by adding national literatures one after the other.

   5.1. The focus on space has resulted in an attempt at mapping literary regions.

      5.1.1. Literary regions are usually identified with international sets, such as sub-Saharan Africa, the Caribbean, East-Central Europe, or the Iberian peninsula.

★

As has been mentioned on several occasions, the comparative literary histories under the aegis of the AILC/ICLA Coordinating Committee do not exhaust the entire field of comparative literary history. In fact, Arturo Casas has listed this set of projects as one of the existing four models of comparative literary history, though, as we have tried to show here, the Coordinating Committee's model is quite multifaceted and constantly evolving. As for the other three models listed by Casas, they are the interliterary, the systemic, and the subaltern.

The reason why we have not included the interliterary model here is that it has already been discussed in Chapter 2, for its historiographical applications are but one possibility within a general theory, namely, the theory of the interliterary process, which aims at challenging the disciplinary divide implied by comparative literature. The reader, therefore, may re-read Chapter 2 and explore what the interliterary theory offers to comparative literary history. As for the "Braudelian–Valdés model," we have discussed it as part of the Coordinating Committee's model. We have already mentioned that, even though the volume *Literary Cultures of Latin America* was not finally included in the Coordinating Committee's series, Valdés was the fourth president of the Committee and he wrote the "General Preface" for some of the volumes. Moreover, both the literary history of Latin America by Valdés and Kadir and the literary history of East-Central Europe by Cornis-Pope and Neubauer form part of the "Literary History Project," of which Valdés was the general editor ("Preface" xiii). There are reasons, therefore, for and against considering the "Braudelian–Valdés model" an independent one.

The systemic model is no less multifaceted than the Coordinating Committee's model. In fact, Dionýz Ďurišin's interliterary theory is a variety of the systemic model as characterized by Casas in terms of functional and dynamic structuralism (59). Casas includes within the systemic model Itamar Even-Zohar's polysystem theory, Siegfried J. Schmidt's empirical study of literature, and Steven Tötösy de Zepetnek's comparative cultural studies. All these theories have much to offer to comparative literary history, yet none of them has produced a comparative literary history as such. The reader will find these outstanding contributions mentioned elsewhere in this book.

Casas's fourth model—subaltern studies—is an entirely different case. Though initially this term named a group of—mainly Indian—historians interested in "the general attribute of subordination in South Asian society whether this is expressed in terms of class, caste, age, gender and office or in any other way" (Guha, "Preface" vii), today subaltern studies is a global academic pursuit whose research agenda transcends regional and disciplinary boundaries (see Chaturvedi). The above-mentioned difference lies in the fact that subaltern studies aimed at revising the elitist historiography of colonialists or neo-colonialists in India and South Asia. A case in point in terms of the critique of the rationale of Western philosophy of history is Ranajit Guha's 2002 *History at the Limit of World-History*, in which he addresses the "giant" Hegel and his world-historical project wherein the ascent of Europe is "rationally" justified. As for a "subaltern history," Guha's 1983 *Elementary Aspects of Peasant Insurgency in Colonial India* and Dipesh Chakrabarty's *Provincializing Europe* are also exemplary. Despite the fact that subaltern theorists have turned to language and literature produced during the colonial era, a subaltern literary history has not been written as yet. We have already discussed this, as well as the case of Latin American subaltern studies, in Chapter 3.

Comparative literary history has many challenges to face yet. A very important one is to abandon the presupposed autarky of literatures in European languages, though advocating the autarky of literatures in non-European languages will not, of course, be a good solution. (Post)colonial settings are obvious sites to be analyzed by literary and cultural comparatists, but this is not the only area in which comparative perspectives can offer a new dimension of analysis. Consider the case of global (labor) migration flows and how they challenge any attempt at treating languages as identical to nations and peoples. The Arab population in Europe is currently estimated at approximately five million, and as a result Arabic is now "one of the many minority languages that, together with the local standard languages, make up the modern European 'linguistic market'" (Boumans and de Ruiter 259). Galician has around 3.2 million speakers, Welsh around 720,000, Basque around the same number—making them, therefore, "minor" languages in Europe compared to Arabic. One might speak, therefore, of "Eurarabic" literature were it not for the radical and xenophobic overtones of the coinage "Eurabia." One wonders, analogously, what a comparative history of literatures in Papua New Guinea, where more than 800 languages are spoken, would look like.

Another important restriction that comparative literary history needs to overcome is the selection of transnational areas. Cities and intra-national regions lend themselves to transnational study, since both small and large objects are subject to theorization when local processes are examined in a national and international sphere and various levels of change operating in the local area are analyzed. There is much work to de done as well with alternative historiographical models, overcoming of Eurocentric literary periods, inter-literary and inter-artistic "dysrhythmias," inter-periodology, literary years, mapping of literary regions, comparative history of typological literary phenomena, literary statistics, inclusion of orature and translation, collaboration between literary studies and linguistics (especially comparative linguistics and sociolinguistics), and digital humanities, to name but a few areas of theoretical opportunity. Whether as method or perspective, the "comparative" in "comparative literary history" should stress the narrative dimension of literary history, a perspectival vision, the dialectic of past and present as seen from the present, and, last but not least, the contention that no comparative literary history could go beyond national limits and adequately represent inter-literary processes if what is shared globally is not contemplated from the site of its local/regional/national idiosyncrasy. World literature is no more abstract than a (trans-)national, regional or local literature. Conversely, the latter are no more empirically specific than world literature. As Doreen Massey (129) has warned, to hold the opposite would be akin to confusing "geographical scale with processes of abstraction in thought."

Gibraltar: an area for a comparative literary history?

Gibraltar is a British Overseas Territory located in the southern end of the Iberian peninsula at the entrance of the Mediterranean. It has an area of 2.3 square miles. An Anglo-Dutch force captured Gibraltar from Spain in 1704 during the War of the Spanish Succession. The territory was subsequently ceded to Britain under the Treaty of Utrecht in 1713. Its strategic importance as the gate of the Mediterranean is obvious. The sovereignty of Gibraltar has long been a major point of contention in Anglo-Spanish relations. Unlike the other twelve British Overseas Territories, Gibraltar is the only "colonial" territory left in continental Europe, to which Akrotiri and Dhekelia on the island of Cyprus may be added. In a way, Gibraltar's status is similar to French overseas territories, which are an integral part of the European Union.

As for literature, Gibraltar is a clear case of a no man's land or, better said, the place of no man's *national literature*. There is not a single reference to "Gibraltarian literature" in any history of Spanish or British literature except, in the case of the latter, as a collateral issue (as an instance of postcolonial literature). In fact, for the poet Trino Cruz Seruya, Gibraltarian literature is a literature *nonata* (not born yet), which is paradoxical, given that the history of the colony and its official bilingualism (but are its inhabitants really speakers of English and Spanish only?) should have favored the emergence of literary expression.

When one approaches Gibraltar comparatively, the situation proves to be much more complex. There is a plurilingual literature in Gibraltar, written in English (Rock English), Spanish, Creole (Yanito), Ladino, Maltese, and Moroccan-Arabic. And yet there have been very few attempts to systematize Gibraltarian literature. Eduardo Fierro Cubiella includes in Section 2 of *Gibraltar* a chapter devoted to literature, situating its institutional recognition around 1990, through a list of Spanish-language (Alberto Pizzarello), English-language (Eric Chipulina, Joseph Patron, Leopold Sanguinetti), or bilingual Spanish–English (Mario Arroyo, Luis Bruzon) and English–Yanito (Elio Cruz) writers. Another interesting perspective is that of Domingo F. Faílde García, who introduces the problem of "literary reintegrationism" in the sense that in his reading of poetry produced in the Campo de Gibraltar (a county in the province of Cádiz where former inhabitants of Gibraltar settled down after 1713), he defends the need to contrast literatures from either side of the border by the symbolic role played by the British colony (singled out in Diego Bautista Prieto and Lola Peche Andrade's work).

None of these approaches by Spanish critics shares Philip Dennis and Anne Taylor's framework (the one we mentioned above as "collateral"), namely, Gibraltarian literature as postcolonial literature written in English. In fact, the English-language Gibraltarian poet Leopold Sanguinetti had already claimed his collection of poems, *The Calpean Sonnets* (1957), to be "a Gibraltarian contribution to the literature of the Commonwealth" (cited in Fierro Cubiella 76). Adopting the geopolitical viewpoint that makes Gibraltar "a British dependency at the western end of the Mediterranean," Dennis and Taylor's imperial key (585) places the birth of Gibraltarian literature in 1704. In linguistic terms, they consider Spanish to be an instrument of the past, while English "has become the language most often used by Gibraltarian writers" (586).

Is not Gibraltar as an object for comparative literary history good proof, on one hand, that "what gives life and particular character to comparative literature"—as Claudio Guillén puts it (*The Challenge* 19)—"is a complex of problems which it alone can and wishes to confront" and, on the other hand, that the discipline is always at odds with simplification?

Notes

1 The following passage from Georg Brandes's 1899 "World Literature" is illustrative: "Of all writers of Denmark in the nineteenth century, only one, Hans Christian Andersen, has achieved world fame. This has caused much amazement in Denmark. Among us Andersen is thought of as one among many, nothing more" (64–65; see Chapter 4).

2 The reason lies in the fact that comparative literature restricts itself, for Van Tieghem, to binary connections, whereas general literature addresses "literary phenomena that belong at the same time to several literatures" (Van Tieghem 175).

3 Comparative literary history is not, of course, a mid-twentieth-century creation. The first French comparatists were, in fact, comparative historians in accordance with the already quoted definition of Ampère's second branch of literary studies. Ampère himself wrote an unfinished *Histoire de la littérature française au Moyen Âge comparée aux littératures étrangères* (1833), whose aim was to assess the distinctiveness of medieval French literature by comparing it with other European literatures. A similar enterprise was undertaken by Abel-François Villemain with *Tableau de la littérature au Moyen Âge en France, en Italie, en Espagne et en Angleterre* (1846), which the author presented as "the first time that in a French chair a comparative analysis of modern literatures is carried out" (1: i). These nineteenth-century transnational literary histories have as their minimal unit national literatures, which are independently dealt one after the other. One has to conclude, therefore, that the comparative act is implicitly required from readers, who will find the possible connections. A different method—synchronic cross-cultural comparisons—was applied by English historians, such as Joseph Berington's *The Literary History of the Middle Ages* (1814) and Henry Hallam's *View of the State of Europe during the Middle Ages* (1835). An intermediate model was adopted by Friedrich Schlegel in *Geschichte der alten und neuen Literatur* (1815).

4 In 1986 Albert S. Gérard published a two-volume history devoted to sub-Saharan Africa, and between 1994 and 1997 A. James Arnold published a three-volume history on the Caribbean.

8

INTERARTISTIC COMPARISON

In Chapter 1 we identified the foundation of comparative literature with the universal faculty of language, and the aesthetic use of this faculty that is literature. We also adduced that the origin of the arts lies in the Aristotelian principle of *mimesis*, and that human nature is fundamentally mimetic. All the arts are imitative and the object of imitation is always the same: human and natural reality. But each art imitates in different ways, and this divergence in artistic means is the reason that interartistic studies are essential to comparative literature. Reflection on the nature of imitation allows us to understand why comparative literature not only has as its object of study the comparison of literatures written in different languages, but also the comparison of arts understood in terms of the different media that they employ.

There is another Aristotelian principle that structures this interartistic comparison, that of *catharsis*, which describes the psychological dimension of the aesthetic, the emotions that the artwork provokes in the receptor. Already in 1719, the Abbé Du Bos, in his *Réflexions critiques sur la poésie et sur la peinture* (Critical Reflections on Poetry and Painting), claimed that the greatest value of poetry and painting lay in their capacity to imitate interesting objects, and that poems and pictures can only be evaluated in terms of the extent to which they impress or affect us. Theodor Lipps (1903), for his part, spoke of a sympathetic fusion—*Einfühlung*—between work and receptor, in the context of a truly subjectivist aesthetic, valid both for literature and for the other five arts of the classical system.

These reflections traditionally form part of a specific philosophical discipline, aesthetics. Their abstraction does not allow us to consider more down-to-earth issues, such as the different techniques, procedures, and resources of each art. Imitation of reality is common to all of them, but the means by which they carry out this imitation is specific to each. Comparison therefore becomes an absolutely necessary tool for a full comprehension of the mimetic impulse of the varieties of artistic expression. In more contemporary terminology, we could say that these varieties correspond to different languages, in the sense that "language" is understood in European tradition, following on from Ferdinand de Saussure's work in semiology, or what Charles Sanders Peirce termed "semiotics." The distinction that the American philosopher draws between three types of sign—symbol, icon, and index—points to the ways in which each of the arts imitates reality. It is fundamental, then, to approach the field of interartistic studies in terms of what André-Michel Rousseau (50) calls "*un univers global de signes*" (a global universe of signs). Hegel, in his *Aesthetics*, placed poetry (*Dichtung*) at the top of his hierarchy of the arts, ahead of architecture, sculpture, painting, music, and dance. Literature, for the German philosopher, was a *universal art*, because in it the imagination is constitutive, and the imagination is the foundation of all art.

In response to the query of Claudio Guillén (*The Challenge* 124) as to whether today the study of the relations between literature and other arts should fall under the remit of comparative literature, Emilia Pantini constructs an interesting argument. She argues that comparative literature is the adequate sphere for these inquiries, as literature is word-based and the links between arts need to be verbalized. Pantini admits that literature is not totalizing, nor can it grant itself the status of a super-art. But, ultimately, it is through language, which is the medium through which thought and communication among humans is organized, that reflection on the arts is produced.

In this regard, the consolidation of this interartistic sphere as proper to comparative literature in such works as those of Henry H.H. Remak ("Comparative Literature") or A. Owen Aldridge, which were cited in the opening chapter, mirrors the self-critical reflection which René Wellek, speaking at the second congress of the AILC/ICLA, deemed essential to comparative literature. The study of the relationship between the arts becomes then a central aspect of comparative literature, but Wellek's imperative, outlined in his speech of 1958, is not surprising, given the wider context of his work. The entire eleventh chapter of the influential *Theory of Literature*, co-written by Wellek and Austin Warren in 1949, was dedicated to the relationship between literature and the other arts, and the Czech critic had already published an article dealing with the parallels between the arts soon after his arrival in the US (Wellek "The Parallelism").

From the early 1960s onwards, a considerable increase in this type of study is visible. C.S. Brown's fundamental study, *Music and Literature: A Comparison of the Arts*, for example, dates from 1963; at this time, the *MLA Bibliography* included interartistic study as one of its "General Topics," and in 1968 *A Bibliography on the Relations of Literature and the Other Arts, 1952–1967* (Brown) was published.

The "Bernheimer Report" confirms the currency of these approaches in its claim that "the space of comparison today involves comparisons between artistic productions usually studied by different disciplines," and this is still true at the start of the twenty-first century. The more recent report of Haun Saussy includes a text by Christopher Braider on comparative literature and visual arts in early modern studies, which paraphrases the title of an article by Erwin Panofsky published in 1955, affirming that comparative literature is also a humanistic discipline because of its attention not only to literary works but also to the "aesthetic artifacts" of the other arts.

The reciprocal illumination of the arts

The writings of the German neo-classicist Gotthold Ephraim Lessing, especially his work of comparative literature *avant la lettre*—*Laokoon, oder Über die Grenzen der Malerei und Poesie* (*Laocoön. An Essay on the Limits of Painting and Poetry*), published in Berlin in 1766—are fundamental in this regard. Lessing attempts to correct the hermeneutic confusions or misreadings of the famous lines from Horace's poetics— *"ut pictura, poesis: erit quae, si propius stes / te capiat magis, et quaedam, si longius abstes"* (361–62; As painting, so poetry: there will be one that seizes you more if you stand closer and another if you stand farther off)—which had often been taken as a declaration of the submission of poetry to painting.

Lessing adopts, on the other hand, an attitude that could be compared to what today is called "reception theory," as he recognizes in his prologue the similar effects that a painting, sculpture, or literary work can have on a "man of refined taste." In each case, the artist or writer places before us absent realities as if they were present, giving us appearance for reality, cheating but at the same time consoling us. At the same time, Lessing defends the absolute autonomy of the means with which each art achieves its goals. Painting and sculpture are static, as they work with figures and colors that are distributed in space, and the signs with which they work are "natural"—icons in semiotic terms—whereas literature is an art in which articulated sounds succeed each other in time and are grouped together to form words, that is, arbitrary and conventional signs. Because of this, literature can represent actions with facility, something painters can only feebly attempt in the representation of their natural objects, bodies.

Returning to debates (the main protagonist of which was Johann Joachim Winckelmann) that centered on the Alexandrine sculptures attributed to Hagesandros, Polydoros, and Athanadoros, sculptures that represent the Trojan priest Laocoön and his children in their struggle with the two monstrous serpents sent by the goddess Minerva, and taking into account the second canto of Virgil's *Aeneid*, which describes this terrible scene, Lessing defends the aesthetic autonomy with which the sculptors represented this struggle in stone. Lessing is vehement in his rejection of the confusion of the two arts, in which poetry would become a descriptive mania, and painting would descend to the level of allegory, in which case there would be created a monstrous "speaking picture" and "mute poetry."

It is worthwhile to consider here the importance that this issue has from both a theoretical and semiotic perspective, as well as from the perspective of comparative literature, starting from the essential distinction that Lessing develops in Chapter 16 of *Laocoön* in his phenomenology of two forms of aesthetic expression: that of the spatial arts (painting, but also sculpture and architecture), and the temporal arts (literature, but also music and dance).

At the start of the nineteenth century, at the moment of the great expansion of comparatism as method in various spheres of knowledge, Jean François Sobry published his *Cours de peinture et littérature comparées* (1810; Course of Comparative Painting and Literature). But it would be a disciple of the great art historian

Heinrich Wölfflin, Oskar Walzel, who in a programmatic conference of 1919 would coin the expression that best reflects this comparative modality: "the reciprocal illumination of the arts" (*Wechselseitige Erhellung der Künste*), a happy formulation that complements the notion of "double talents," creative artists such as Michelangelo, Blake, Hoffmann, Wagner, Rossetti, Almada Negreiros, Dalí, Pier Paolo Pasolini, or Federico García Lorca, who expressed themselves through multiple artistic means.

The seven arts of modernity

It is true that in the study of interartistic relationships it is easy to fall into the trap of superficial comparisons without rigor, but it is also true that semiotics, understood as a general theory of signs, can lend the comparatist methodological instruments and conceptual precision. On a primary level we encounter purely thematic comparisons, which are not without interest, especially if they are developed in terms of the "iconology" of Erwin Panofsky, inheritor of the *Philosophy of Symbolic Forms* of Ernst Cassirer. Mixed forms, such as emblems or the opera, also open a vast field of study. Studies of forms and structures are also relevant and, building on the work of Mario Praz and others, there has been some very interesting research on the homology of models of musical composition, such as the sonata, symphony, fugue, and counterpoint, and literary forms. It is in this context that we can see how a comparative approach to the study of cinema, for example, can yield results of real value (Brunel and Chevrel 263–98).

Apollinaire was in France one of the pioneers in the recognition of cinema as art, like Nicholas Vachel Lindsay in the US (*The Art of the Moving Picture*, 1915). Initially, these defenses of cinema were expressed with a certain timidity, apart from the writing of Riccioto Canudo, whose "Manifesto of the Seven Arts" dates from 1911, and the followers of Marinetti, who in the ninth edition of *L'Italia futurista* of September 1916 published their manifesto "La Cinematografia futurista."

Ricciotto Canudo (8), while using arguments that reveal a certain distant inspiration in the dichotomy established between the spatial and temporal arts in the eighteenth century by Lessing, had expressed himself with certainty: "*Nous avons besoin du Cinéma pour créer l'art total vers lequel tous les autres, depuis toujours, ont tendu*" (We need cinema in order to create that total art towards which all the others, since their origins, have tended). On the screen, because of the harmonious merging of science and art, one could finally "capture and fix the rhythms of light," and this "marriage of light and sound around an incomparable bonfire" represented for Canudo a perfect emblem of "our new modern spirit" (Romaguera and Alsina Thevenet 16, 18).

Cinema signified the meeting point of space and time. It possesses a powerful plastic and descriptive dimension, which allows it to integrate in full aesthetic harmony pictorial, sculptural, and architectonic elements (one could recall here the collaboration of architects such as Kettelhut, Hunte, or Vollbrecht with Fritz Lang, the director of *Metropolis*). It also has an immense narrative potential, similar to that of the novel or drama, as well as the capacity to incorporate music and dance. It is, then, a syncretic and modern art, which enriches itself at the cost of the six arts of antiquity, becoming in some ways the most complete and fertile synthesis of these. And its privilege extends today even in the era of digital media according to, for example, Lev Manovich.

In 1971 the film-maker Luchino Visconti premiered his *Morte a Venezia* (Death in Venice), based on Thomas Mann's novella, published in 1911 as *Der Tod in Venedig*, but also on another work of the German Nobel Prize winner, *Doktor Faustus*, from 1947. The Italian director, who wrote the script conjointly with Nichola Badalucco, not only places the emphasis, as he does in the majority of his films, on the images and settings of the city that so fascinated Canaletto, but also transforms Mann's protagonist, Gustav von Aschenbach, into a musician. Behind Gustav von Aschenbach we can see the figure of Gustav Mahler, whose music is a fundamental element of the film. Its soundtrack includes the fourth movement from Mahler's fourth symphony, as well as the contralto solo entitled "O Mensch" of the third symphony, which plays over a wonderfully vivid scene on Lido beach, filled with the families of the Central-European upper-middle classes. The "Adagietto" of the fifth movement acts as a *Leitmotiv* throughout the film. This means that Mahler's compositions, as well as contributing to the musical decoration of the film, are also diegetic elements that form part of the narrative development of the story, which in general is faithful to the original literary text, but allows for the addition of the musician Alfred, a disciple of von Aschenbach in the same way that Arnold Schoenberg was a disciple of Mahler.

Transposition, hypertextuality, postprocessing

In the same year in which Visconti was making his film, the English composer Benjamin Britten was creating an opera in two acts, with an English-language libretto written by Myfanway Piper based on *Death in Venice*. His vision and interpretation of the novel were not influenced by Visconti's film, though the ballet of John Neumeier, which premiered in 2003, surely was. This American choreographer is a specialist in bringing literary works to dance, and has brought various of Shakespeare's works—*A Midsummer Night's Dream*, *Hamlet*, *Othello*, and *As You Like It*—to ballet. He has also adapted Henrik Ibsen's *Peer Gynt*, and in Athens in 1995 premiered his version of the *Odyssey*.

These adaptations are what Roman Jakobson ("On Linguistic Aspects") defined as "intersemiotic transposition from one sign-system to another": a concept that has recently been designated with the term "transduction." Originally used in the field of biochemistry to refer to the transmission of genetic material from one bacterium to another, the term appeared in Lubomir Doležel's 1986 article "Semiotics of Literary Communications," giving it the double meaning of *transmission* and *transformation* in the posterior processing of literary works.

As Doležel reiterates in his *Occidental Poetics: Tradition and Progress*, transduction is today one of the highpoints of any semiotics of literary communication. The concept includes many diverse phenomena and activities: from the insertion of one text in another to genre transformation (the adaptation of a novel into a drama, for example). But translation, critical paraphrase, or the plastic, musical, or filmic transduction of a hypotext would also come under this conceptual framing. This latter practice is especially characteristic of our information and communication society, as we will later show.

Complementary to this work is Gérard Genette's study of the different facets of transtextuality elaborated in his *Palimpsests*. For the French narratologist, hypertextuality should be understood as the relation between a text B (hypertext) and another, anterior, text A (hypotext), the former deriving from the latter in an operation that he terms "transformation," and this term defines perfectly the commerce between the arts to which we are referring.

But, as we showed in Chapter 1, what Norbert Groeben terms *Empirische Literaturwissenschaft* (Empirical study of literature) considers literature in a basic context of communicative and social actions that begins with creation and reading, but which also includes the distinct forms of mediation and transformation that constitute both the literary products and those derived from it. This does not lead inevitably to the consideration of other artistic discourses and the specific codes that are inherent to these.

With regard to the practice of transduction characteristic of the "reciprocal illumination of the arts," the importance of the phase posterior to creation is key, the mediation and the reception of texts that another member of the German group NIKOL ("nicht-konservative Literaturwissenschaft", non-conservative literary science), Götz Wienold, terms *Textverarbeitung*, which has been translated as "postprocessing" (in a meaning quite different from how this word is employed in film studies) or simply "transformation of literary messages," in consonance with the terminology of Genette's hypertextuality. This has to do, obviously, with re-creation, the transductive reading of the literary hypotext that occurs in the form of criticism, interpretation, commentary, parody, paraphrase, adaptation, change of genre, comic, painting, sculpture, opera, musical, film or TV version, etc.

In the theory of the NIKOL group and of their leader, Siegfried J. Schmidt, this "literary system" is entirely interdependent: it constitutes a conditioning structure in which each element, phase, or agent participates with, or depends upon, every other element. The "producer," for example, in the aforementioned example of Thomas Mann, is the agent whose action results in the work; the "transformer," "postprocessor," or "recreator" is the agent who reacts to the reception of the work, elaborating another product relative to this first. This is the role taken by film-makers such as Visconti, composers such as Britten, or choreographers such as Neumeier within the literary system, whose work is realized in the resultant *Textverarbeitung*.

We believe it is necessary to include in the theoretical framework of an empirical study of the contemporary literary system other activities of transduction, such as the elaboration of a musical score, a dance performance, or an audiovisual script from a literary text. The posterior incorporation of these hyper/hypotexts to film entails a complex postprocessing that would result in a final filmic hypertext, the ultimate origin of which would be the literary hypotext.

Music and literature

One of Marshall McLuhan's final reflections in his *The Gutenberg Galaxy* sets out the claim that the separation of poetry and music was first made visible in the printed page. This would be another of the consequences of the implementation of a new technology, that of the mobile printing press in the service of phonetic writing, a process that has its origins in Mesopotamia around 3,500 BCE. Before the phonetic alphabet, communication was fundamentally oral, and the move from tribal to so-called civil society would not have been possible without this new system of fixing and transmitting content.

As L. Kramer recalls in a book dedicated to this theme, song is at the origin of the transmission of memorable information, and the identification of music and poetry is founded in the fact that both are arts that are dependent on the immediate and tangible organization of the passage of time. In this order, the structural foundation is the same, although the author of *Music and Poetry* immediately recognizes that not only have we advanced slowly in the search for an interdisciplinary method for their comparative study, but that even in 1984, when Kramer wrote his work, there was no such language available.

However, Nicolas Ruwet's book from 1972 on language, music, and poetry is a valuable point of reference for the analytic study of musical and literary work from a methodological common principle. Ruwet starts from a linguistic basis formulated by Roman Jakobson, that of the projection of the paradigmatic over the syntagmatic axis, which in the case of poetical sequencing produces an intense concentration of recurrences or "couplings." It can be concluded from this that the phenomena of repetition and variation are determinant in any structural configuration that has, as in the case of literary and musical texts, a development in time, an idea that similarly underlies the work of Brown (*Music and Literature*).

Steven P. Scher's speech to the ninth congress of the ICLA/AILC, held in Innsbruck, which included a call for a semiological approach to the relations between both arts, was the prologue to a series of interesting contributions to the theme, such as those of Isabelle Piette or Jean-Pierre Barricelli, not to mention the volumes edited by Nancy Anne Cluck, Wendy Steiner, and Raphaël Célis.

The identification of music and poetry cannot, however, be considered in any way exclusive of that which occurs between poetry and painting much before the appearance of the printing press. In the same way in which the disposition of words, pauses, accents, vowels, and consonants, as well as the distribution of poetic sequences in hemistiches, verses, strophes, or compositions such as the sonnet, obey rhythmical principles based fundamentally on repetition and variation, so one can manipulate the verbal flow of the poem in order to achieve plastic and visual harmonies. Phrases and enunciations are lyrical in many cases because of the suggestiveness of their meanings, and the music and rhythms of their words and sequences, but alongside these elements even the very distribution of printed words on a page can be significant, as in the case in the *calligrammes* of Guillaume Apollinaire. Apollinaire's compositions derive a lyrically coherent meaning not only from the significance of their words, but also from the ways in which the distribution of these on the page suggests a picture that has to do with the meaning of the poem, as in the case of the poem "Coeur, couronne et miroir."

Following on from Apollinaire's work, similar experiments were elaborated in what has been termed "concrete" or "visual" poetry, cultivated for example by the Brazilian group *Noigandres*, whose leading members, Haroldo and Augusto de Campos, as well as Décio Pignatari, authored in 1954 the manifesto "Plan piloto para a poesía concreta" (Initial Plan for Concrete Poetry), the European derivation of which would be found in the work of the Bolivian/Swiss poet Eugen Gomringer, whose own manifesto would be titled "Vom vers zur konstellation."

Though one can identify the development of these tendencies in the twentieth century *avant-garde*, as a matter of fact they have a much longer history, going back to what the Greeks called *technopaignía*, literally "artful games" or what in Latin was called *carmina figurata* or figurative poems. The well known poem of Simmias of Rhodes, which reproduces the wings of Eros, is a good example of this type of work, which in the classical and Hellenic worlds often had a pragmatic use as votive offerings to determined gods.

The relationship between poetry and music was tackled in Gioseffo Zarlino's *Institutioni harmoniche* from 1558, and like him, contemporary thinkers tended to approach the problem from three complementary perspectives. The first has to do with purely rhythmic and euphonic concerns; the second with what the rhetorical tradition termed the *dispositio* (what we might term the "structure") of the work, as there are forms of composition of musical origin that can be applied both to narrative and lyric expression; and finally, the difficult question of the meaning of poetic and musical signs and words, which are both arbitrary and conventional symbols, except in the case of the musician's harmonic imitation of the sounds of nature, or the poet's use of onomatopoeia.

This being the case, the identification of poetical and musical signs that Peirce defines as symbolic does not prevent us from distinguishing between these in terms of their arbitrary, conventional, and ambiguous nature. The relationship between signifier and signified is semantically much more telling in the case of literature than in music. As Eero Tarasti (30) points out, paraphrasing Claude Lévi-Strauss, music is a language without a signified, which does not imply a radical, lack of meaning. In fact, the opposite is true, as music has such a capacity to so involve the listener emotionally that s/he projects on the sounds of the song, sonata, or symphony a meaning that is not necessarily the same as that of other listeners.

This perspective is very similar to that of Roman Ingarden's literary phenomenology, which describes the process through which the reader of a literary text recreates the text in all its plenitude, filling in, so to speak, the blanks and "indeterminacies" that characterize the work as the pure linguistic construct—of arbitrary signs—that in reality it is. There is a large margin of discretion in the reading that any of us can make of a given novel or poem, to which we intentionally grant a meaning that derives from our own sensibility, experience, and cultural horizons.

But for all the range of this particularity of reception, literature can never achieve the profound ambiguity of meaning that characterizes music.

Close to this phenomenological notion of intentionality is what François Delalande describes as "narrative listening behaviour patterns," a concept from which Jean-Jacques Nattiez ("Can Someone Speak") justifies the possibility of musical narrative and diegesis. For Nattiez, if we can speak of a musical tale, it is because music shares with literature a syntactic or temporal dimension, but at the same time it is the listener who constructs the narrative development from a given musical piece. This means that a musical work can be the starting point for a narrative impulse, but does not in itself constitute a story.

The most natural and genuine link between music and poetry, however, can be found at the origins of the lyric, when the poem was song. This union has never ceased to be an important part of our culture, as evidenced by the popularity of contemporary singer-songwriters, but it has had moments of particular splendor, such as the German *Lieder* cycles, from the vast corpus of which stand out the musical settings of the poems of Goethe by Mozart, Beethoven, Schubert, Schumann, and Liszt. Opera, a genre that deserves much more attention than the length of this chapter allows, also establishes a fertile dialog between music and the theatrical text understood as both literature and spectacle.

We could also mention here musical works that originate as a response to a poetic text, such as Claude Debussy's "Prélude à l'après-midi d'un faune," which derives from an eclogue of Stéphane Mallarmé. The strategy of closing with maximum intensity the development of a large orchestral work with the incorporation of a literary text at the symphonic climax is another important element of the relationship between music and poetry, and we could mention here Beethoven's ninth symphony and the use of Schiller's "Ode an die Freude" or Franz Liszt's "Eine Faust-Symphonie in drei Charakterbildern," as well as the contralto solo "O Mensch! Gib acht!" which Gustav Mahler takes from Nietzsche's *Thus Spoke Zarathustra* to illuminate the fourth movement of his third symphony.

Conversely, music can provide a compositional scheme for poets and novelists, as Nancy Anne Cluck argues. The examples here are numerous, from the *Four Quartets* of T.S. Eliot, or novels such as André Gide's *La Symphonie Pastorale* (1919), or Armando Palacio Valdés's *Sinfonía pastoral* (1931). Anthony Burgess, too, shows the influence of music in his *Napoleon Symphony: A Novel in Four Movements*, and, of course, in *A Clockwork Orange*, where Beethoven's ninth symphony plays a major part, and this centrality of music is reflected in Stanley Kubrick's 1971 film version of the novel. Leo Tolstoy's *The Kreutzer Sonata* (1889) is inspired by Beethoven's score for piano and violin, and this musical form is also at the base of Ramón de Valle Inclán's novels of Spanish *modernismo*, *Sonata de otoño* (1902), *Sonata de estío* (1903), *Sonata de primavera* (1904), and *Sonata de invierno* (1905). This is also the case in Thomas Mann's *Tonio Kröger* (1903) and Herman Hesse's *Steppenwolf* (1927).

Nattiez ("Récit musical") has analyzed in detail the composition, based on the musical model of the fugue, of Hubert Aquin's 1965 novel *Prochain épisode*, and

Leiling Chang that of the "musical novel" *Concierto barroco* (1974), whose Cuban author, Alejo Carpentier, a renowned musicologist, admits to having composed on the tripartite structure of the sonata and the concerto, although both forms can also have four movements.

Musical inspiration is at the heart of the profound renewal of the novel that characterizes international modernism, a movement in which we would include the aforementioned authors Valle Inclán and André Gide. In the third chapter of the second part of *Les Faux-Monnayeurs* (1925), titled "Eduard discusses his ideas on the novel," Eduard, a novelist, claims, during a conversation on Bach with his music teacher La Pérouse, that what he would like to do in narrative is "*quelque chose qui serait comme* L'Art de la fugue" (something that would be like the *Art of the Fugue*). It is important to recall, in this regard, one of the other major modernist works, the title of which is in itself telling: Aldous Huxley's *Point Counter Point* (1928). The story begins with a concert in Tantamount House in which Bach's "Suite in C minor" is played. The narrator observes that each instrument interprets the score in a different way, an observation that serves as a pretext to a theorization of the relativity of reality and the multi-perspectivalism of the novel. *Point Counter Point* is structured, then, on the musical form that gives it its title, and elaborates its themes, based on the duality of this form, in an exploration of the antitheses of passion/reason, body/spirit, which were for Huxley of fundamental interest. Here we can see the influence of D.H. Lawrence, for whom happiness lay in the capacity to harmoniously reconcile these opposites.

This fertile cross-pollination of music and novel, to which Brown (*Music and Literature*) pays special attention, is also present in writers such as Milan Kundera and his *The Book of Laughter and Forgetting* (1979) or *The Unbearable Lightness of Being* (1984). With these, and countless other examples, we might argue that contemporary narrative exemplifies Walter Pater's famous *dictum* included in his study *The Renaissance* (1873): "All art constantly aspires towards the condition of music."

Literature and the plastic arts: ekphrasis

Plutarch attributed to Simonides of Ceos the statement that painting was "silent poetry" and that poetry was "speaking painting," an analogy that was also expressed in the East by the twelfth-century poet Su Dongpo, who, referring to another poet and also painter of the Tang dynasty (the eighth century in Western terms)—Wang Wei—claimed "There is poetry in his painting and painting in his poetry" (cited in Weinberger 230).

The idea of the mutual convertibility of the two became a cliché from Lessing's "misreading" on, as the Polish researcher Henryk Markiewicz has shown. These are analogical comparisons that do not amount to a literal equivalence of two artistic systems that are in fact distinct. Painting is based on icons, signs that maintain a relation of similarity with the object or reality that they represent. Literature, on the other hand, works with words, which in Peirce's terminology are symbolic, conventional signs.

Lessing approached the theme of the boundaries between poetry and painting concentrating, paradoxically, on the Alexandrine sculptures that represent the mythological story of the death of Laocoön and his sons at the hands of the goddess Minerva. Given that this episode is described in the second canto of Virgil's *Aeneid*, the German philosopher proposes three possible options: that the sculptor's figures were inspired by the poet; that Virgil was inspired by a figurative rendering of the scene; and finally, that the poet and the sculptors were inspired by the same classical sources, which the Roman grammarian Macrobius attributed to the epic poetry of the Greek, Pisander.

These options raise one of the central issues in the consideration of the possible transductions between the plastic arts and literary creation. We are referring, of course, to ekphrasis (Krieger). From Dionysius of Halicarnassus on, for classical rhetoric ekphrasis is a figure that is comparable to *hypotyposis*, and understood as a vivid and intense description that attempts to make a material reality visible through words. This conception implies a certain inferiority of literature with respect to the plastic arts, as the images of literature, its signs, are artificial and conventional, as opposed to the "natural" icons with which a painter describes reality. By the eighteenth century, however, the meaning of the term ekphrasis underwent a significant restriction, coming to designate a description in a literary text of a plastic work of art, whether this was sculptural, architectural, a drawing, or a painting. It becomes, as James A.W. Heffernan points out, the verbal representation of a visual representation.

One of the most cited examples of ekphrasis is the description of Achilles' shield in Book 18, verses 478–608 of Homer's *Iliad*. But even in classical antiquity it is possible to propose the existence of an "inverse ekphrasis," in which a literary work or fragment is transduced in the form of painting or sculpture. In this context we can appreciate the series of Etruscan alabaster funerary ornaments, housed since the eighteenth century in the Guarnacci Museum of Volterra, which depict in exquisite reliefs the adventures of Ulysses and other Homeric episodes. In the English-speaking world, John Keats's famous ekphrastic poem "Ode on a Grecian Urn" stands out, as does William Carlos Williams's *Pictures from Brueghel*. More recently, and in a Hispanic context, the *"Botines con lazos*, de Vincent Van Gogh" of the Argentine writer Olga Orozco is a fine example of ekphrasis.

As a modern example of inverse ekphrasis we could highlight the cinematic version of Walt Whitman's descriptive New York poetry, the 1920 film *Manhatta*. The film-makers, Paul Strand and Charles Sheeler, both reputed photographers and painters, were members of Alfred Stieglitz's New York circle, and their short piece, which premiered in the Rialto Theater in 1921, has been recognized as the first *avant-garde* North American film. It consists in a paraphrase in cinematic images of twelve lines from Whitman's *Leaves of Grass*. Discussing the concept of ekphrasis, Michel Riffaterre speaks of a "double mimesis" in the way in which an ekphrastic text represents in words a plastic representation. But Strand and Sheeler's film reveals the innovative possibilities of inverse ekphrasis, as in it plastic cinematic images attempt to translate the verbal images of Whitman's poetry: *Ut poesis, pictura*.

In sum: *Manhatta* is an ekphrastic visual poem based not only on the poem of the same title—the section that Whitman wrote as "Mannahatta"—but on various verses from other sections of *Leaves of Grass*, in which the textuality of the writing, reproduced in posters at the start of each of the sequences, measures the rhythm of the film and gives it its meaning. The choice of texts and, above all, their positioning gain great importance. In some ways we could say that these texts are the script of the film, the action of which is structured in the succession of twelve instants between dawn and dusk, between which there are an equal number of blanks or ellipses.

Images of *Don Quixote*

Cervantes's great novel *Don Quijote* contains many prescient moments which seem to foretell the work's fertile afterlife in its reception by the plastic arts. At the start of the first adventure of the Knight of the Woeful Countenance (I, 2) he proclaims: "Fortunate the time and blessed the age when my famous deeds will come to light, worthy of being carved in bronze, sculpted in marble, and painted on tablets as a remembrance for the future" (25).

The first known images of the figure of Don Quijote, his squire, and other characters from the novel date from 1614, even before the publication of the second part of the novel. It seems that these iconographical representations, attributed to Andreas Bretschneider, are related to other early derivations from the novel, the Cervantine figures that formed part of the parades and pantomimes of the Baroque festivals.

Baroque theatre immediately responded to the unlimited representational potential of the Cervantine characters, and even within the first year of the publication of *El Quijote* the Valencian dramatist, Guillén de Castro, premiered a comedy titled *Don Quixote de la Mancha*, which nonetheless told the story of the amorous adventures of Cardenio, Luscinda, Dorotea, and don Fernando. The same story interested William Shakespeare, who with John Fletcher wrote *The History of Cardenio*, played twice before the English court in 1613 and since lost.

These examples serve to form the basis of the long career of Don Quijote on the stage, a career that would also include the ballets of Marius Petipa, Alexander Gorsky, Nureyev, and George Balanchine; and the operas of Salieri, Caldara, Paisiello, Mendelssohn, Massenet, Cristóbal Halffter, and José Luis Turina. Music, too, has taken on the figure of Don Quijote, and we could mention here the symphonic poem *Don Quijote*, premiered by Richard Strauss in 1898; Manuel de Falla's *El retablo de Maese Pedro* (1923); and other works of Spanish musicians such as Jesús Guridi, Óscar Esplá, Gerardo Gombau, Ernesto Halffter, and Joaquín Rodrigo.

The illustrations accompanying the successive editions of *El Quijote* deserve close attention. The first of these appear in a German edition of the work published in Frankfurt in 1648, in the Dutch translation of Jacob Savery published in Dordrecht in 1657, and in the Spanish edition that Juan

Monmartre printed in Brussels in 1662. This is the start of a large series of inverse ekphrases based on the novel that would continue up to the brilliant illustrations of Salvador Dalí for the Parisian edition of Joseph Foret in 1957.

The Cervantes Project and the Cushing Library of Texas A&M University do not ignore the iconographic tradition of El Quijote as a key element in the canonization of the text and of the transformation of Don Quijote into a cultural icon. New information technologies allow us to consult online (www.qbi2005.com) the QBI (1605—1905), the image bank of El Quijote directed by José Manuel Lucía Megías, which at the end of 2013 spanned 550 editions and 17,603 images.

These illustrated editions are only one of the many streams that make up the flood of iconographic images based on El Quijote, which will also include the paintings and drawings of Domenicus van Wynen, Fragonard, William Turner, Goya, Leslie, Camille Corot, Honoré Daumier, Paul Cézanne, Pablo Picasso, Paul Klee, Marcel Duchamp, George Grosz, Edward Hopper, Jackson Pollock, the photographs of Luis de Ocharán, and, of course, films.

The imagistic potential of Cervantes's descriptions explains the attention given to his work by illustrators, engravers, painters, and even advertising executives, but this abiding characteristic, allied with the extraordinary dynamism of the narrative syntax, at the same time justifies the various cinematographic adaptations of El Quijote.

Building on a brief scene based on El Quijote filmed in 1898 for the Gaumont film company, the fertile relationship between literature and cinema had a foundational milestone in 1903, with Ferdinand Zecca and Lucien Non-guet's showing in Washington of their Les Aventures de Don Quichotte de la Manche, filmed for the great French producers Pathé. Among the 150 film and television versions of El Quijote, there are works of very uneven commercial and aesthetic achievement. Some of these, however, have become part of the history of cinema. The 1932 versions of the German expressionist Georg Wilhelm Pabst, or that of Rafael Gil in 1948, have certainly reached this level. The version by a disciple of Eisenstein, Grigori Kozintzev, a Soviet super-production filmed in Crimea in 1957, is also notable.

Orson Welles's attempts to bring El Quijote to the screen deserve a separate treatment. Welles, one of the greatest adaptors of Shakespeare, with his expressionist Macbeth of 1948, his Othello of 1952, and Chimes at Midnight (based on the character of Falstaff) of 1966, wrote a screenplay based on El Quijote and until his death was involved in the attempt to realize his cinematic vision of the film, an attempt that survives only in fragmentary form. Finally, the work of the Spanish director Manuel Gutiérrez Aragón is especially interesting. In 1991 Aragón filmed a television version of the novel in five episodes and with a total duration of more than five hours. Later, in 2002, he would make a film version, which covers the second half of the novel in the space of two hours.

FIGURE 8.1 Plate 30. Don Quixote conquers the Gentleman of the White Moon, Part II, I take IV, chapter LXIV, page 273 © Antonio Carnicero & J. Fabregat/RAE 1780

Pre-cinema

Edward C. Riley, author of the notable *Cervantes's Theory of the Novel*, also considered *El Quijote* to be a novel conceived in fundamentally visual terms, and that the problems of visual perception were basic to the structure of the book itself. Riley was not the only critic to approach the novel in these terms. In 1981, Diane Chaffe studied the techniques of portrait, picture, still-life, and landscape put into play by Cervantes, whom she defines as "the painter of *Don Quijote*." Chaffe's observations are similar to those of Henri Suhamy with regard to the theater of Shakespeare, according to whom objects—instruments, utensils, documents, books, liquids, jewels, food, and clothes—as well as the place and physicality of the characters— the obesity of Falstaff, the warts on the face of Bardolph, the thinness of Pinch or Cassius, or the imposing figure of Charles in *As You Like It*—are in themselves protagonists of each scene.

The fact that Helena Percas de Ponsetti titles one of her later works on Cervantes, *Cervantes Writer and Painter of 'Q'*, is indicative of her approach. She describes a Cervantine ekphrastic tendency that she terms "pictorial writing techniques," precursor in many ways of the painterly techniques of the impressionists, expressionists, and surrealists of later centuries.

These discussions help us to understand the extraordinary attraction that *El Quijote* has always exercised on artists of the image, whether these are painters or film-makers. If the novel organizes verbal reality, and film effects the same organization with visual reality, one could advance the argument that in *El Quijote* there is a deliberate verbal predetermination of the visual, not only in those elements that have to do with the purely aesthetic, pictorial, or descriptive, but also in terms of those that are dynamic, relational, and cinematic. This verbal predetermination of the visual facilitates screenwriters' and film-makers' adaptations of Cervantes's work, but also allows us to speak of a "pre-cinematography" in *El Quixote*.

The birth of cinema in the last decade of the nineteenth century was thanks to two paths of development that can be traced quite a way back in time. On one hand, there is the scientific and technological progress that allowed the Lumière brothers in France, as well as other inventors in various countries, to capture and afterwards project images in movement. But no less importance, on the other hand, should be given to the aesthetic evolution of spatial, figurative, or narrative forms over various centuries. From its very origin, then, cinema will include two complementary dimensions: technical innovation and the synthesis of diverse art-forms. Canudo spoke, in this regard, of "*ce nouveau-né fabuleux de la Machine et du Séntiment*" (cited in Romaguera and Alsina Thevenet 15; a prodigy born of the machine and sentiment).

For this reason, the term "pre-cinema" can be understood in two ways. The more common acceptance today is that which refers to the period before 1895 and the devices that were used prior to this date to animate and project images. In this context one has to take into account devices such as the "magic-lantern" illustrated by the German Jesuit Athanasius Kircher, who in the tenth book of his *Ars Magna Lucis et Umbrae in Mundo*, published in 1646, thirty years after the death of Cervantes, discusses what he calls "parastatics" or "representative magic," and recognizes the advances made in this area by the Danish mathematician Thomas Walgenstein.

Today, however, the tendency to understand pre-cinema in purely technical terms seems to have been superseded in favor of a cultural and interdisciplinary contextualization of what has been termed the "pre-cinematographic universe."

This approach covers not only the modes of visual representation before the end of the nineteenth century, but also iconographic traditions, popular entertainment, theatre and other scenic arts, and notably, stories and narrative literature, with the understanding that there is a considerable amount of interference and transmission between all these arts. Sandra Machetti (33) considers pre-cinema to be all that which is before cinema, and which at the same time explains it, and therefore argues that it is necessary to take into account the history of art, theatre, literature, and culture in general when discussing film. She argues that it is impossible to exclude the narrative tradition from a history of visual perception that leads necessarily to cinematography.

We might remember here the pioneering work of Paul Leglise, who over fifty years ago studied Virgil's *Aeneid* as a work of pre-cinema. Already in the International Congress of Film Studies held at the Sorbonne in 1955, Pierre Francastel had found in classic literary texts elements that for him presaged the arrival of film. These had to do with certain ways of articulating narratives and associations from the multiplicity of natural images that pass before our eyes. Leglise (23) identifies the ways in which Virgil's work can be understood as visual art, and even goes so far as to claim that the *Aeneid* "*soutient un rythme filmique d'une extraordinaire et éclatante pureté*" (25; maintains a cinematic rhythm of extraordinary and astounding purity). This "filmic art" of the pre-cinematographic writers consists in making animated paintings, enriching them with all the artifices of vision, and placing them on different planes that are linked together in accordance with an artistic syntax that combines the continuity of the action with a rhythm that is pleasing to the reader's visual imagination.

We do not believe that these arguments imply an understanding of film as a derivative form of literature, a relationship that would go beyond that which the film-makers such as Griffith and Eisenstein identified in the early history of cinema, but rather that each of these two languages, the language of literature and the language of cinema, provides solutions to narrative difficulties that are in many ways comparable. These similarities have their basis in the natural relationship between a reality that can be narrated and the perspective of a determined viewpoint (or "ear-point," as François Jost calls it in a book from 1987), and can create the corresponding relation of events and descriptions of landscapes, objects, and people.

Shakespeare

Leglise's interpretation of the *Aeneid* was not long in provoking a reaction amongst experts in the work of William Shakespeare, perhaps the classic writer to whom cinema is most indebted, in qualitative if not quantitative terms. We will not delve into the entire history of all the cinematographic adaptations of Shakespeare's plays, which have been collected in a study by Kenneth S. Rothwell, but rather focus on the ways in which the pre-cinematographic is of great interest for the study of Shakespeare's work. In this regard, Henri

Lemaitre writes in 1960 about what he terms the "pre-cinematographic nature of Shakespearean drama" (Lemaitre 27), and René Lalou defines the author of *Macbeth*, a tragedy of which there have been at least thirty versions, as a true "precursor of cinema."

French studies of pre-cinema focus on *Henry V* (1598–99). Of special importance here is the role of the chorus, which voices a fascinating prologue to the play with an exploration of questions that will be repeated throughout the work. These questions have to do with the limits of the power of theater to represent a tale of heroism filled with spectacular scenes, events, and figures. The chorus of *Henry V* provokes the audience, encouraging them to use their imagination to compensate for the deficiencies of the scenic apparatus of a playhouse such as the Globe, deficiencies that were also present in the contemporary Spanish theaters or *corrales*, in which Lope de Vega and other Spanish comedic playwrights presented their works:

> Can this cock-pit hold
> The vasty fields of France? or may we cram
> Within this wooden O the very casques
> That did affright the air at Agincourt?
> O, pardon! since a crooked figure may
> Attest in little place a million;
> And let us, ciphers to this great accompt,
> On your imaginary forces work.
>
> (*Shakespeare 1966: 363*)

We can note here a subtle and *avant la lettre* semiological argumentation: the author takes advantage of the very conventionality of the language at his disposal and the imagination of the audience in order to compensate for the necessarily schematic representation of great battles and diplomatic intrigues that take place in both France and England. The chorus addresses us in the imperative, in a genuinely perlocutionary linguistic act that directly influences our behavior. The audience becomes complicit in the re-creation of the court and military worlds. In the third act we can read: "CHORUS: Thus with imagin'd wing our swift scenes flies / In motion of no less celerity / Than that of thought" (Shakespeare 389). And in the prologue to the fourth act: "Yet sit and see; / Minding true things by what their mockeries be" (409). The plea to the audience to actively cooperate in the filling in of the gaps and indeterminacies of the dramatic text is repeated in the prologue to *The Famous History of the Life of King Henry the Eighth*: "Therefore, for goodness' sake / […] think ye see / The very persons of our noble story / As they were living; think you see them great, / And follow'd with the general throng and sweat / Of thousand friends; then, in a moment see / How soon this mightiness meets misery" (855–56).

We can make no objection to the claim that Shakespeare was a potential film-maker, as Suhamy argues. The characteristics of his writing are in consonance with this claim, as is his desire to transcend the technical and expressive limits that the scenic apparatus of his time imposed upon him. In consequence, we could add the achievement of pre-cinematographic works to the many qualities of Shakespeare that have inspired so much debate amongst critics and researchers. This phenomenon, which came to light more than half a century ago with the study of Virgil's *Aeneid*, allows for another approach to the relationship between literature and film that further enriches the classic comparative theme of the reciprocal illumination of the arts.

9

THE RETURN OF LITERATURE

Is comparative literature a "metadiscipline"? This is a venturesome claim, but it is at least possible to imagine a future for comparative literature within literary studies as "an art of the in-between, a diplomacy of disciplines, a clearinghouse for cultural specificities" (Saussy, "Exquisite Cadavers" 20).

Such an optimistic stance with regard to the future of comparative literature may seem misguided, given the historical, economic, technological, and social circumstances in which we find ourselves at the beginning of the new millennium. There is a sense of the end of an era—above all in what concerns the literary and humanistic tradition which has been part of the Western experience since well before the advent of so-called postmodernity. If Nietzsche proclaimed the death of God in 1883, the following century would echo his claims, with much philosophical thought taking on the air of elegy. Francis Fukuyama would follow this trend with his announcement of the end of history, which had allegedly reached its arrival point with liberal democracy and the market economy. Fukuyama would, however, qualify his claims, admitting that history would not entirely end until advances in biotechnology had altered human beings to such a degree that we would enter a new post-human era. Damian Thompson, studying contemporary millenarianism, has also contemplated this "end of times," in the same way that J.H. Plumb had explored the "death of the past." Compared with these grand deaths, the end of the novel seems a minor matter, as does George Steiner's *The Death of Tragedy*, or Roland Barthes's famous "death of the author" explained in *Le Bruissement de la langue*.

It is within this apocalyptic context that we should place Susan Bassnett's claim, already mentioned in the first chapter, that "[t]oday, comparative literature is in one sense dead" (47). Bassnett linked this decline of comparative literature to the decrease in the number of university chairs dedicated to the discipline, the recuperation of the study of English Literature to the detriment of literary theory in the United States, the impact of cultural studies, and the exposure of Eurocentric bias by postcolonial studies. We also mentioned Gayatri Chakravorty Spivak's description in the year 2000, in her "Wellek Library Lectures in Critical Theory" in Irvine, of the final "gasp of a dying discipline," which she also saw as the result of the predominance of the postcolonial in cultural and social thought. This is hardly a promising diagnosis when it comes to enlivening comparative literature at the start of a new century, and it is similar in tone to the prologue to the second edition of Claudio Guillén's introduction to the discipline—"La Literatura comparada y la crisis de las humanidades" (Comparative Literature and the Crisis of the Humanities).

In this text Guillén transmits a general sense of uncertainty, given that the golden age of comparatism, which ran from the conclusion of World War II to the middle of the 1980s, seemed to have come to an end. Guillen's ideas are not far from those which Edward W. Said (9) put forth in his final work, *Humanism and Democratic Criticism*. The "Saussy Report" (*Comparative Literature in an Age of Globalization*), in its turn, takes a far more optimistic view with regard to the opportunities and possibilities for contemporary comparative literature both as an academic discipline and as a field of investigation.

On the level of university humanities departments, J. Hillis Miller (2–3) baldly states that the time of the study of literature is "over," first because of the after-effects of the deconstructive wave of which Hillis Miller was himself part, and also because of the growing influence of cultural studies. Literature, for Hillis Miller, is a category that has progressively lost its specificity in the broader categories of "discourse," "textuality," and "information." In his judgment, which is no less cruel than the situation warrants, literature is deprived of the power that would be taken for granted if it were an intimate part of a single homogeneous culture in which the citizens of a given nation reside (4).

As a corollary to the various deaths and extinctions that we have already mentioned, the Princeton professor Alvin Kernan published in 1990 a much discussed text: *The Death of Literature*. Kernan describes how and why that which since the Romantics we have termed literature is losing attraction as a category, disappearing both from the social world and from the consciousness of individuals. Both endogenous and exogenous elements play a part in this process, and Kernan views the effects of deconstruction and television as equally damaging to the continuity of literature. The latter, television, is for Kernan an emblem of the technological revolution that McLuhan identified as the death knell of the Gutenberg Galaxy. Deconstruction, blazing a spectacular trail through the American university system with its insistence on the absence of stable meanings of language and texts, had left the road open to a radical literary relativism, the liquidation of the canon, and, ultimately, to the discrediting of the ways in which literature had traditionally been studied as a privileged fount of knowledge and aesthetic education. Two scholars of the old school—both coincidentally named Bloom: Allan and Harold—stand out in their denunciation of this humanistic apocalypse, with works as significant as *The Closing of the American Mind* and *The Western Canon*, respectively.

The North American critic Sven Birkerts would be even more radical, publishing in 1994 *The Gutenberg Elegies*, a work in which he explains his pessimistic stance towards the future of reading in the electronic era. Birkerts strings together a series of arguments for how the new technologies can distort the human condition, fragmenting our identity and eroding the profundity of our consciousness. He adds, then, to the various dangers to humanism identified by Guillén, Hillis Miller, Said, or George Steiner, the no less terrible consequences of new technologies.

But the nub of the question lies not so much in how new communicative technologies are going to end the state of things in our field of interest, which is cultural and literary, but in which way they are going to fundamentally alter these as we move forward. The much heralded death of the book is not inexorable or definitive, for all that, in the coming years, the digital library might coexist with, or even replace, traditional forms of reading. And by the same reasoning, rather than focusing on the death of literature, we should imagine the possibilities and limits of cyberliterature, or, better still, the ways in which literature will change as a result of the digital era, becoming what could be termed "postliterature."

Kernan takes "literature" in its widest sense, a stance that is easily justifiable given the history of our civilization. For Kernan, the great works form a literary system of printed culture, and to a great degree its institutional power lies in the strength of the mechanical means that Gutenberg put at the service of an older technological revolution, the invention of the written alphabet discovered by the Sumerians between 3,000 and 4,000 BCE (cf. Chapter 3). It is important to note the extent to which the technologies of alphabetization and movable type echo and need one another, in their atomizing approach to language and their centralizing mode of production and distribution. To the industrial character of European printing, one might contrast the East Asian book, which, produced from carved wooden blocks, retained its roots in calligraphy, handicraft, and domestic industry.

The Gutenberg Galaxy

In this regard, a disciple of McLuhan, Walter Ong, pointed out how the second revolution (the printing press) gave an extraordinary push to the first (the phonetic alphabet), as it was printing and not writing that reified the word, and with it communication and intellectual activity.

More than thirty years ago, just as postcolonial studies began to make an impact in the academic world, McLuhan died. A professor of literature at the University of Toronto and expert in, among others, Tennyson, Pope, Coleridge, Poe, Mallarmé, Joyce, Pound, and John Dos Passos, in 1962 McLuhan published a work that would have an enormous influence on thought in the last third of the twentieth century: *The Gutenberg Galaxy: The Making of Typographic Man*. When McLuhan coined this phrase—Gutenberg Galaxy—which would go on to have such success, and which referred to the cycle of modernity marked by the invention of the printing press, he defined it against two preceding galaxies: that of orality, and that of manuscript. His work also meant that his name would be used to identify our contemporary era as that which is characterized by "electric" communication technologies, inaugurated in the nineteenth century with the pioneering invention of the telegraph, which was followed by Graham Bell's telephone, Edison's phonograph, the Lumière brothers' cinematograph, the radio of De Forest and Marconi, and finally the television, which was already a viable technology in the 1930s but would become universally available only at the end of World War II.

In the three decades that followed his death, events have occurred that are profoundly significant from the perspective that McLuhan made his own. In his writings he mentioned the computer as an instrument for the electronic storing of data, and from a contemporary viewpoint his writings seem prophetic. When he writes about how electronic interdependency recreates the world as a global village, in which information will be stored in a giant electronic brain rather than an enormous Alexandrian library, or describes the way in which, as our consciousness becomes exteriorized, Big Brother invades our interiority, it seems that he was able to predict quite accurately many aspects of our interconnected era.

Some years after *The Gutenberg Galaxy*, in an extensive interview with *Playboy* magazine, McLuhan expresses a premonition with regard to computers which in that moment could only have been a dream, but which is today the most important aspect of what, with Manuel Castells, we will term the "Internet Galaxy," or what others such as Neil Postman (22) prefer to call "the Age of Electronic Communication." According to McLuhan, the computer suggests the promise of technologically engendering a state of universal understanding and unity, a state of absorption in the world which could unite all of humanity within one family and create perpetual collective harmony and peace. This would be the appropriate— *real* in McLuhan's word—use of the computer, according to his criteria, as opposed to its employment as an instrument of marketing or for the resolution of technical problems (McLuhan and Zingrone).

Manuel Castells (31) argues, however, that despite the fact that the internet was conceivable by computer experts from the start of the 1960s, for individuals, companies, and society in general, the world wide web was born in 1995. That is to say, we have still not surpassed the formative period—the "incunabulum"—of what could be called our new Internet culture. Sufficient time has passed, however, to ask ourselves to what extent we can identify its effects on the human condition. Or, perhaps of lesser general importance, but for us a question that is not without interest: its relevance to the survival of literature.

Word and technology: intermediality

McLuhan liked to refer to "TV children" as the protagonists of the Gutenberg Galaxy, but we have now arrived at the Internet Galaxy, and to reflect this change Nicholas Negroponte uses the phrase "digital kids," a coining that prefigures Marc Prensky's "digital natives." Though McLuhan calculated that his TV children would enter kindergarten with 4,000 hours of exposure to television already accumulated, he thought that it was still possible that there could be a creative mixture of the alphabetic-Gutenberg and what he termed the "electric" culture.

We should avoid easy stereotypes here. Placing television as the origin of all the ills of our culture is still a commonplace among intellectuals, but it is also a huge simplification. In fact, television has provoked much worthwhile reflection among contemporary thinkers in literature and communication studies. Pierre Bourdieu (54–55), for example, described the way in which the state television of the 1950s used its monopoly to attempt to form the tastes of the public through cultural products such as documentaries, adaptations of classic works, cultural debates, etc. For Bourdieu, the television of the 1990s, on the other hand, pandered to the tastes of its audience and offered simple slices of life—talk shows, exhibitionism—designed to satisfy voyeuristic impulses. These conclusions are worth noting: the paternalist, pedagogical television of the past has given way to a demagogical submission to the lowest common denominator.

At the same time, Raymond Williams, one of the founders of the Birmingham circle and a key exponent of the Marxist sociology that is at the base of New Historicism and cultural studies, wrote an important essay on the relationship between television and cultural form. In contrast to other scholars' disdain for television, Williams, who was a television reviewer between 1968 and 1972 for the BBC's monthly magazine *The Listener*, saw television as a powerful cultural instrument, shared by elites and ordinary people, commercial and public interests, the state and private individuals. Williams rejects, above all, any form of technological determinism. For him, the new advances in communicative infrastructures are not autonomous, nor do they derive from intrinsic developments within science, but respond to the necessities thrown up by processes of historical, economic, political, social, and cultural change. Television is born, then, from "a complex of inventions and developments in electricity, telegraph, photography and motion picture, and radio" (Williams 7), but also from the exploitation and transformation of "received forms of other kinds of cultural and social activity [...]: the newspaper, the public meeting, the educational class, the theatre, the cinema, the sports stadium, the advertising columns and billboards" (39).

What seems, in any case, necessary for the development of comparative literature in our time is a rejection of the prejudices that can be identified with the elitism of the "happy few" capable of transcending the limits of a sole language or literature. These prejudices inform the rejection of translation as a means of access to texts in other languages, and also the strict division between the popular and the highbrow as objects of academic attention.

It is in this context that we can understand the growing importance within comparative literature of interartistic comparisons, to which the previous chapter was dedicated. In this regard, note the attention paid to interartistic comparison in the "Bernheimer Report" (45): "Comparative Literature should include comparisons between media, from early manuscripts to television, hypertext, and virtual realities. The material form that has constituted our object of study for centuries, the book, is in the process of being transformed through computer technology and the communications revolution. As a privileged locus for cross-cultural reflection, comparative literature should analyze the material possibilities of cultural expression, both phenomenal and discursive, in their different epistemological, economic, and political contexts. This wider focus involves studying not only the business of bookmaking but also the cultural place and function of reading and writings and the physical properties of newer communicative media."

Similarly, and around the same time, Douwe W. Fokkema ("Comparative Literature and the Problem") proposed a moderation of the exclusive focus on the literary in the discipline, and encourages comparison between the literary and the non-literary—musical, historical, philosophical, and legal texts. The treatment of these as comparable "discursive systems" is perfectly compatible with definitions of comparative literature such as those of Remak and Aldridge, cited in Chapter 1.

We do not lack precedents for the undermining of apocalyptic positions taken in the light of cultural revolutions. Humanity has always shown tremendous assimilative capacities with regard to new technologies, including those that Ong terms the "technologies of the word." We might remember here the Greek distrust of the letter as articulated in the Socratic dialogues. In the *Phaedrus*, Plato has Socrates tell the story of the invention of writing by the Egyptian god Theuth. As is well known, when Theuth presents his invention to the king Thamus/Amon, the latter casts suspicion on writing, citing its harmful effects on memory, and puts it into opposition with true knowledge, which can only be learned from the spoken words of the masters. Socrates, the creator of maieutics, concords with this vision. For him, written words were dead letters, mere simulacra of authentic, living discourse which, once written on the soul of the student, allowed him both to defend himself, and to know when it was appropriate to speak and when to stay silent.

As with writing, so disdained by Socrates, or with the invention of the printing press, which McLuhan links to schizophrenia and alienation (McLuhan and Zingrone), we might, following Sven Birkerts, consider the extent to which new media change us, and whether these changes are for the good. For Birkerts, the answers to these questions are exclusively negative: the new media are alienating forces, dividing us from the world and from ourselves.

Postman (12) denounces similar tendencies in his *Technopoly*, which discusses the surrender of technology to culture and the ways in which the new possibilities offered by technology fundamentally changed what we consider "knowledge" or "truth," and in consequence the basic structures through which a culture makes sense of reality. Postman defines Technopoly as a cultural state which founds its legitimacy in technology, and in which it finds its realization and direction (71).

Orality, writing, print

It seems logical that the future of literature—understood in its widest acceptance as the totality of knowledge transmitted through the word, and in the narrower and relatively recent sense of texts having a fundamentally aesthetic conception and functionality—should have become the preoccupation of intellectuals, humanists, students, and creators. Florence Dupont sheds light on some of these future possibilities in her indispensable *The Invention of Literature*, which deals with the foundation of our conceptions of literature, and their relation to the conflict between orality and writing.

Dupont, recalling the great philosophical and aesthetic works of the Greco-Roman world, postulates a "foundational alterity" in these, which she links to their original orality. Dupont's championing of the foundational orality of much of what we conceive to be literature allows us to imagine a future of a reinvented orality that would not constitute a break with our past. For Dupont, that future lies in the recycling of the written, its transformation into living energy, recuperating the meaning of Greco-Roman "literature" *avant la lettre*, a literature that was in reality nothing more than a spoken word in search of a speech act. McLuhan had himself highlighted the rebirth of orality in the global village thanks to the galaxy of electric communication media, a galaxy to which he had given his own name.

Another text that is especially informative with regard to the transformations of contemporary media arises from the experience of Janet Murray, who, after failing to find funding for a doctorate in English literature, became a systems programmer for IBM in the 1970s. When she did manage to achieve her academic ambitions, she became a member of MIT's "Laboratory for Advanced Technology in Humanities," an institution that counted Nicholas Negroponte among its professors. Murray, a brilliant Harvard-trained scholar, found herself not only at the vanguard of cybernetics in MIT, but also among a group of excellent hackers who filled their leisure time immersed in role-playing games on multi-user-domain networks. Murray, observing these games, noticed the applicability of narrative theory to them, with the *agon* that characterized the games corresponding to the earliest narrative forms.

The ludic foundations of art, literature, fiction, and the "willing suspension of disbelief," explicit in Schiller and in Coleridge, and attributed to the essence of the human condition by Huizinga, strengthen the argument that we are entering an age of digital narrative, the aesthetic of which is found in the immersive storylines and experiences provided by certain computer games. This would make them part of a new genre, what we could term "cyberdrama," which would not be the transformation of an already existing genre, but the reinvention of narrative art for the new digital era.

The key question is whether cyberdrama can progress from the realm of entertainment to that of art. For Murray, this is only a question of time. Murray also explores the roles of the "cyberauthor" or the "cyberbard," who would no longer be the communicators of a lineal cybertext that would be susceptible to the hermeneutic variations of readers, but would be rather the creators of schematic foundations and rules upon which users could develop. Agency, therefore, is more important than authorship, and these new artifacts would lack the stability and temporal and intersubjective durability of the texts that we categorize as literary today.

Postman (118) agrees that the printing press, in replacing manuscript, created new forms of literature, and that electronic writing has the potential to do the same. He defines three principal genres that would make up the universe of cyberliterature. After the already cited cyberdrama, there would be hypertextual narration, which would be made up of chains of stories that would be connected together through links that could also include multimedial elements such as sound or image. The third genre would be cyberpoetry, which is often linked with graphic design or visual art, an example of which was given in the electronic calligram in Chapter 8. Another distinctive phenomenon however is the, so to speak, "conventional" literature that is diffused through electronic platforms. This new and problematic scenario should not be ignored in a revision of the past, present, and future of comparative literature that we are attempting to describe.

Internet galaxy

We are immersed in a new communications revolution that the author of the *Gutenberg Galaxy* was not able to imagine, or live. The progress in the two long decades that succeeded his death, which occurred just at the start of the predominance of personal and home computers, has been so great as to appear literally unimaginable. But, paradoxically, all of this represents a recuperation of writing and its concomitant visuality: elements supposedly to be lost in the return to orality envisioned by McLuhan. It seems that the sequences of galaxies, as we have tried to demonstrate, do not represent fixed compartments or irreversible changes.

Umberto Eco reflects on these paradoxes, arguing that the computer is in fact characterized by a new syncreticism. It is similar in appearance to the great enemy of written culture, the television, but its screens bear evidence to an ever-increasing presence of letters and numbers. Another paradox we might mention here is the presence of the voice and listening as fundamental elements of the culture of the twentieth century, an insight that is more obvious if we remember that television is constructed on the generic basis of radio, to the point that some theorists of communication speak in this respect of "audiovision" (see Chion). A similar inversion is visible in the relationship between the Gutenberg and Internet Galaxies. Ted Nelson, one of the gurus of hypertext, reflects this in his coining of the term "literary machines" to describe computers.

It is possible to conclude, in light of these seeming contradictions, that the past millennium has been characterized by compatibility rather than exclusion, and that if writing did not eradicate orality, nor did printing eradicate manuscript, then the arena of cyberspace should be able to accommodate the communicative procedures that humans have developed throughout history in order to relate to one another intersubjectively. These communicative procedures have allowed us to transmit the range of our knowledge and culture; what we have come to know as literature is a fundamental part of these processes.

Despite the apocalyptic prognoses of some thinkers, the book today is in good health. Never throughout history have we written, printed, distributed, sold, plagiarized, explained, criticized, and read books to such a degree, and there is no sign that this activity is decreasing. A considerable proportion of these books belong to what we continue to define as literature. These facts, and the considerable cultural status attached to books, as well as our inveterate habits of reading, mean that we should be cautious in proclaiming the death of the printed word, and along with it the death of literature and its comparative study.

The making of the modern canon

There is a fundamental strength of literature. This has to do with the fact that there are more books than ever, and this in a double sense: in purely quantitative and material terms, as we have already mentioned; but also in a qualitative, artistic, and intellectual sense. Even if never again were another novel, poem, drama, or essay written, we would still be left, thanks to the inexhaustible amount of literary production that our cultures have accrued, with a surfeit of literature. The absurd hypothesis of the eradication of contemporary literature reminds us of our dependence on literatures past, and brings us to the great and polemical question of the so-called canon, an idea the genesis of which, as applied to literature, has been studied by Jan Gorak, moving on from previous essays (Gombrich, Frye, Kermode, and Said) prior to Harold Bloom's controversial *The Western Canon*.

But, as strategy theorists warn, that which can be considered a strength in a given institutional context can also, as paradoxical as it may seem, be a weakness. It is in this sense that we can understand the problem of "too many books" identified by the poet, engineer, and essayist Gabriel Zaid (52).[1] For every book that is published, there is a greater difference between what we read and what we could potentially read. According to Zaid, "the problem of the book is not limited to the millions in poverty who can barely read and write, but also applies to the millions of university students who do not want to read but to write" (52). He proposes, as a solution to this difficulty, a literary welfare state in which artistic geishas would be charged with reading, praising, and consoling the legions of writers frustrated by their lack of a public.

Zaid's ideas coincide with one of the aspects of Technopoly that Postman (69–70) describes. According to Postman, in this world there is a gap between information and human necessity. Information appears indiscriminately, directed to no one in particular, in enormous volume and speed, and without relation to any theory, meaning, or necessity.

We are flooded with information, to such an extent that one of the ways of defining Technopoly is to say that it is what happens when a society's defenses are washed away by an excess of information. Traditionally, courts, schools, and families were the institutions that controlled information. Concerning literature, the canon, with its basis firmly in academia, was a method for imposing order on the proliferation of information. The technician of this method was what Postman calls the "expert," whether a critic or a professor of literature. This expert would be more effective the greater her/his knowledge of written works in a variety of languages and eras, the gaining of which knowledge coincides with the requisites of comparative literature.

Julien Gracq, in his pamphlet *La littérature à l'estomac* (Literature of the Stomach), already warned in 1950 of a tendency that has been increasing in the past sixty years: what he describes as the "drama of the yearly book," a rate of productivity that he linked to the French author's desire to be talked of more than read. The result is the frenetic production of books of fiction conceived with the aim of massive and immediate sales, a phenomenon favored by the global publishing industry. Many of these best-sellers are characterized by a strange deliteralization. Their non-style reflects an attitude according to which prose that takes advantage of its poetic possibilities would be the great enemy of story-telling.

Surprising, in this regard, is the sincere and reiterated praise that Mario Vargas Llosa heaps on the extremely popular work of Stieg Larsson. The Peruvian Nobel Prize winner underlines a virtue of the Swedish writer that he too enjoys, the capacity to narrate, but Vargas Llosa does not mention Larsson's obvious failings. He argues that it is possible to write a novel that is at the same time formally imperfect and exceptional, similar perhaps to the "*escritura desatada*" (unstitched writing) that the Canon of Toledo in *El Quijote* attributes to books of chivalry.

Vargas Llosa's own work, the twenty-one novels that run from *Los jefes* (The Cubs) to *El héroe discreto* (The Discreet Hero), represents a stunning example of the harmonious alliance that can exist between the richness of the stories told and the sumptuousness of the language in which they exist. With Vargas Llosa, the conflict that Eco established at the time of the publishing of *La ciudad y los perros* (The Time of the Hero) between popular and elite culture does not exist. Much to the contrary, in his work he has been able to seduce a large readership through story-telling in a prose that is as beautiful as it is effective, and with a mastery of narrative strategies deriving from the techniques that the modernist writers of the first third of the twentieth century invented in order to surpass another prodigious way of making novels, that of the realism and naturalism of the previous century.

If we take into account the pre-, sub-, or para-literature of the scribblers that Gracq unmasks, and also that of those others who, as Zaid puts it, write without having read, we are confronted with the avalanche of what we could call, adapting a phrase of Gianni Vattimo referring to thought, *letteratura debole* (weak literature). Another term for this writing could be "postliterature."

In the context of the present situation of literary studies in particular, and the humanities in general, we might imagine the need to recuperate the role of the critic that Terry Eagleton found lacking when he compared our present to the situation at the start of the eighteenth century in England. Compared with the social role of critics such as Addison or Steele, at the end of the twentieth century, literary criticism seems either a mere academic matter, such as Steiner ridiculed, or—what is even worse—a part of the publicity arm of the book industry, fulfilling the function of consecrating works that are far from fulfilling the important role that the Spanish poet Antonio Machado reserved for literature as "*palabra esencial en el tiempo*" (Machado 1802; the essential word in time).

Another great menace for the future of literature could well be the tyranny of the public, which is often manipulated by powerful publicity machines. Postman (136) has observed that, in the same way as politicians make decisions in terms of the polls, so popular literature depends on the tastes of the public rather than the creativity of the artist. The result is a disposable literature, or literature as bluff or swindle, what Gracq calls a "*littérature au culot*" (literature of the dregs) or "*à l'esbroufe*" (cod literature).

One of the most damaging aspects of the destruction of the canon is precisely the attitude of those who write without having read. H. Bloom, on the other hand, constructs his theory of literature on reading (or misreading) the works that have had the most importance in the history of literature. His skepticism with regard to the continued reading of these works among new generations places him very close to other apocalyptic prophets. Shocked by the proliferation of new technologies that fill up our leisure time, he feels surrounded by negators of the canon, among whom he counts some of his own Yale disciples.

Although H. Bloom considers the task of teaching how to read almost impossible, asking himself whether, if "real reading is a lonely activity," then the impossible task of the teacher is to "teach solitude" (*The Western Canon* 519), this does not undermine the "elegiac conclusion" to his 1994 book, which tells us "neither what to read nor how to read it, only what I have read and think worthy of rereading, which may be the only pragmatic test for the canonical" (518). H. Bloom is right in at least one of his less extreme views: that there is no vigorous or creative writing without the process of literary influence—a difficult process to understand because the great writers do not choose their precursors, but are chosen by them.

As opposed to those who sustain that the canon—in origin a religious concept—is a system of texts in a struggle for survival that is mediated by social groups, educational institutions, and critical traditions, H. Bloom insists that the key is in decisions taken by writers who feel chosen by their precursors. Against the idea that aesthetic values depend on class dynamics, H. Bloom believes in the individual as the only method and only barometer of aesthetic value, and fears that we are destroying all the aesthetic and intellectual criteria of the humanities in the name of social justice.

Despite the various excesses in his theories, H. Bloom does recognize the obvious: it is impossible to control what Goethe termed *Weltliteratur*, and, if this is the case, it is fantastical to imagine that a specific individual or group can impose a canon of presences and exclusions. Nobody has the authority to tell us what will make up the Western canon, but at the same time, it does exist as an intellectual and pragmatic entity that is the fruit of the elective affinities of social groups (what Stanley Fish called "interpretive communities"), the action of educational systems, the tradition of criticism, and above all the "anxiety of influence," which is the voluntary adscription of writers to determined literary precursors, a theme that H. Bloom (*The Anxiety*) had studied before the publication of his work on the canon.

For Gerald Gillespie ("Rhinoceros"), polysystems theory could contribute to this debate on the canon, with its non-manichean approach to international literary relations and the neutralization of anti-Eurocentrism—the "ritual of condemnation of the European contribution to human affairs"—that characterizes much multiculturalist discourse. Insights such as this are shared by all those convinced that today the contrastive study of literary polysystems constitutes a space of transaction and exchange between comparative literature and the best of cultural studies.

Literature and time

In any argument that explores the various communicative galaxies, the essence and phenomenology of literature and its canon, and the sedimentation of readings throughout the centuries, the central importance of time is ever-present. Time can be conceived in terms of durability, and as such is a configuring agent of the canon. It is related to both media and the form of literary messages. Whereas orality, with its flexibility and openness, consigned literary survival to the memory of the oral reciter and his audiences, writing increased the stability of the textual form and thereby its durability, though this could be undermined by textual errors or misreadings. Gutenberg's revolution resulted in a certain democratization of writing and reading, just as it opened the Pandora's box of the economic and industrial mediation of the literary text. Today, however, we have seen the return of flexibility, with the hypertextuality and interactivity of the internet experience challenging our previous understandings of authorship. In this latter case, as in the proliferation of books and their increasing ephemerality, we could indeed find arguments to support Kernan's sounding of the death knell for literature in 1990.

Comparative literature is an intellectual and methodological perspective founded precisely on wide temporal (and spatial) horizons. It considers literature as a system of simultaneous relations, stable but also dynamic, a system that possesses its own meaning but also grants significance to each of its elements. This is literature without spatial or temporal boundaries, which transcends the barriers of different languages thanks to the circulation of texts, translation and multilingualism, and especially thanks to creators, mediators, and receptors.

What is at stake in light of the current situation of literature referred to above is something fundamental: the survival of literature as a language beyond the restrictions of space and time. This durability of literature is inherent as it constitutes the very texture of its discourse, its literariness, the condensation of an intangible message that is divorced from its original enunciative context but as such is open to any reader from any era who can make the text her/his own, and find his- or herself within it. Today's situation, on the other hand, might best be described not as Machado's "essential word in time," but as the banal word of the passing moment.

Writing conceived with the acceptance by its author of its short life-span would, under this perspective, cease to be literary, becoming something else—the pap of the leisure industry served up by a powerful industrial machine. The risk, then, lies in supplanting literature for something that would be a pale substitute, in which writers would become simple operatives within the cultural production line of Technopoly. To the question whether we are entering a period of "postliterature," comparative literature should give a strong response. This question constitutes one of the major challenges our era imposes on the discipline, but one for which it is sufficiently prepared, with the answer lying in two elements that are essential to comparative literature both in the present and in the future: education and ethics.

Reading and education

The "struggle of texts" from which we derive literary value is a debate that occurs in the texts themselves, in the reader, in language, and in discussions within society, but also, and with no less importance, in the classroom.

Poetry, the novel, theatre, and the essay reveal a genuine sense of who we are, and that which surrounds us, and also act as vital instruments in the education of our sensibility and in the correct formation of our intellect. In the pages of true literature there is also an irreplaceable resource for the full development of linguistic competency, an essential aid in the ability of citizens to act within society.

That is to say, it would be profoundly contradictory for professors of literature to be "anti-canonical." We cannot imagine how this could be the case among researchers and readers who are, both through duty and through enthusiasm, tireless readers, but also because the literature that we have studied is structured on a continuum that stretches from the origins of the aesthetic use of language, in all languages and cultures, and which orients us throughout our lives as readers. As H. Bloom himself argues, the canon is the true art of memory, the true base of cultural thought. To the same extent that it seems impossible to study literature without reference to comparative evaluation within a historic context, it would also be excessively limiting to reduce our study to a single literature.

T.S. Eliot's essay "Tradition and the Individual Talent," which we cited in our first chapter, confirms this. For the Nobel Prize winner from St. Louis, no poet, nor any artist in any field, finds his or her full meaning in themselves, but rather, this is revealed "for contrast and comparison, among the dead" (49). For all that, it is also important to pay attention to the programmatic formulation of the "Bernheimer Report" (44): "Comparative Literature should be actively engaged in the comparative study of canon formation and in reconceiving the canon. Attention should also be paid to the role of non-canonical readings of canonical texts, readings from various contestatory, marginal, or subaltern perspectives." The relevance of this debate on the canon for contemporary culture is reflected in the compilation of Jan Gorak published in 2001.

Similarly, Edward W. Said has left an important legacy in his call, in a posthumous work, for a "return to philology" as a foundation for an "idea of humanistic culture as coexistence and sharing" (*Humanism* xvi). In order to achieve such an objective, reading, a skill that can be taught and learned, is essential. This is reading as "reading for meaning" (*Humanism* 70), of texts that may be culturally or linguistically distant, for which, as René Étiemble held, translation as cultural practice, and even as object of investigation for comparatists, is absolutely necessary.

As opposed to such catastrophic visions as Samuel Huntington's "Clash of Civilizations," Said reminds us that the word *Koran* in Arabic means "reading," and that the practice of *ijtihad*—personal and lengthy reading, what we might term "close reading"—coincides in Islam with a profound humanistic commitment, to which comparative literature has much to contribute, especially in its capacity to teach how to read well, which today means participating in literary tradition without, however, ignoring the culture of the Other. George Steiner, too, would have liked to be remembered as an attentive reader, and we might recall here that Said claimed, a short time before his death, that his work as a humanist was the reading of fundamental texts, whatever their precedence. Teaching, for Said, was teaching how to read, just as reading well was the path to learning.

Gayatri Chakravorty Spivak (*Death* 13), for her part, despite her recognition of the difficulties of a "dying discipline," argues not only that comparatists should "cross borders" in the search for pluridiscursive and interdisciplinary perspectives, but also that the skills of reading should be recuperated: "It is my belief that initiation into cultural explanation is a species of such a training in reading. By abandoning our commitment of reading, we unmoor the connection between the humanities and cultural instruction" (72).

The new galaxies of information and communication require new pedagogical frameworks, some of which have to do with an education in the new technology. This is the great challenge for those who were not born as "digital children" and who today write, teach, research, and govern. The teaching of literature has to partake of a constant effort to recuperate the phenomenological basis of the literary fact, that is to say, the relation of the reader to the text. From the moment such a relation weakens, or even disappears, any further teaching of literature will become absurd. As Steiner put it in 1979, in a discussion of the proliferation of theories, methods, and new proposals with regard to the teaching of literature: "what we need are places, i.e., a table with some chairs around it, in which we can learn again how to read, how to read together" ("'Critic'/'Reader'" 452). This reading together is, some decades later, the best strategy for comparative literature, and could perhaps work as a slogan to describe its functioning: the reading together of the texts of various traditions, the most significant examples of world literature.

Perhaps the most immediate and urgent question in the teaching of literature is this return to reading, learning to read literature once more. Because, paradoxically, this competence is fading, and there is a strange contradiction in the fact that the most developed and educated societies are also those in which the capacity of the people to read complex texts on leaving the educational system seems to progressively worsen. Literature will cease to exist as such if there are no longer individuals who know how to read it and understand the complexity of the two codes of which it consists: the linguistic code, and, above this, the special code of properly literary conventions that have to be both known and practiced. But the most efficient and complete scenario for the reading of texts is one without frontiers, through which we move as readers with a comparatist perspective.

Literature and globalization

It is very significant, in this respect, that the concept of *Weltliteratur* coined by Goethe in 1827 is now, almost two centuries after his death, gaining a renewed relevance. The rapid evolution of contemporary society, caused in large degree by the prodigious developments in communications technology, has changed the world into a "global village" and explains perhaps why literary studies have recuperated the old idea of the German writer. The duality, so beloved of Claudio Guillén, of the "one" and the "multiple" underlies both the North American constitution of 1778 with its *E pluribus unum*, and the *Treaty Establishing a Constitution for Europe* signed in Rome on 29 October, 2004.

Already in the preamble to this treaty, Europe is mentioned as "unified in diversity," an idea taken up in article I, 3, which lists among the objectives of the European Union that "It shall respect its rich cultural and linguistic diversity, and shall ensure that Europe's cultural heritage is safeguarded and enhanced." This notion of the respectful meeting of differences is a running thread through all the text. In part II, in which the fundamental rights of the union are laid out, an important proportion of these have to do with "respecting the diversity of the cultures and traditions of the peoples of Europe," an attitude that is repeated in article II, 82 and in article III, 280: "The Union shall contribute to the flowering of the cultures of the Member States, while respecting their national and regional diversity and at the same time bringing the common cultural heritage to the fore."

This historical new configuration of Europe, which is not without a host of difficulties and contradictions, contextualizes, as was the case 200 years ago, the youngest of the literary disciplines. As we know, however, comparative literature should have as its guiding aim that of definitively abandoning Eurocentrism for the broader horizons of *Weltliteratur* evoked by Goethe. More than ever in its 200 years of existence, the primary function of this type of literary study should be to contribute to the multicultural recontextualization of European, Anglo-American, Oriental, and African perspectives. This does not mean simply negating these, but rather questioning their dominance, as proposed by Fokkema ("Comparative Literature and the Problem of Canon Formation") in his work on comparative literature and the problem of the formation of the canon.

In the context of a world made small by new communication media, in which the reduction of the dimensions of space and time have broken down the once almost insuperable barriers between individuals, cultures, and peoples, a new concept has come into being, the glocal—the global (diverse) and the local (one)—a concept that finds its origins in the area of Japanese economics, and which was later developed by the German sociologist Ulrich Beck and his British counterpart Roland Robertson. This idea was taken on in literary studies by Mary Louise Pratt ("Comparative Literature" 64), who argued more than twenty years ago for a literary comparatism that would include not only horizontal comparison, between "case A" and "case B," but also a vertical "relating the global and the local."

According to Pratt (59), comparative literature cannot ignore three historical processes that are transforming "the way literature and culture are conceived and studied in the academy": democratization in favor of minorities; decolonization; and, above all, globalization understood as "the increasing integration of the planet." From these three processes emerges a sense of "global citizenship" which supposes "the need for people who have deep familiarity with more than one language, literature, and culture" (Pratt 63). She requires of scholars the study of "literary and cultural formations relationally," reading "across the imperial divide," or studying "the interplay of hegemonic and counterhegemonic forms of expression, or the interaction of media." In any case, and without discarding the potential of translation, comparative literature "should remain the home for polyglots; multilingualism and polyglossia should remain its calling card."

The most fertile orientation of postcolonial studies operates in a similar vein, with its "contrapuntal analysis" (Said, *Culture* 66–67) paying due attention to peripheral or ignored literatures. As Guillén (*Entre lo uno* 23) remarks: "the imperial mentality is not only political; it is cultural and coincides morally with pride. We live in plural worlds and our great enemy is simplification. No vision has complete hegemony over the terrain that it contemplates. No culture is monolithic. No one of us is simply one thing."

A similar idea animates one of the most impassioned themes in Said's *Humanism and Democratic Criticism*. In this work, Said argues for the revitalization of one of the most politicized aspects of comparative literature, which, beyond academia, has always been fundamental in the minds of its founders and cultivators. Convinced that academic humanism should be both a theoretical and a practical endeavor, Said proposes to revive "a different kind of humanism that was cosmopolitan and text-and-language-bound in ways that absorbed the great lessons of the past" (11).

A cosmopolitan ethic

Ulf Hannerz, like Robertson or Betz, distinguishes between "cosmopolitans" and "locals," and supports a cosmopolitanism which would concede maximum relevance to those who, like Diogenes, consider themselves citizens of the world. For Hannerz (239), "cosmopolitanism in a stricter sense includes a stance toward the coexistence of cultures in the individual experience[.] It is an intellectual and aesthetic stance of openness toward divergent cultural experiences."

This is the cosmopolitanism that Fokkema ("Comparative Literature and the Problem") links to one of the fundamental tasks of comparative literature, the investigation of canon formation, or, better, the formation of the various canons elaborated by the interpretative communities of different cultural worlds. Any of these canons can be understood as an anthology of well known texts which are considered useful, are used in educational processes, and serve as a constant reference for critics and students of literature. This is the canon according to Fokkema, but his definition omits a basic point: the texts of the canon are chosen above all by writers, who before they become authors are diligent readers. For all the legitimate need to diversify the canon, it is important to remember the "expansive" capacity of some of these, their capacity to extend to very distant cultures and territories.

Fokkema's political convictions include a concept of cosmopolitanism based on the universality of the human condition, an ethics based on the rights inherent to all that can compete with any reductive identity politics, to which we will refer below. We human beings have something in common that differentiates us from other animals: the desire to break free from natural, biological, or material conditions. But this does not mean that we have overcome the possibility of wars over not only geopolitical, economic, or strategic issues, but also cultural, religious, and identitarian differences. Wars, even, between canons, as Henry Louis Gates pointed out in his 1992 book.

We can speak, then, of a truly "cosmopolitan reading" as does Kwame Anthony Appiah (*Cosmopolitanism*). If his cosmopolitanism consists in a formula as simple as "universalism plus difference," "cosmopolitan reading" is that in which this difference is enacted. When Appiah (204) adds that "cosmopolitan reading presupposes a world in which novels […] travel between places where they are understood differently, because people are different and welcome to their difference," he could be thinking of, without citing them, "global" writers such as the Japanese Haruki Murakami, the Anglo-Caribbean of Indian descent Vidiadhar Surajprasad Naipaul, or the Albanian Ismail Kadaré. In terms of Fish, this cosmopolitan reading consists simply in the multiplication of "interpretative communities" which would act simultaneously, a possibility that is viable today given the globalization of the literary polysystem, the internationalization of the culture industry, and the generalized mediation of translators. This would invariably give rise to many "misreadings," but this is always the case for any literary work that survives beyond its most immediate readership.

We have claimed that the universality of the human condition is consubstantial with the idea of comparative literature since its foundation, from the thought of Juan Andrés, Madame de Staël, and Goethe to Jean-Jacques Ampère, Abel-François Villemain, and Hugo Meltzl de Lomnitz, and which has gained renewed relevance today in a cosmopolitanism that can be understood in terms of Kwame Anthony Appiah's "ethics in the world of strangers."

To understand this point, we might recall that there are two possible meanings of a word that has always been related to literature: identity. It can be taken, and perhaps too often, in an individualistic sense, according to which identity is "the fact of being who or what a person or thing is: the characteristics determining who or what a person or thing is." To this definition, sometimes affirmed with great vigor, according to which a person has to be similar to or different from others, we should add another sense no less legitimate, which refers rather to "a close similarity of affinity," identity in the sense of identical, "similar in every detail, exactly alike." This total identification can never occur between human beings, but at the same time, we do sense, and this conviction is often strengthened through travel and reading, that the great themes and passions that go to the heart of our human condition, from our birth to our death and in our hatreds and our loves, are fundamental and common to all.

This idea, which demands all kinds of nuances and inspires simultaneously deep reflection, is perfectly explained in these accurate words of the Polish writer and Nobel Prize winner, Wisława Szymborska, with which she concludes her poem *Nic dwa razy* ("Nothing twice"):

> With smiles and kisses, we prefer
> to seek accord beneath our star,
> although we're different (we concur)
> just as two drops of water are.

(20)

It is necessary, too, to recuperate the belief that literature is a social and aesthetic institution of the first importance, and that the teaching of literature is not a mere adornment of educational systems dedicated primarily to more "serious" concerns. The teaching of literature plays an irreplaceable part in the formation of pluralist, democratic, and cosmopolitan citizens. In this regard, it is very probable, as Ed Ahearn and Arnold Weinstein argue (80), that "comparative literature is arguably the sole humanistic discipline equipped to meet this educational and ideological challenge."

Note

1 In the world of companies and large corporations there is a well trusted strategic tool designed in order to find out the real situation of an organization and take decisions that would safeguard its future. This is the SWOT (strengths, weaknesses, opportunites, threats) method of analysis. We trust that the methodological application of such a resource to an entity as complex as literature will not be considered gratuitous.

GLOSSARY

This glossary provides clear and short definitions of key concepts of comparative literature. It lists only concepts that have been elaborated from within comparative literature, notwithstanding the relevance for the discipline of concepts elaborated by other disciplines and fields. The purpose of this lexicon is to provide the reader with a picture of comparative literature's basic conceptual map. Differing ways in which terms are used, their ancestry, and the reasons why they are relevant in current debates in the discipline go beyond its scope.

Abduction It is a kind of inference characterized by probability and, as such, is linked to creativity, for it is responsible for introducing new ideas in research.

Alienation A canon of comparability that consists of introducing something kindred but unconnected historically with the phenomenon under research.

Comparative literary history A field within comparative literature that consists of building narratives on the networks of interactions among several literatures in time.

Comparative literature One of the four main literary disciplines that replicate the experience of the common reader with the aim of understanding the workings of world literature by way of abduction.

Comparative poetics A field within comparative literature that analyzes similarities and differences between explicit poetics across the world.

East/West studies A field within comparative literature that researches similarities/ differences between Eastern and Western literary cultures.

Formal affinity A canon of comparability that consists of taking as object of study a literary phenomenon that is formally identical in more than one literary culture.

Genetic contact Literary similarity that is due to a factual connection between two works (at least) of distinct literatures.

Homology A canon of comparability that analyzes different literary elements that serve the same function in different literary cultures.

Interarts A field within comparative literature that researches the relations of literature and other arts.

Interdiscourse A field within comparative literature that researches the relations of literatures and other fields of human expression.

Interliterary centrism Regional bodies larger than interliterary communities or communities that play a large-scale integrative role.

Interliterary community Coexistence of several literary systems whose level of integration is due to linguistic, historical, geographical, and/or political-administrative factors.

Interliterary theory A comparatist theory that addresses the literary growth through two main paths—genetic contacts and typological affinities.

Intermediality This term embraces both the interaction of several media within a single work and the passage of a work from one medium to another.

Literary comparison Search of a relationship between two (at least) literary works or parts of them with the aim of identifying similarities and differences.

Transduction Transformation of literary elements when they are introduced in communicative networks.

Typological affinity Literary similarity between two works (at least) that cannot be explained by contact.

Weltliteratur Concept coined by Goethe to refer to the field of literary interactions that go beyond the limits of the nation and which points to a worldwide literary communication.

World literary knowledge Alternative way of conceptualizing and analyzing literary production.

World literature Historically understood as all literary works in the world, the canon of masterpieces, or the network of genetic and typological relations.

FURTHER READING

1. Comparative literature and the future of literary studies

a) *What Does the Comparative Do?* Special issue of *PMLA* 128.3 (2013). (It includes twelve short contributions which discuss the cross-fertilization between comparative literature and other disciplines and fields, such as area studies, world literature, cosmopolitanism, ecocriticism, literary history, translation, literary theory, and postcolonial studies.)

b) Felski, Rita and Susan Stanford Friedman, eds. *Comparison. Theories, Approaches, Uses*. Baltimore: Johns Hopkins University Press, 2013. (This collective book brings together sixteen essays that argue for the importance of greater self-reflexivity about the politics and methods of comparison in teaching and in research.)

c) Behdad Ali and Dominic Thomas, eds. *A Companion to Comparative Literature*. Oxford: Wiley-Blackwell, 2011. (This is a collective volume that brings together several contributions around six topics: road maps, theoretical directions, disciplinary intersections, linguistic trajectories, postcolonial mobilities, and global connections.)

d) Damrosch, David, Natalie Melas and Mbongiseni Buthelezi, eds. *The Princeton Sourcebook in Comparative Literature. From the European Enlightenment to the Global Present*. Princeton: Princeton University Press, 2009. (This collection brings together thirty-two pieces, from foundational statements by Herder, Madame de Staël, and Nietzsche to work by a range of influential comparatists, such as Lawrence Venuti, Gayatri Chakravorty Spivak, and Franco Moretti.)

e) Saussy, Haun, ed. *Comparative Literature in an Age of Globalization*. Baltimore: Johns Hopkins University Press, 2006. (This is the decennial ACLA Report. It includes contributions on the state of the discipline mainly from a US perspective, though its discussions are extremely valuable for other academic locations.)

2. Comparative literature as interliterary theory

a) Domínguez, César. "Dionýz Ďurišin and a Systemic Theory of World Literature." *The Routledge Companion to World Literature*. Ed. Theo D'haen, David Damrosch and Djelal Kadir. London: Routledge, 2012. 99–107. (A survey on interliterary theory and discussion of future directions.)

b) Vajdová, Libuša and Róbert Gáfrik, eds. *New Imagined Communities. Identity Making in Eastern and South-Eastern Europe*. Bratislava: Kalligram – Ústav Svetovej Literatúry, SAV, 2010. (This collective volume focuses on the process of identity-making in Central, Eastern and South-Eastern Europe. Some of Dionýz Ďurišin's concepts are discussed.)

c) *World Literature Studies* 18.2 (2009). (This issue of the journal published by the Institute of World Literature at Bratislava includes contributions related to interliterary theory.)

d) Koška, Ján and Pavol Koprda, eds. *Koncepcie svetovej literatúry v epoche globalizácie/Concepts of World Literature in the Age of Globalisation*. Bratislava: Institute of World Literature – Slovak Academy of Sciences, 2003. (Collective book that addresses the tenets of interliterary theory within the context of globalization, with a special focus on world literature, interliterary communities, and reception.)

e) Ďurišin, Dionýz and Armando Gnisci, eds. *Il Mediterraneo. Una rete interletteraria/La Méditerranée. Un réseau interlittéraire/Stredomorie medziliterárna siet*. Rome: Bulzoni, 2000. (This collective volume addresses one of the last projects by Ďurišin, the study of literary centrisms—here the Mediterranean.)

3. Comparative literature and decoloniality

a) Santos, Boaventura de Sousa. *Epistemologies of the South. Justice against Epistemicide*. Boulder: Paradigm, 2014. (Though Santos is not properly speaking a decolonial thinker, the *Grupo Modernidad/Colonialidad* claims the relevance of his contribution. In a world of multiple injustices, Santos calls attention to "cognitive injustice," meaning the failure to recognize different ways of knowing.)

b) Special issue of *Cultural Studies* 21.2–3 (2007). (This special issue is devoted to decolonial studies and includes seminal essays translated into English for the first time, as well as new contributions by Walter D. Mignolo, Catherine Walsh, and Freya Schiwy, among others.)

c) Mignolo, Walter D. *Local Histories/Global Designs. Coloniality, Subaltern Knowledges, and Border Thinking*. Princeton: Princeton University Press, 2000. (This book remains the most important contribution to decolonial studies. Though it does not address comparative literature *per se*, its discussions of Occidentalism, the relocation of languages and knowledges, and border thinking prove instrumental for new directions in comparative literature.)

d) Gaonkar, Dilip Parameshwar, ed. *Alternative Modernities*. Durham, NC: Duke University Press, 2001. (The essays in this collection approach the dilemmas of modernity from transnational and transcultural perspectives. The language and lessons of Western modernity are comparatively analyzed from such sites as China, Russia, India, Trinidad, and Mexico.)

e) Dussel, Enrique. *The Underside of Modernity: Apel, Ricoeur, Rorty, and Taylor and the Philosophy of Liberation*. Trans. Eduardo Mendieta. Atlantic Highlands, NJ: Humanities Press, 1996. (In this book Dussel discusses what he calls the "developmental fallacy," that is, the belief that there is a linear sequence that moves from the premodern, underdeveloped to the modern, developed and industrialized.)

4. World literature as a comparative practice

a) Damorsch, David, ed. *World Literature in Theory*. Oxford: Wiley, 2014. (This reader is split into four parts which examine the origins and seminal formulations of world literature, world literature in the age of globalization, contemporary debates on world literature, and localized versions of world literature.)

b) D'haen, Theo, César Domínguez and Mads Rosendahl Thomsen, eds. *World Literature. A Reader*. London: Routledge, 2013. (This reader brings together thirty essential readings which display the theoretical foundations of world literature, as well as showing its conceptual development over a 200-year period.)

c) D'haen, Theo. *The Routledge Concise History of World Literature*. London: Routledge, 2012. (A remarkable and informative overview on world literature, which traces the term from its earliest roots and situates it within a number of relevant contexts from postcolonialism to postmodernism.)

d) D'haen, Theo, David Damrosch and Djelal Kadir, eds. *The Routledge Companion to World Literature*. London: Routledge, 2012. (This book includes four key sections: the history of world literature, the disciplinary relationship of world literature to other fields, theoretical issues on world literature, and a global perspective on the politics of world literature.)

e) Thomsen, Mads Rosendahl. *Mapping World Literature. International Canonization and Transnational Literatures*. London: Continuum, 2008. (This is a study of literature and literary history in the light of globalization, which argues that international canonization of books and authors can be used as an instrument for textual analysis of world literature.)

5. Comparing themes and images

a) Jockers, Matthew L. *Macroanalysis: Digital Methods and Literary History*. Urbana: University of Illinois Press, 2013. (This book introduces readers to large-scale literary computing and the potential of macroanalysis. By using computational analysis to retrieve key words, phrases, and linguistic patterns, a new approach to thematic studies is possible.)

b) Zacharasiewicz, Waldemar. *Imagology Revisited*. Amsterdam: Rodopi, 2010. (This book traces the emergence of national and ethnic stereotypes in the early modern age and studies their evolution and multiple functions in a wide range of texts, from travelogues and diaries to novels, plays and poetry, produced between the sixteenth and twentieth centuries.)

c) Wilkinson, Martha. *Antigone's Daughters. Gender, Family and Expression in the Modern Novel*. Bern: Peter Lang, 2008. (This book can be read as an example of thematic analysis. Each chapter isolates an aspect of Antigone's struggle within both public and domestic spheres as she negotiates her independence and asserts her voice.)

d) Beller, Manfred and Joep Leerssen, eds. *Imagology. The Cultural Construction and Literary Representation of National Characters. A Critical Survey*. Amsterdam: Rodopi, 2007. (The most updated and comprehensive collective book for the study of national stereotypes.)

e) Sollors, Werner, ed. *The Return of Thematic Criticism*. Cambridge, MA: Harvard University Press, 1993. (A seminal book reasserting the validity of the thematic approach to literature. The essays collected come out of such diverse traditions as Russian film theory, narratology, linguistics, and psychoanalytic criticism, among others.)

6. Comparative literature and translation

a) Pym, Anthony. *Exploring Translation Theories*. London: Routledge, 2010. (This book builds on Western theories of translation, starting with a survey of the classical twentieth-century linguistic approaches before moving on to more recent models such as cultural translation. Each central paradigm and its associated theories are addressed in turn, including equivalence, purpose, description, uncertainty, localization, and cultural translation.)

b) Apter, Emily. *The Translation Zone. A New Comparative Literature*. Princeton: Princeton University Press, 2006. (This book examines the vital role of translation studies in the "invention" of comparative literature as a discipline.)

c) Munday, Jeremy. *Introducing Translation Studies. Theories and Applications*. London: Routledge, 2001. (This textbook brings together translation theory and practice by applying each approach to texts from a broad range of languages.)

d) Venuti, Lawrence. *The Translator's Invisibility: A History of Translation*. London: Routledge, 1995. (This book, which provides a fascinating history of translation from the seventeenth century to the present day, is one of the best introductions to the field of literary studies.)

e) Steiner, George. *After Babel: Aspects of Language and Translation*. Oxford: Oxford University Press, 1975. (Though published in 1975, Steiner's book remains a classic in translation studies.)

7. Comparative literary history

a) Cornis-Pope, Marcel and John Neubauer, eds. *History of the Literary Cultures of East-Central Europe: Junctures and Disjunctures in the Nineteenth and Twentieth Centuries*. 4 vols. Amsterdam: John Benjamins, 2004–10. (This comparative history constitutes an outstanding example of the AILC/ICLA Coordinating

Committee's research on the field, especially with regard to the new regional approach.)

b) Krishnaswamy, Revathi and John C. Hawley, eds. *The Postcolonial and the Global*. Minneapolis: University of Minnesota Press, 2008. (This collective book brings the humanities and social sciences into dialogue by examining issues such as globalized capital, discourses on antiterrorism, and identity politics, with a special focus on postcolonial studies.)

c) Lindberg-Wada, Gunilla, ed. *Studying Transcultural Literary History*. Berlin: Walter de Gruyter, 2006. (This collective book brings together contributions on the possibilities for transcultural literary history, the objects of literary history, rethinking world literature, the practice of writing transnational and translingual literary history, literature in circulation, and translating cultures and literatures.)

d) Manning, Patrick. *Navigating World History. Historians Create a Global Past*. New York: Palgrave Macmillan, 2003. (Though this book does not address literary issues, it provides the reader with an informative introduction to world history as narrative and technique.)

e) Hutcheon, Linda and Mario J. Valdés, eds. *Rethinking Literary History. A Dialogue on Theory*. Oxford: Oxford University Press, 2002. (This collective book revisits literary history as it has been developed over the last two decades of the twentieth century, including issues such as the national model, racial memory, and the colonial model.)

8. Interartistic comparison

a) Spurr, David Anton. *Architecture and Modern Literature*. Ann Arbor: University of Michigan Press, 2012. (This book explores the representation and interpretation of architectural space in modern literature from the early nineteenth century to the present, with the aim of showing how literary production and architectural construction are related as cultural forms in the historical context of modernity.)

b) Corrigan, Timothy, ed. *Film and Literature: An Introduction and Reader*. London: Routledge, 2011. (This book offers an introduction to the contentious relationship between literature and film, with selected readings that cover influential approaches to this area of study.)

c) Chekee, Stephen. *Writing for Art: The Aesthetics of Ekphrasis*. Manchester: Manchester University Press, 2011. (This is a general survey of the philosophical and theoretical questions arising from the encounter of literary texts and artworks. It covers a broad range of writing and theory about the relation of literary text to visual arts.)

d) Cahir, Linda Costanzo. *Literature into Film: Theory and Practical Approaches*. Jefferson: McFarland, 2006. (An introductory textbook on movie adaptations of literary texts, including novels, short stories, and plays.)

e) Correa, Delia da Sousa, ed. *Phrase and Subject. Studies in Literature and Music*. Oxford: Legenda, 2006. (This collection of interdisciplinary essays provides a valuable introduction to literature and music studies, mapping the contours of recent research and investigating the mutual aesthetic influence of the two arts.)

9. The return of literature

a) Jay, Paul. *The Humanities "Crisis" and the Future of Literary Studies.* New York: Palgrave Macmillan, 2014. (This book explores the idea that the humanities seem to be in a perpetual state of crisis. Jay argues that the real humanities crisis is not intellectual but budgetary, and it can be opposed most effectively by taking a multifaceted approach to explaining their value in twenty-first-century higher education.)

b) Pressman, Jessica. *Digital Modernism. Making It New in New Media.* Oxford: Oxford University Press, 2014. (This book examines how and why some of the most innovative works of online electronic literature adapt and allude to literary modernism.)

c) Brown, Garrett Wallace and David Held, eds. *The Cosmopolitanism Reader.* Cambridge: Polity, 2010. (This volume brings together twenty-five seminal essays in the development of cosmopolitan thought.)

d) Gupta, Suman. *Globalization and Literature.* Cambridge: Polity, 2009. (This book presents a state-of-the-art overview of the relationship between globalization studies and literature and literary studies, and discusses the impact of globalization on the production and reception of literary texts.)

e) Kolbas, E. Dean. *Critical Theory and the Literary Canon.* Boulder: Westview, 2001. (Kolbas discusses the conservative humanist and liberal pluralist positions on the canon, which either assiduously avoid any sociological explanation of the canon or treat texts as stand-ins for particular ideologies.)

BIBLIOGRAPHY

Abu-Lughod, Janet L. *Before European Hegemony: The World System A.D. 1250–1350*. New York: Oxford University Press, 1989.

Ahearn, Ed and Arnold Weinstein. "The Function of Criticism at the Present Time: The Promise of Comparative Literature." *Comparative Literature in the Age of Multiculturalism*. Ed. Charles Bernheimer. Baltimore, MD: Johns Hopkins University Press, 1995. 77–85.

Aldridge, A. Owen, ed. *Comparative Literature: Matter and Method*. Urbana: University of Illinois Press, 1969.

Amin, Samir. *Delinking. Towards a Polycentric World*. Trans. Michael Wolfers. London: Zed Books, 1985.

Ampère, Jean-Jacques. *De l'histoire de la poésie*. Marseille: Feissat aîné et Demonchy, 1830.

——*Histoire de la littérature française au Moyen Âge comparée aux littératures étrangères. Introduction: Histoire de la formation de la langue française*. Paris: Just Tessier, 1841.

——*La Grèce, Rome et Dante. Études littéraires d'après nature*. 7th edn. Paris: Didier, 1870.

Anderson, Benedict. *Imagined Communities. Reflections on the Origin and Spread of Nationalism*. Rev. and exp. edn. London: Verso, 1991.

Appiah, K. Anthony. "*Geist* Stories." *Comparative Literature in the Age of Multiculturalism*. Ed. Charles Bernheimer. Baltimore, MD: Johns Hopkins University Press, 1995. 51–57.

——"Cosmopolitan Readings." *Cosmopolitan Geographies. New Locations in Literature and Culture*. Ed. Vinay Dharwadker. New York: Routledge, 2001. 197–227.

——*The Ethics of Identity*. Princeton: Princeton University Press, 2005.

——*Cosmopolitanism. Ethics in a World of Strangers*. New York: W.W. Norton, 2006.

Apter, Emily. *Against World Literature: On the Politics of Untranslatability*. London: Verso, 2013.

Aristotle. *Poetics*. Trans. Stephen Halliwell. Cambridge, MA: Harvard University Press, 2005.

Arnold, A. James, ed. *A History of Literature in the Caribbean*. 3 vols. Amsterdam: John Benjamins, 1994–97.

Ashcroft, Bill, Gareth Griffiths and Helen Tiffin. *The Empire Writes Back. Theory and Practice in Post-Colonial Literatures*. 2nd edn. London: Routledge, 2002.

Auerbach, Erich. "Philology and *Weltliteratur*." Trans. M. and E.W. Said. *The Princeton Sourcebook in Comparative Literature. From the European Enlightenment to the Global Present*. Ed. David Damrosch, Natalie Melas and Mbongiseni Buthelezi. Princeton: Princeton University Press, 2009. 126–38.

Austin, Peter K. and Julia Sallabank. "Introduction." *The Cambridge Handbook of Endangered Languages*. Ed. Peter K. Austin and Julia Sallabank. Cambridge: Cambridge University Press, 2011. 1–24.

Backès, Jean-Louis. *Littérature et musique*. Paris: PUF, 1994.

Bacon, Francis. *The Philosophical Works of Francis Bacon*. Ed. John M. Robertson. London: Routledge, 1905.

Bagno, Vsevolod Jevgenijevič. "Vzájomná komplementárnos' v systéme medziliterárneho spoločenstva. Na materiáli mnohonárodnej literatúry Španielska." Dionýz Ďurišin et al. *Osobitné medziliteráme spoločenstvá*. Bratislava: VEDA-Ústav svetavej literatúry, 1987. 1: 170–83.

Bakhtin, Mikhail M. *Rabelais and His World*. Trans. Hélène Iswolsky. Bloomington: Indiana University Press, 1984.

Baldensperger, Fernand. "Littérature comparée: le mot et la chose." *Revue de Littérature comparée* 1 (1921): 5–29.

Barricelli, Jean-Pierre. *Melopoiesis: Approaches to the Study of Literature and Music*. New York: New York University Press, 1988.

Barricelli, Jean-Pierre and Joseph Gibaldi, eds. *Interrelations of Literature*. New York: The Modern Language Association of America, 1982.

Barthes, Roland. *Le Bruissement de la langue*. Paris: Seuil, 1984.

Bassnett, Susan. *Comparative Literature: A Critical Introduction*. Oxford: Blackwell, 1993.

Beck, Ulrich. *Cosmopolitan Vision*. Cambridge: Polity Press, 2006.

Beecroft, Alexander. "World Literature without a Hyphen. Towards a Typology of Literary Systems." *New Left Review* 54 (2008): 87–100.

Bergard, Laird W. *The Comparative Histories of Slavery in Brazil, Cuba, and the United States*. Cambridge: Cambridge University Press, 2007.

Bermann, Sandra and Michael Wood, eds. *Nation, Language, and the Ethics of Translation*. Princeton: Princeton University Press, 2005.

Bernabé, Jean, Patrick Chamoiseau and Raphaël Confiant. *Éloge de la créolité/In Praise of Creoleness*. Paris: Gallimard, 1989.

Bernheimer, Charles. "Introduction. The Anxieties of Comparison." *Comparative Literature in the Age of Multiculturalism*. Ed. Charles Bernheimer. Baltimore, MD: Johns Hopkins University Press, 1995. 1–17.

Bernheimer, Charles. "The Bernheimer Report, 1993. Comparative Literature at the Turn of the Century." *Comparative Literature in the Age of Multiculturalism*. Ed. Charles Bernheimer. Baltimore, MD: Johns Hopkins University Press, 1995. 39–48.

Bernheimer, Charles, ed. *Comparative Literature in the Age of Multiculturalism*. Baltimore, MD: Johns Hopkins University Press, 1995.

Betz, Hang-Georg. *Radical Right-Wing Populism in Western Europe*. London: Macmillan, 1994.

Birkerts, Sven. *The Gutenberg Elegies. The Fate of Reading in the Electronic Age*. Boston: Faber & Faber, 1994.

Bloch, Marc. "A Contribution towards a Comparative History of European Societies." *Land and Work in Medieval Europe*. Berkeley: University of California Press, 1967. 44–81.

Bloom, Allan. *The Closing of the American Mind*. New York: Simon & Schuster, 1987.

Bloom, Harold. *The Anxiety of Influence*. New York: Oxford University Press, 1973.

——*The Western Canon. The Books and Schools of the Ages*. New York: Harcourt Brace, 1994.

Borges, Jorge Luis. *Labyrinths. Selected Stories & Other Writings*. New York: New Directions, 2007.

Bortolussi, Marisa and Peter Dixon. *Psychonarratology: Foundations for the Empirical Study of Literary Response*. New York: Routledge, 2003.

Boumans, Louis and Jan Jaap de Ruiter. "Moroccan Arabic in the European Diaspora." *Language Contact and Language Conflict in Arabic. Variations on a Sociolinguistic Theme*. Ed. Aleya Rouchdy. London: Routledge, 2002. 259–85.

Bourdieu, Pierre. *Sur la télévision*. Paris: Liber-Raison d'agir, 1996.

Braider, Christopher. "Of Monuments and Documents: Comparative Literature and the Visual Arts in Early Modern Studies, or The Art of Historical Tact." *Comparative Literature in an Age of Globalization*. Ed. Haun Saussy. Baltimore, MD: Johns Hopkins University Press, 2006. 155–74.

Brandes, Georg. "World Literature." Trans. Haun Saussy. *The Princeton Sourcebook in Comparative Literature.* Ed. David Damrosch, Natalie Melas and Mbongiseni Buthelezi. Princeton: Princeton University Press, 2009. 61–66.

Braudel, Ferdinand. *The Structures of Everyday Life. The Limits of the Possible.* Trans. Siân Reynolds. Vol. 1 of *Civilization and Capitalism 15th–18th Century.* London: William Collins, 1985.

——*The Mediterranean and the Mediterranean World in the Age of Philip II.* Trans. Siân Reynolds. Vol. 1. Berkeley: University of California Press, 1996.

Brown, Calvin S. *Music and Literature. A Comparison of the Arts.* Athens, GA: The University of Georgia Press, 1963.

——*A Bibliography on the Relations of Literature and the Other Arts, 1952–1967.* New York: AMS, 1968.

Brunel, Pierre and Yves Chevrel, eds. *Précis de littérature comparée.* Paris: Presses Universitaires de France, 1989.

Bruner, Jerome S. *Actual Minds, Possible Worlds.* Cambridge, MA: Harvard University Press, 1986.

Bryson, Norman, Michael Ann Holly and Keith Moxey, eds. *Visual Culture: Images and Interpretations.* Hanover, NH: University Press of New England, 1994.

Burke, Kenneth. "Literature as Equipment for Living." *The Philosophy of Literary Form: Studies in Symbolic Action.* Baton Rouge: Louisiana State University Press, 1941. 253–62.

Cabo Aseguinolaza, Fernando, Anxo Abuín González and César Domínguez, eds. *A Comparative History of Literatures in the Iberian Peninsula.* Vol. 1. Amsterdam: John Benjamins, 2010.

Canudo, Ricciotto. *Manifeste des Septs Arts.* Paris: Séguier, 1955.

Cao Shunqing. *The Variation Theory of Comparative Literature.* Berlin: Springer, 2013.

Cao Shunqing and Zhi Yu. "The Principles and Ways of the Dialogues between Chinese–Western Literary Theories." *Comparative Literature: East & West* 5.1 (2003): 84–106.

Cao Xueqin and Gao E. *Honglou meng.* Ed. Zhongguo yishu yanjiuyuan "Honglou meng" yanjiu suo. 2 vols. Beijing: Renmin wenxue chubanshe, 2002.

Cao Xueqin and Gao E. *The Story of the Stone.* Trans. David Hawkes and John Minford. 5 vols. Harmondsworth: Penguin, 1973–86.

Casanova, Pascale. *The World Republic of Letters.* Trans. M.B. DeBevoise. Cambridge, MA: Harvard University Press, 2004.

Casas, Arturo. "Catro modelos para a nova Historia literaria comparada. Unha aproximación epistemolóxica." *Bases metodolóxicas para unha historia comparada das literaturas na península Ibérica.* Ed. Anxo Abuín González and Anxo Tarrío Varela. Santiago de Compostela: Universidade de Santiago de Compostela, 2004. 45–71.

Cassin, Barbara, ed. *Dictionary of Untranslatables: A Philosophical Lexicon.* Trans. and ed. Emily Apter, Jacques Lezra and Michael Wood. Princeton: Princeton University Press, 2013.

Castells, Manuel. *La Galaxia Internet. Reflexiones sobre Internet, empresa y sociedad.* Barcelona: Plaza & Janés, 2001.

Célis, Raphaël, ed. *Littérature et musique.* Brussels: Facultés Universitaires Saint-Louis, 1982.

Cervantes, Miguel de. *Don Quixote.* Trans. Edith Grossman. London: Vintage, 2005.

Chadwick, Nora K. and Victor Zhirmunsky. *Oral Epics of Central Asia.* Cambridge: Cambridge University Press, 1969.

Chaffe, Diane: "Pictures and Portraits in Literature: Cervantes as the Painter of *Don Quijote.*" *Anales Cervantinos* 19 (1981): 49–56.

Chakrabarty, Dipesh. *Provincializing Europe. Postcolonial Thought and Historical Difference.* Princeton: Princeton University Press, 2008.

Chang, Leiling. *La Présence de la musique dans "Concert baroque" d'Alejo Carpentier.* Montreal: Université de Montréal, 1997.

Chaturvedi, Vinayak. "Introduction." *Mapping Subaltern Studies and the Postcolonial.* Ed. Vinayak Chaturvedi. London: Verso, 2012. vii–xviii.

Chion, Michel. *L'Audio-vision*. Paris: Nathan, 1990.

Clements, Robert. J. *Comparative Literature as Academic Discipline. A Statement of Principles, Praxis, Standards*. New York: The Modern Language Association of America, 1978.

Clifford, James. *The Predicament of Culture: Twentieth-Century Ethnography, Literature, and Art*. Cambridge, MA: Harvard University Press, 1988.

——*Routes: Travel and Translation in the Late Twentieth Century*. Cambridge, MA: Harvard University Press, 1997.

Cluck, Nancy Anne, ed. *Literature and Music*. Provo: Brigham Young University Press, 1981.

Cohen, Tom, ed. *Jacques Derrida and the Humanities. A Critical Reader*. Cambridge: Cambridge University Press, 2001.

Collins, Randall. *The Sociology of Philosophies: A Global Theory of Intellectual Change*. Cambridge, MA: Harvard University Press, 1998.

Cooke, Brett and Frederick Turner, eds. *Biopoetics: Evolutionary Explorations in the Arts*. Lexington, KY: ICUS, 1999.

Cornis-Pope, Marcel and John Neubauer. *Towards a History of the Literary Cultures in East-Central Europe: Theoretical Reflections*. New York: American Council of Learned Societies, 2002.

——"Literary Nodes of Political Time." *History of the Literary Cultures of East-Central Europe: Junctures and Disjunctures in the 19th and 20th Centuries*. Ed. Marcel Cornis-Pope and John Neubauer. Vol. 1. Amsterdam: John Benjamins, 2004. 33–38.

——"General Introduction." *History of the Literary Cultures of East-Central Europe: Junctures and Disjunctures in the 19th and 20th Centuries*. Ed. Marcel Cornis-Pope and John Neubauer. Vol. 4. Amsterdam: John Benjamins, 2010. 1–9.

Coutinho, Eduardo F. and Victoria Peralta. "The Cultural Centers of Latin America. Introduction." *Literary Cultures of Latin America. A Comparative History*. Ed. Mario J. Valdés and Djelal Kadir. Vol. 2. Oxford: Oxford University Press, 2004. 307–11.

Crane, Mary Thomas. *Shakespeare's Brain: Reading with Cognitive Theory*. Princeton: Princeton University Press, 2001.

Crary, Jonathan. *Techniques of the Observer. On Vision and Modernity in the Nineteenth Century*, Cambridge, MA: The MIT Press, 1992.

Cruz Seruya, Trino. "El bilingüismo gibraltareño: aproximación a una literatura que se resiste a nacer." *III Congreso Internacional de la Lengua Española, Rosario*. 2004. <http://congresosdelalengua.es/rosario/ponencias/identidad/cruz_t.htm>.

Crystal, David. *English as a Global Language*. 2nd edn. Cambridge: Cambridge University Press, 2003.

Culler, Jonathan. "Comparative Literature and Literary Theory." *Michigan Germanic Studies* 5.2 (1979): 170–84.

——"Comparative Literature, at Last." *Comparative Literature in an Age of Globalization*. Ed. Haun Saussy. Baltimore, MD: Johns Hopkins University Press, 2006. 237–48.

——*Literary Theory. A Very Short Introduction*. Oxford: Oxford University Press, 2011.

Curtius, Ernst Robert. *European Literature and the Latin Middle Ages*. Tr. Willard R. Trask. Princeton: Princeton University Press, 1953.

D'haen, Theo, David Damrosch and Djelal Kadir, eds. *The Routledge Companion to World Literature*. London: Routledge, 2012.

D'haen, Theo, César Domínguez and Mads Rosendahl Thomsen, eds. *World Literature. A Reader*. London & New York: Routledge, 2013.

Damrosch, David. *What Is World Literature?* Princeton: Princeton University Press, 2003.

——"World Literature in a Postcanonical, Hypercanonical Age." *Comparative Literature in an Age of Globalization*. Ed. Haun Saussy. Baltimore, MD: Johns Hopkins University Press, 2006. 43–53.

Damrosch, David, Natalie Melas and Mbongiseni Buthelezi, eds. *The Princeton Sourcebook in Comparative Literature*. Princeton: Princeton University Press, 2009.

Davidson, Donald. "A Nice Derangement of Epitaphs." *Truth and Interpretation: Perspectives on the Philosophy of Donald Davidson*. Ed. Ernest Lepore. Oxford: Blackwell, 1986. 443–46.

——"On the Very Idea of a Conceptual Scheme." *Inquiries into Truth and Interpretation.* Oxford: Clarendon Press, 2001. 183–98.

Delalande, Francois. "Music Analysis and Reception Behaviours: Sommeil by Pierre Henry". *Journal of New Music Research* 27-1-2 (1998): 13–66.

Dennis, Philip and Anne Taylor. "Gibraltar." *Encyclopedia of Post-Colonial Literatures in English.* Ed. Eugene Benson and L.W. Conolly. Vol. 1. London: Routledge, 1994. 585–87.

Derrida, Jacques. "Signature événement contexte." *Marges de la philosophie.* Paris: Minuit, 1972. 367–93.

——*Limited Inc.* Trans. Samuel Weber and Jeffrey Mehlman. Evanston, IL: Northwestern University Press, 1988.

——"The Future of the Profession or the University without Condition (Thanks to the 'Humanities,' What *Could Take Place* Tomorrow)." *Jacques Derrida and the Humanities. A Critical Reader.* Ed. Tom Cohen. Cambridge: Cambridge University Press, 2001. 24–57.

——"Who or What Is Compared? The Concept of Comparative Literature and the Theoretical Problems of Translation." Trans. Eric Prenowitz. *Discourse* 30.1–2 (2008): 22–53.

Dilthey, Wilhelm. *Einleitung in die Geisteswissenschaften. Versuch einer Grundlegung für das Studium der Gesellschaft und der Geschichte.* Leipzig: Duncker & Humblot, 1883.

Dobrenko, Evgeny. "Literary Criticism and the Institution of Literature in the Era of War and Late Stalinism." *A History of Russian Literary Theory and Criticism. The Soviet Age and Beyond.* Ed. Evgeny Dobrenko and Galin Tihanov. Pittsburgh: University of Pittsburgh Press, 2011. 163–83.

Doležel, Lubomír. "Semiotics of Literary Communication." *Strumenti Critici* 1.1 (1986): 5–48.

——"Literary Transduction: Prague School Approach." *The Prague School and its Legacy in Linguistics, Literature, Semiotics, Folklore and the Arts.* Ed. Yishai Tobin. Philadelphia: John Benjamins, 1988. 165–76.

——*Occidental Poetics. Tradition and Progress.* Lincoln: University of Nebraska Press, 1990.

Domínguez, César. "Literary Emergence as a Case Study of Theory in Comparative Literature." *CLCWeb: Comparative Literature and Culture* 8.2 (2006): <http://dx.doi.org/10.7771/1481-4374.1304>.

——ed. *Literatura europea comparada.* Madrid: Arco Libros, 2013.

Donne, John. *The Complete English Poems.* Harmondsworth: Penguin, 1976.

Dupont, Florence. *L'Invention de la littérature. De l'ivresse grecque au texte latin.* Paris: La Découverte, 1994.

Ďurišin, Dionýz. *Sources and Systematics of Comparative Literature.* Trans. Peter Tkáč. Bratislava: Univerzita Komenského, 1974.

——*Theory of Literary Comparatistics.* Trans. Jessie Kocmanová. Bratislava: VEDA, 1984.

——"Aspects ontologiques du processus interlittéraire." *Slavica Slovaca* 20.1 (1985): 1–22.

——*Theory of Interliterary Process.* Trans. Jessie Kocmanová. Bratislava: VEDA, 1989.

——*Čo je svetová literatúra.* Bratislava: Vydavateľstvo Obzor, 1992.

——*Notions et principes.* Trans. Alena Anettová. Vol. 6 of *Communautés interlittéraires spécifiques.* Bratislava: Institut de Littérature Mondiale, 1993.

Ďurišin, Dionýz et al. *Osobitné medziliterárne spoločenstvá.* 6 vols. Bratislava: VEDA-Ústav svetavej literatúry, 1987–93.

Ďurišin, Dionýz and Armando Gnisci, eds. *Il Mediterraneo. Una rete interletteraria.* Rome: Bulzoni, 2000.

Durkheim, Émile. "Préface." *L'Année sociologique* 1 (1898 [1896–97]): i–vii.

Eagleton, Terry. *The Function of Criticism. From "The Spectator" to Post-Structuralism.* London: Verso, 1994.

Eco, Umberto. "Afterword." *The Future of the Book.* Ed. Geoffrey Nunberg. Berkeley: University of California Press, 1996. 295–306.

Eckermann, Johann Peter. *Gespräche mit Goethe in den letzen Jahren seines Lebens.* Berlin: Aufbau, 1982.

Einstein, Albert. "Fundamental Ideas and Problems of the Theory of Relativity." Lecture delivered to the Nordic Assembly of Naturalists at Gothenburg. July 11, 1923. <http://www.nobelprize.org/nobel_prizes/physics/laureates/1921/einstein-lecture.pdf>.

Eliot, T.S. "Tradition and the Individual Talent." *The Sacred Wood. Essays on Poetry and Criticism*. London: Methuen, 1972. 47–53.

Escobar, Arturo. "Worlds and Knowledges Otherwise. The Latin American Modernity/Coloniality Research Program." *Cultural Studies* 21.2–3 (2007): 179–210.

Espagne, Michel. *Le Paradigme de l'étranger. Les chaires de littérature étrangère au XIXe siècle*. Paris: Cerf, 1993.

Étiemble, René. *Hygiène des lettres: Savoir et goût*. Paris: Gallimard, 1958.

——*Comparaison n'est pas raison. La crise de la Littérature Comparée*. Paris: Gallimard, 1963.

——*Essais de littérature (vraiment) générale*. Paris: Gallimard, 1974.

——*Ouverture(s) sur un comparatisme planétaire*. Paris: Christian Bourgois, 1988.

——"Do We Have to Revise the Notion of World Literature?" Trans. Theo D'haen. *World Literature. A Reader*. Ed. Theo D'haen, César Domínguez and Mads Rosendahl Thomsen. London: Routledge, 2013. 93–103. Orig. pub. 1964.

Even-Zohar, Itamar. "Polysystem Theory." *Poetics Today* 1 (1979): 287–310.

——"Interference in Dependent Literary Polysystems." *Actes du VIIIe Congrès de l'Association Internationale de Littérature Comparée/Proceedings of the International Comparative Literature Association*. Ed. B. Köpeczi and G.M. Vajda. Vol. 2. Stuttgart: Erich Bieber, 1980. 617–22.

——"Laws of Literary Interference." *Poetics Today* 11.1 (1990: *Polysystem Studies*): 53–72.

——"The Position of Translated Literature Within the Literary Polysystem." *Poetics Today* 11.1 (1990): 45–51.

——"The Role of Russian and Yiddish in the Crystallization of Modern Hebrew." *Studies in Jewish Culture in Honour of Chone Shmeruk*. Ed. Israel Bartal, Ezra Mendelsohn, and Chava Turniansky. Jerusalem: The Zalman Shazar Center for Jewish History, 1993. 105–18.

Fernández Retamar, Roberto. *Para una teoría de la literatura hispanoamericana*. Santafé de Bogotá: Instituto Caro y Cuervo, 1995.

Fierro Cubiella, Eduardo. *Gibraltar: aproximación a un estudio sociolingüístico y cultural de la Roca*. Cádiz: Universidad de Cádiz, 1997.

Fish, Stanley. *Is There A Text in This Class? The Authority of Interpretative Communities*. Cambridge, MA: Harvard University Press, 1980.

Fokkema, Douwe W. "Method and Programme of Comparative Literature." *Synthesis* 1 (1974): 51–62.

——"Comparative Literature and the New Paradigm." *Canadian Review of Comparative Literature/Revue Canadienne de Littérature Comparée* 9 (1982): 1–18.

——"Cultural Relativism Reconsidered: Comparative Literature and Intercultural Relations." *Douze cas d'interaction culturelle dans l'Europe ancienne et l'Orient proche ou lointain*. Paris: Organisation des Nations Unies pour l'Éducation, la Science et la Culture, 1984. 239–55.

——"Comparative Literature and the Problem of Canon Formation." *Canadian Review of Comparative Literature/Revue Canadienne de Littérature Comparée* 23.1 (1996): 51–66.

Foley, John Miles. *The Theory of Oral Composition: History and Methodology*. Bloomington: Indiana University Press, 1988.

——*How to Read an Oral Poem*. Urbana, IL: University of Illinois Press, 2002.

——*Oral Tradition and the Internet: Pathways of the Mind*. Urbana, IL: University of Illinois Press, 2012.

Foucault, Michel. "What is an Author?" *The Book History Reader*. Ed. David Finkelstein and Alistair McCleery. London: Routledge, 2002. 225–30.

Freud, Sigmund. *The Psychopathology of Everyday Life*. London: Penguin, 2003.

Frye, Northrop. *The Critical Path. An Essay on the Social Context of Literary Criticism*. Bloomington: Indiana University Press, 1973.

——"The Responsibilities of the Critic." *Modern Language Notes* 91 (1976): 797–813.

Fukuyama, Francis. "The End of History?" *The National Interest* 16 (1989): 3–18.

Gadamer, Hans-Georg. *Truth and Method*. Trans. Joel Weinsheimer and Donald G. Marshall. London: Bloomsbury, 2013.

Galli Mastrodonato, Paola, ed. *Ai confini dell'impero. Le letterature emergenti. Atti del Convegno di Macerata, 17–18 maggio 1994*. Rome: Vecchiarelli, [1996].

Gamsa, Mark. *The Chinese Translation of Russian Literature. Three Studies*. Leiden: Brill, 2008.

Garrett, Mary. "Some Elementary Methodological Reflections on the Study of the Chinese Rhetorical Tradition." *International and Intercultural Communication Annual* 22 (1999): 53–63.

Gates, Henry Louis. *Loose Canons: Notes on the Cultural Wars*. New York: Oxford University Press, 1992.

Gemelli, Giuliana. *Fernand Braudel*. Trans. Brigitte Pasquet and Béatrice Propetto Marzi. Paris: Odile Jacob, 1995.

Genette, Gerard. *Palimpsests. Literature in the Second Degree*. Trans. Channa Newman and Claude Doubinsky. Lincoln, NE: University of Nebraska Press, 1997.

Gérard, Albert S., ed. *European-Language Writing in Sub-Saharan Africa*. 2 vols. Budapest: Akadémiai Kiadó, 1986.

Gillespie, Gerald. "Rhinoceros, Unicorn, or Chimera? A Polysystemic View of Possible Kinds of Comparative Literature in the New Century." *Journal of Intercultural Studies* 19 (1992): 14–21.

——*By Way of Comparison. Reflections on the Theory and Practice of Comparative Literature*. Paris: Honoré Champion, 2004.

Glotz, Gustave. "Réflexions sur le but et la méthode de l'histoire." *Revue internationale de l'enseignement* 54 (1907): 481–95.

Gnisci, Armando, ed. *Introduzione alla letteratura comparata*. Milan: Bruno Mondadori, 1999.

——*Via della Decolonizzazione europea*. Isernia: Cosmo Iannone, 2004.

Godzich, Wlad. "Emergent Literature and the Field of Comparative Literature." *The Comparative Perspective on Literature: Approaches to Theory and Practice*. Ed. Clayton Koelb and Susan Noakes. New York: Columbia University Press, 1988. 18–36.

Goethe, Johann Wolfgang von. *Goethes Gespräche mit J. P. Eckermann*. Ed. Johann Peter Eckermann. Leipzig: Insel, 1908.

——"On World Literature." *World Literature. A Reader*. Ed. Theo D'haen, César Domínguez and Mads Rosendahl Thomsen. London: Routledge, 2013. 9–15.

Goodman, Nelson. *Ways of Worldmaking*. Indianapolis: Hackett, 1988.

Gorak, Jan. *The Making of the Modern Canon. Genesis and Crisis of a Literary Idea*. London: Atholone, 1991.

——ed. *Canon vs. Culture. Reflections on the Current Debate*. New York: Garland, 2001.

Gracq, Julien. *La Littérature à l'estomac*. Paris: Jose Corti, 1950.

Grassin, Jean-Marie. "Introduction: The Problematics of Emergence in Comparative Literary History." *Littératures émergentes/Emerging Literatures*. Ed. Jean-Marie Grassin. Vol. 10 of *Actes du XIe Congrès de l'Association Internationale de Littérature Comparée (Paris, 20–24 août 1985)/Proceedings of the XIth Congress of the International Comparative Literature Association (Paris, 20–24 August, 1985)*. Bern: Peter Lang, 1996. 5–16.

Groeben, Norbert. *Rezeptionsforschung als empirische Literaturwissenschaft*. Kromber: Scriptor, 1977.

Guha, Ranajit. "Preface." *Subaltern Studies: Writings on South Asian History and Society*. Ed. Ranajit Guha, Vol. 1. Delhi: Oxford University Press, 1982. vii–viii.

——*Elementary Aspects of Peasant Insurgency in Colonial India*. Delhi: Oxford University Press, 1983.

——*History at the Limit of World-History*. New York: Columbia University Press, 2002.

Guillén, Claudio. "Literatura como sistema." *Filologia Romanza* 4 (1957): 1–29.

——*Literature as System. Toward the Theory of Literary History*. Princeton: Princeton University Press, 1971.

——"Emerging Literatures: Critical Questionings of a Historical Concept." *Emerging Literatures*. Ed. Reingard Nethersole. Bern: Peter Lang, 1990. 1–23.

——*The Challenge of Comparative Literature*. Trans. Cola Franzen. Cambridge, MA: Harvard University Press, 1993.

——*Entre el saber y el conocer. Moradas del estudio literario*. Valladolid: Universidad de Valladolid Cátedra – Jorge Guillén, 2001.

——"La Literatura Comparada y la crisis de las humanidades." *Entre lo uno y lo diverso. Introducción a la Literatura Comparada (Ayer y hoy)*. Barcelona: Tusquets, 2005. 11–24.

——*Entre lo uno y lo diverso. Introducción a la Literatura Comparada (Ayer y hoy)*. Barcelona: Tusquets, 2005.

Gumbrecht, Hans Ulrich. *In 1926: Living at the Edge of Time*. Cambridge, MA: Harvard University Press, 1997.

Guyard, Marius-François. *La Littérature comparée*. Paris: Presses Universitaires de France, 1965.

Hannerz, Ulf. "Cosmopolitans and Locals in World Culture." *Theory, Culture and Society* 7.2–3 (1990): 295–310.

Hannick, Jean-Marie. "Brève histoire de l'histoire comparée." *Le Comparatisme dans les sciences de l'homme. Approches pluridisciplinaires*. Ed. Guy Jucquois and Christophe Vielle. Brussels: De Boeck Université, 2000. 301–27.

Haring, Lee. "What Would a True Comparative Literature Look Like?" *Teaching Oral Traditions*. Ed. John Miles Foley. New York: The Modern Language Association, 1998. 34–45.

Hassan, Waïl S. and Rebecca Saunders. "Introduction." *Comparative Studies of South Asia, Africa and the Middle East* 23.1–2 (2003): 18–31.

Hayot, Eric. *On Literary Worlds*. New York: Oxford University Press, 2012.

Heffernan, James A.W. *Museum of Words: The Poetics of Ekphrasis from Homer to Ashbery*. Chicago: University of Chicago Press, 1993.

Henríquez Ureña, Pedro. *Literary Currents in Hispanic America*. Cambridge, MA: Harvard University Press, 1945.

Herskovits, Melville J. *Acculturation: The Study of Cultural Contact*. New York: J.J. Augustin, 1938.

Higonnet, Margaret. "Comparative History of Literatures in European Languages." *A Comparative History of Literatures in the Iberian Peninsula*. Ed. Fernando Cabo Aseguinolaza, Anxo Abuín González and César Domínguez. Vol. 1. Amsterdam: John Benjamins, 2010. i–ix.

Hillis Miller, J. "Will Comparative Literature Survive the Globalization of the University and the New Regime of Telecommunications?" *Tamkang Review* 31.1 (2000): 1–21.

Hoesel-Uhlig, Stefan. "Changing Fields: The Directions of Goethe's *Weltliteratur*." *Debating World Literature*. Ed. Christopher Prendergast. London: Verso, 2004. 26–53.

Hogan, Patrick Colm. *Cognitive Science, Literature, and the Arts: A Guide for Humanists*. New York: Routledge, 2003.

Hollier, Denis, ed. *A New History of French Literature*. Cambridge, MA: Harvard University Press, 1989.

Horace. *Epistles Book II and Ars poetica*. Ed. Niall Rudd. Cambridge: Cambridge University Press, 1989.

Howell, James. *Instructions for Forreine Travell*. [1642] Westminster: Constable, 1895.

Huntington, Samuel P. *The Clash of Civilizations and the Remaking of World Order*. New York: Touchstone, 1997.

Ingarden, Roman. *Das literarische Kunstwerk*. 3rd edn. Tübingen: Max Niemeyer, 1931.

Iriye, Akira. *Global Interdependence: The World After 1945*. Cambridge, MA: Harvard University Press, 2014.

Iser, Wolfgang. *The Act of Reading: A Theory of Aesthetic Response*. Baltimore, MD: Johns Hopkins University Press, 1978.

Jackson, Russell, ed. *The Cambridge Companion to Shakespeare on Film*. Cambridge: Cambridge University Press, 2000.

Jakobson, Roman. "Über die phonologischen Sprachbünde." *Travaux du Cercle linguistique de Prague* 4 (1931): 234–40.

——"On Linguistic Aspects of Translation." *Selected Writings II*. The Hague: Mouton, 1971. 260–66.

Jameson, Fredric. "Third World Literature in the Era of Multinational Capitalism." *Social Text* 15 (1986): 65–88.

Jardine, Alexander. *Letters from Barbary, France, Spain, Portugal, & c.* Vol. 2. London: T. Cadell, 1788.

Jauss, Hans Robert. "Esthétique de la réception et communication littéraire." *Critique: Revue générale des publications françaises et étrangères* 413 (1981): 1116–30.

Jolles, André. *Einfache Formen: Legende, Sage, Mythe, Rätsel, Spruch, Kasus, Memorabile, Märchen, Witz.* Tübingen: Max Niemeyer, 1982.

Jorgens, Jack J. *Shakespeare on Film.* Bloomington: Indiana University Press, 1977.

Jost, François. *L'Œil-caméra. Entre film et roman.* 2nd edn. Lyon: Presses Universitaires de Lyon, 1987.

Joyce, James. *Ulysses.* New York: Random House, 1961.

Jucquois, Guy. *Généalogie d'une méthode.* Vol. 1 of *Le Comparatisme.* Louvain-la-Neuve: Peeters, 1989.

——"Le Comparatisme. Éléments pour une théorie." *Le Comparatisme dans les sciences de l'homme. Approches pluridisciplinaires.* Ed. Guy Jucquois and Christophe Vielle. Brussels: De Boeck Université, 2000. 17–46.

Kennedy, George A. *Comparative Rhetoric. An Historical and Cross-Cultural Introduction.* New York: Oxford University Press, 1998.

Kernan, Alvin. *The Death of Literature.* New Haven, CT: Yale University Press, 1990.

Kircher, Atanasio. *Ars Magna Lucis et Umbrae. Liber Decimus.* Ed. José Luis Couceiro Pérez. Trans. Inés Verde Pena and Ma Liliana Martínez Calvo. Santiago de Compostela: Universidade de Santiago de Compostela, 2000.

Klátic, Zlatko. *Štúrovci a Juhoslovania: príspevok k dejinám slovensko-juhoslovanských literárnych vzťahov.* Bratislava: SAV, 1965.

Klooster, Wim. *Revolutions in the Atlantic World. A Comparative History.* New York: New York University Press, 2009.

Konstantinović, Zoran et al, eds. *Proceedings of the IXth Congress of the International Comparative Literature Association/Actes du IXe Congrès de l'Association Internationale de Littérature Comparée.* 3 vols. 3. Innsbruck: Institut für Sprachwissenschaft der Universität, 1980.

Koška, Ján and Pavol Koprda, eds. *Koncepcie svetovej literatúry v epoche globalizácie.* Bratislava: Ústav svetovej literatúry – Slovenskej akadémie, 2003.

Kottak, Conrad Phillip. *Mirror for Humanity. A Concise Introduction to Cultural Anthropology.* 7th edn. New York: McGraw-Hill, 2010.

Kramer, L. *Music and Poetry.* Berkeley: University of California Press, 1984.

Krieger, Murray. *Ekphrasis: The Illusion of the Natural Sign.* Baltimore, MD: Johns Hopkins University Press, 1992.

Krishnaswamy, Revathi. "Toward World Literary Knowledges: Theory in the Age of Globalization." *Comparative Literature* 62.4 (2010): 399–419.

Kuhn, Thomas S. *The Structure of Scientific Revolutions.* Chicago: University of Chicago Press, 1962.

Kujundžić, Dragan. *The Returns of History. Russian Nietzscheans after Modernity.* Albany: State University of New York Press, 1997.

Lagerroth, Ulla-Britta, Hans Lund and Erik Hedling, eds. *Interart Poetics: Essays on the Interrelation of the Arts and Media.* Amsterdam: Rodopi, 1997.

Lalou, René. "Shakespeare, précurseur du cinéma." *L'Âge Nouveau* 109 (1960): 70–74.

Lambert, José. "Plaidoyer pour un programme des études comparatistes. Littérature comparée et théorie du polysystème." *Orientations de recherches et méthodes en Littérature comparée.* Montpellier: Société Française de Littérature Générale et Comparée – Université Paul Valéry, 1984. 59–69.

——"Les Relations littéraires internationales comme problème de réception." *Oeuvres & Critiques* 11.2 (1986): 173–89.

——"Un modèle descriptif pour l'étude de la littérature. La littérature comme polysystème." *Contextos* 9 (1987): 47–67.

——"Itamar Even-Zohar's Polysystem Studies: An interdisciplinary Perspective on Cultural Research." *Canadian Review of Comparative Literature/Revue Canadienne de Littérature Comparée* 24.1 (1997): 7–14.

Lampert-Weissig, Lisa. *Medieval Literature and Postcolonial Studies*. Edinburgh: Edinburgh University Press, 2010.

Le Blanc, Claudine. "Littératures orales, littérature et littérature comparée: une discipline pour penser l'oralité littéraire." *Comparer l'étranger. Enjeux du comparatisme en littérature*. Ed. Émilienne Baneth-Nouailhetas and Claire Joubert. Rennes: Presses Universitaires de Rennes, 2006. 111–27.

Legge, James, trans. *The Life and Works of Mencius*. London: Trübner, 1875.

Leglise, Paul. *Une Œuvre de pre-cinéma: L'Eneide. Essai d'analyse filmique du premier chant*. Paris: Debresse, 1958.

Lemaitre, Henry. "Shakespeare, the Imaginary Cinema, and the Pre-Cinema". *Focus on Shakespearean Films*. Ed. and trans. Charles W. Eckert. Englewood Cliffs: Prentice-Halls, 1972. 27–36.

Lessing, Gotthold Ephraim. *Laocoön. An Essay on the Limits of Painting and Poetry*. Trans. Edward Allen McCormick. Baltimore, MD: Johns Hopkins University Press, 1984.

Li, Yu [Li Yu]. *The Carnal Prayer Mat*. Trans. Patrick Hanan. Honolulu: University of Hawaii Press, 1990.

Lipps, Theodor. *Grundlegung der Ästhetik*. Vol. 1 of *Ästhetik: Psychologie des Schönen und der Kunst*. Hamburg: Voss, 1903.

Liu, James J.Y. *The Art of Chinese Poetry*. Chicago: University of Chicago Press, 1962.

——*Chinese Theories of Literature*. Chicago: University of Chicago Press, 1975.

Lodge, David. *Small World*. London: Vintage, 2011.

Lolo, Begoña, ed. *Cervantes y El Quijote en la música. Estudios sobre la recepción de un mito*. Madrid: Centro de Estudios Cervantinos, 2007.

Loomba, Ania. *Colonialism/Postcolonialism*. London: Routledge, 1998.

Lu, Xing [Lu Xing]. *Rhetoric in Ancient China Fifth to Third Century B.C.E.: A Comparison with Classical Greek Rhetoric*. Columbia: University of South Carolina Press, 1998.

Lucía Megías, José Manuel. *Leer el Quijote en imágenes. Hacia una teoría de los modelos icono-gráficos*. Madrid: Calambur, 2006.

Machado, Antonio. *Poesía y prosa*. Ed. Oreste Macri. Vol. 3. Madrid: Espasa Calpe, 1989.

Machetti, Sandro. *Què és el precinema? Bases metodològiques per a l'estudi del precinema*. Girona: Fundació Museo del Cinema – Ajuntament de Girona, 2000.

Magris, Claudio. *Danube*. Trans. Patrick Creagh. New York: Farrar Straus Giroux, 2008.

Mair, Victor H. and Tsu-Lin Mei, "The Sanskrit Origins of Recent Style Prosody." *Harvard Journal of Asiatic Studies* 51 (1991): 375–470.

Malinowski, Bronislaw. *The Dynamics of Culture Change: An Inquiry into Race Relations in Africa*. New Haven, CT: Yale University Press, 1945.

de Man, Paul. *Aesthetic Ideology*. Ed. Andrzej Warminski. Minneapolis: University of Minnesota Press, 1996.

Manovich, Lev. *The Language of New Media*. Cambridge, MA: The MIT Press, 2001.

Mao, LuMing [Mao LuMing]. "Reflective Encounters: Illustrating Comparative Rhetoric." *Style* 37.4 (2003): 401–25.

Marino, Adrian. "Repenser la littérature comparée." *Synthesis* 7 (1980): 9–38.

——*Comparatisme et théorie de la littérature*. Paris: Presses Universitaires de France, 1988.

Markiewicz, Henryk. "*Ut pictura poesis. Dzieje toposu i problem.*" *Wymiary dziela literackiego*. Cracow: Taiwpn Universitas, 1996. 7–42.

Martin, Serge. *Le Langage musical. Sémiotique des systems*. Paris: Klinscksieck, 1978.

Marx, Karl and Friedrich Engels. *Manifesto of the Communist Party*. New York: International Publishers, 1948.

Massey, Doreen. *Space, Place and Gender*. Cambridge: Polity Press, 2003.

McLuhan, Marshall. *The Gutenberg Galaxy: The Making of Typographic Man*. Toronto: University of Toronto Press, 1962.

——*Understanding Media. The Extensions of Man*. Cambridge, MA: The MIT Press, 1994.

McLuhan, Marshall and Frank Zingrone, eds. *Essential McLuhan*. Concord, ONT: Anansi, 1995.

Meltzl, Hugo. "Present Tasks of Comparative Literature." *World Literature. A Reader*. Ed. Theo D'haen, César Domínguez and Mads Rosendahl Thomsen. London: Routledge, 2013. 18–22.

Melville, Herman. *Moby Dick*. Trans. Jean Giono, Lucien Jacques and Joan Smith. Paris: Gallimard, 1941.

Menchú, Rigoberta. *I, Rigoberta Menchú. An Indian Woman in Guatemala*. Trans. Ann Wright. London: Verso, 2009.

Mignolo, Walter D. "Canon and Corpus: An Alternative View of Comparative Literary Studies in Colonial Situations." *Dedalus: Revista Portuguesa de Literatura Comparada* 1 (1991): 219–43.

——"Los límites de la literatura, de la teoría y de la literatura comparada: el desafío de las prácticas semióticas en situaciones coloniales." *Ínsula* 552 (1992): 15–17.

——*The Darker Side of the Renaissance. Literacy, Territoriality, and Colonization*. Ann Arbor: University of Michigan Press, 1995.

——*Local Histories/Global Designs. Coloniality, Subaltern Knowledges, and Border Thinking*. Princeton: Princeton University Press, 2000.

——"Delinking. The Rhetoric of Modernity, the Logic of Coloniality and the Grammar of De-Coloniality." *Cultural Studies* 21.2–3 (2007): 449–514.

——"Epistemic Disobedience, Independent Thought and De-Colonial Freedom." *Theory, Culture & Society* 26.7–8 (2009): 1–23.

——*The Darker Side of Western Modernity. Global Futures, Decolonial Options*. Durham, NC: Duke University Press, 2011.

Mignolo, Walter D. and Madina Tlostanova. "The Logic of Coloniality and the Limits of Postcoloniality." *The Postcolonial and the Global*. Ed. Revathi Krishnaswamy and John C. Hawley. Minneapolis: University of Minnesota Press, 2008. 109–23.

Miner, Earl. "Some Theoretical and Methodological Topics for Comparative Literature." *Poetics Today* 8.1 (1987): 123–40.

——"Études comparées interculturelles." Trans. Jean-Claude Choul. *Théorie littéraire*. Ed. Marc Angenot et al. Paris: Presses Universitaires de France, 1989. 161–79.

——*Comparative Poetics. An Intercultural Essay on Theories of Literature*. Princeton: Princeton University Press, 1990.

——"On the Genesis and Development of Literary Systems II: The Case of India." *Revue de Littérature Comparée* 258 (1991): 143–51.

Ming, Xie [Ming Xie]. "Trying to Be on Both Sides of the Mirror at Once: I.A. Richards, Multiple Definition, and Comparative Method." *Comparative Literature Studies* 44 (2007): 279–97.

Moretti, Franco. *Atlas of the European Novel 1800–1900*. London: Verso, 1998.

——"Conjectures on World Literature." *New Left Review* 1 (2000): 54–68.

Mortier, Roland. "Cent ans de Littérature Comparée: L'acquis, les perspectives." *Proceedings of the IXth Congress of the International Comparative Literature Association/Actes du IXe Congrès de l'Association Internationale de Littérature Comparée*. Ed. Zoran Konstantinović et al. Vol. 1. Innsbruck: Institut für Sprachwissenschaft der Universität, 1980. 11–17.

Możejko, Edward. "Nitra School." *Encyclopedia of Contemporary Literary Theory. Approaches, Scholars, Terms*. Ed. Irena R. Makaryk. Toronto: University of Toronto Press, 1997. 130–33.

Murray, Janet H. *Hamlet on the Holodeck: The Future of Narrative in Cyberspace*. New York: The Free Press, 1997.

Nandwa, Jane and Austin Bukenya. *African Oral Literature for Schools*. Nairobi: Longman, 1983.

Nattiez, Jean-Jacques. *Fondaments d'une sémiologie de la musique*. Paris: Union Générale d'Éditions, 1975.

——"Récit musical et récit littéraire." *Études françaises* 14.1–2 (1978): 93–121.

——*De la sémiologie à la musique*. Montreal: Université du Québec, 1988.

——"Can Someone Speak of Narrativity in Music?" *Journal of the Royal Musical Association*, 115.2 (1990): 240–57.

Navarro, Desiderio. "Un ejemplo de lucha contra el esquematismo eurocentrista en la ciencia literaria de la América Latina y Europa." *Casa de las Américas* 122 (1980): 77–91.

——"Otras reflexiones sobre eurocentrismo y antieurocentrismo en la teoría literaria de la América Latina y Europa." *Casa de las Américas* 150 (1985): 68–78.

Negroponte, Nicholas. *Being Digital*. New York: Alfred A. Knopf, 1995.

Nelson, Theodor Holm. *Literary Machines*. Sausalito: Mindful, 1981.

Nesher, Dan. *On the Truth and the Representation of Reality. A Collection of Inquiries from a Pragmatist Point of View*. Lanham, MD: University Press of America, 2002.

Nietzsche, Friedrich. *Daybreak: Thoughts on the Prejudices of Morality*. Ed. Maudemarie Clark and Brian Leiter. Trans. R.J. Hollingdale. Cambridge: Cambridge University Press, 1997.

Ogden, C.K. and I.A. Richards. *The Meaning of Meaning*. London: Kegan Paul, Trench & Trubner, 1927.

Ong, Walter J. *Orality and Literacy. The Technologizing of the Word*. London: Routledge, 1982.

Ortiz, Fernando. *Cuban Counterpoint: Tobacco and Sugar*. Tr. Harriet de Onís. New York: Knopf, 1947. Reprinted, Durham, NC: Duke University Press, 1993.

Padgen, Anthony. *The Fall of Natural Man. The American Indian and the Origins of Comparative Ethnology*. Cambridge: Cambridge University Press, 1982.

Panikkar, Raimundo. "What Is Comparative Philosophy Comparing?" *Interpreting across Boundaries. New Essays in Comparative Philosophy*. Ed. Gerald James Larson and Eliot Deutsch. Delhi: Motilal Banarsidass, 1989. 116–36.

Panofsky, Erwin. *Meaning in the Visual Arts*. Chicago: University of Chicago Press, 1955.

Pantini, Emilia. "La letteratura e le altri arti." *Introduzione alla letteratura comparata*. Ed. Armando Gnisci. Milan: Bruno Mondadori, 1999. 91–114.

Pater, Walter. *The Renaissance*. Ed. Adam Phillips. Oxford: Oxford University Press, 1988.

Peirce, Charles Sanders. *Peirce on Signs: Writings on Semiotics*. Ed. James Hoopes. Chapel Hill: University of North Carolina Press, 1994.

Percas de Ponseti, Helena. *Cervantes the Writer and Painter of Don Quijote*. Columbia: University of Missouri Press, 1988.

Petöfi, S. János. "Texttheorie-Textverarbeitung. (Bemerkungen zu den Anwendungsmöglichkeiten einer partiellen Texttheorie in der Jurisprudenz)." *Rechstheorie und Linguistik. Referate und Protokolle der Arbeitstagung der Werner-Reimer-Stiftung*. Ed. Hans Brinckmann and Klaus. Kassel: Gehlen, 1974. 137–57.

Piette, Isabelle. *Littérature et musique. Contribution à une orientation théorique (1970–1985)*. Namur: Presses Universitaires de Namur, 1987.

Plato. *Phaedrus and Letters VII and VIII*. Trans. Walter Hamilton. New York: Penguin, 1973.

Plumb, J.H. *The Death of The Past*. London: Macmillan, 1969.

Pollock, Sheldon. *The Language of the Gods in the World of Men. Sanskrit, Culture, and Power in Premodern India*. Berkeley: University of California Press, 2006.

Popovič, Antón. *Dictionary for the Analysis of Literary Translation*. Edmonton: University of Alberta, 1976.

Posnett, Hutcheson Macaulay. *Comparative Literature*. London: Kegan Paul, Trench & Co., 1886.

Pospíšil, Ivo and Miloš Zelenka, eds. *Centrisme interlittéraire des littératures de l'Europe centrale*. Brno: Masarykova Univerzita, 1999.

Postman, Neil. *Technopoly. The Surrender of Culture to Technology*. New York: Vintage Books, 1993.

Pratt, Mary Louise. "Comparative Literature and Global Citizenship." *Comparative Literature in the Age of Multiculturalism*. Ed. Charles Bernheimer. Baltimore, MD: Johns Hopkins University Press, 1995. 58–65.

Praz, Mario. *Mnemosyne. The Parallel between Literature and the Visual Arts*. Princeton: Princeton University Press, 1975.

Prendergast, Christopher, ed. *Debating World Literature*. London: Verso, 2004.

Prensky, Marc. "Digital Natives, Digital Immigrants." *On the Horizon* 9.5 (2001): 1–6.

Qian Zhongshu. *Guan zhui bian* (Essays of the Pipe and Awl) 4 vols. Beijing: Zhonghua shuju, 1979.

——*Limited Views: Essays on Ideas and Letters.* Trans. Ronald Egan. Cambridge, MA: Harvard University Asia Center, 1998.

Quijano, Aníbal. "Coloniality and Modernity/Rationality." Trans. Sonia Therborn. *Cultural Studies* 21.2–3 (2007): 168–78.

Rabelais, François. *Gargantua and Pantagruel. The Works of Rabelais.* Trans. Sir Thomas Urquhart and Peter Anthony Motteux. London: Published for the Trade, n.d.

——*Œuvres complètes.* Ed. Jacques Boulenger. Paris: Gallimard, 1955.

Raßloff, Ute. "Juraj Jánošík." Trans. Jutta Faehndrich. *History of the Literary Cultures of East-Central Europe: Junctures and Disjunctures in the 19th and 20th Centuries.* Ed. Marcel Cornis-Pope and John Neubauer. Vol. 4. Amsterdam: John Benjamins, 2010. 441–56.

Reiss, Timothy J. "Mapping Identities: Literature, Nationalism, Colonialism." *Debating World Literature.* Ed. Charles Prendergast. London: Verso, 2004. 110–47.

Remak, Henry H.H. "Comparative Literature at the Crossroads: Diagnosis, Therapy and Prognosis." *Yearbook of Comparative and General Literature* 9 (1960): 1–28.

——"Comparative Literature: Its Definition and Function." *Comparative Literature: Method and Perspective.* Ed. Newton P. Stallknecht and Horst Frenz. Carbondale: Southern Illinois University Press, 1961. 3–57.

——"The Future of Comparative Literature." *Actes du VIIIe Congrès de l'Association Internationale de Littérature Comparée/Proceedings of the International Comparative Literature Association.* Ed. B. Köpeczi and G.M. Vajda. Vol. 2. Stuttgart: Erich Bieber, 1980. 429–37.

——"General Preface to All Volumes Published as Part of *The Comparative History of Literatures.*" *European-Language Writing in Sub-Saharan Africa.* Ed. Albert S. Gérard. Vol. 1. Budapest: Akadémiai Kiadó, 1986. 5–6.

Riffaterre, Michael. "L'Illusion d'ekphrasis." *La Pensée de l'image: Signification et figuration dans le texte et dans la peinture.* Ed. Gisele Mathieu-Castellani. Vincennes: Presses Universitaires de Vincennes, 1994. 211–29.

Riley, E.C. *Cervantes's Theory of the Novel.* Oxford: Clarendon Press, 1962.

Ritter, Harry. *Dictionary of Concepts in History.* Westport, CT: Greenwood Press, 1986.

Robertson, Roland. *Globalization: Social Theory and Global Culture.* London: Sage, 1992.

Romaguera i Ramió, Joaquim and Homero Alsina Thevenet, eds. *Textos y manifiestos del cine. Etética. Escuelas. Movimientos. Disciplinas. Innovaciones.* 4th edn. Madrid: Cátedra, 2007.

Ropars-Wuilleumier, Marie-Claire. *De la littérature au cinema.* Paris: Armand Colin, 1970.

Rothwell, Kenneth S. *A History of Shakespeare on Screen: A Century of Film and Television.* Cambridge: Cambridge University Press, 1999.

Rousseau, André-Michel. "Arts et Littérature: un état présent et quelques réflexions." *Synthesis* 4 (1977): 31–51.

Ruwet, Nicolas. *Langage, musique, poésie.* Paris: Seuil, 1972.

Said, Edward W. *Orientalism.* New York: Vintage Books, 1979.

——*Culture and Imperialism.* New York: Vintage Books, 1994.

——*Out of Place: A Memoir.* New York: Vintage Books, 1999.

——*The Art of Reading/El arte de leer.* Trans. María Isabel Carrera Suárez. Oviedo: Universidad de Oviedo, 2003.

——*Humanism and Democratic Criticism.* New York: Palgrave Macmillan, 2004.

Saussure, Ferdinand de. *Course in General Linguistics.* New York: The Philosophical Library, 1959.

——*Cours de linguistique générale, édition critique.* Ed. Rudolf Engler. 3 vols. Wiesbaden: Harrassowitz, 1968–74.

Saussy, Haun. "Exquisite Cadavers Stitched from Fresh Nightmares: Of Memes, Hives, and Selfish Genes." *Comparative Literature in an Age of Globalization.* Ed. Haun Saussy. Baltimore, MD: Johns Hopkins University Press, 2006. 3–42.

——ed. *Comparative Literature in an Age of Globalization.* Baltimore, MD: Johns Hopkins University Press, 2006.

Saussy, Haun and Gerald Gillespie, eds. *Intersections, Interferences, Interdisciplines: Literature With Other Arts.* Bern: Peter Lang, 2014.

Scharfstein, Ben-Ami. *A Comparative History of World Philosophy: From the Upanishads to Kant.* Albany: State University of New York, 1998.

Scher, Steven Paul. "Comparing Literature and Music: Current Trends and Prospects in Critical Theory and Methodology." *Proceedings of the IXth Congress of the International Comparative Literature Association/Actes du IXe Congrès de l'Association Internationale de Littérature Comparée.* Ed. Zoran Konstantinović et al. Vol. 3. Innsbruck: Institut für Sprachwissenschaft der Universität, 1980. 215–21.

Schleiermacher, Friedrich. "On the Different Methods of Translating." Trans. Susan Bernofsky. *The Translation Studies Reader.* Ed. Lawrence Venuti. 3rd edn. London: Routledge, 2012. 43–63.

Schmeling, Manfred, ed. *Vergleichende Literaturwissenschaft. Theorie und Praxis.* Wiesbaden: Akademische Verlagsgesellschaft Athenaion, 1981.

Schmidt, Siegfried J. *Foundations for the Empirical Study of Literature. The Components of a Basic Theory.* Trans. R. de Beaugrande. Hamburg: Helmut Buske, 1982.

Shakespeare, William. *Histories and Poems.* Ed. W.J. Craig. New York: Oxford University Press, 1966.

Simonde de Sismondi, J.C.L. *Historical View of the Literature of the South of Europe.* Trans. Thomas Roscoe. 2 vols. London: Henry G. Bohn, 1846.

Sinopoli, Franca. "La storia comparata della letteratura." *Introduzione alla letteratura comparata.* Ed. Armando Gnisci. Milan: Bruno Mondadori, 1999. 1–50.

Sobry, J.-Fr. *Poétique des arts, ou Cours de peinture et de littérature comparées.* Paris: Delaunay, 1810.

Spivak, Gayatri Chakravorty. *Death of a Discipline.* New York: Columbia University Press, 2003.

Spolsky, Ellen. "Darwin and Derrida: Cognitive Literary Theory as a Species of Post-Structuralism." *Poetics Today* 23.1 (2002): 43–62.

St. André, James. "Whither East-West Comparative Literature? Two Recent Answers fom the U.S." *Bulletin of the Chinese Institute of Literature and Philosophy* 22 (2003): 291–302.

Staël, Mme de (Anne-Louise-Germaine Necker). *Germany.* 3 vols. London: John Murray, 1813.

Stallknecht, Newton P. and Horst Frenz, eds. *Comparative Literature: Method and Perspective.* Carbondale: Southern Illinois University Press, 1961.

Steiner, George. *The Death of Tragedy.* London: Faber & Faber, 1961.

——"'Critic'/'Reader'." *New Literary History* 10.3 (1979): 423–52.

——*Real Presences. Is There Anything in What We Say?* London: Faber and Faber, 1989.

——"Roncevaux." *The Return of Thematic Criticism.* Cambridge, MA: Harvard University Press, 1993. 299–300.

——*Lessons of the Masters.* Cambridge, MA: Harvard University Press, 2003.

Steiner, Wendy, ed. *The Sign in Music and Literature.* Austin: University of Texas Press, 1981.

——*The Colors of Rhetoric.* Chicago: University of Chicago Press, 1982.

Suhamy, Henri. "Shakespeare, cinéaste par anticipation." *Études anglaises* 55 (2002): 201–14.

Swiggers, Pierre. "A New Paradigm for Comparative Literature." *Poetics Today* 3.1 (1982): 181–84.

——"Methodological Innovation in the Comparative Study of Literature." *Canadian Review of Comparative Literature/Revue Canadienne de Littérature Comparée* 1 (1982): 19–26.

Szymborska, Wisława. *Poems. New and Collected 1957–1997.* Trans. Stanislaw Barańczak and Clare Cavanagh. San Diego: Harcourt, 1998.

Tarasti, Eero. *Myth and Music.* The Hague: Mouton, 1979.

Taylor, Charles. *Philosophy and the Human Sciences.* Cambridge: Cambridge University Press, 1985.

Teroni, Sandra and Wolfgang Klein, eds. *Pour la défense de la culture.* Dijon: Presses Universitaires de Dijon, 2005.

Texte, Joseph. "Les Études de littérature comparée à l'étranger et en France." *Revue sur l'enseignement* 13 (1893): 253–69.

Théry, Hervé. "The Main Locations of Latin American Literature." *Literary Cultures of Latin America. A Comparative History.* Ed. Mario J. Valdés and Djelal Kadir. Vol. 1. Oxford: Oxford University Press, 2004. 169–77.

Thompson, Damian. *The End of Time: Faith and the Fear in the Shadow of the Millennium.* Hanover, NH: University Press of New England, 1997.

Thomsen, Mads Rosendahl. *Mapping World Literature: International Canonization and Transnational Literatures.* London: Continuum, 2008.

Tötösy de Zepetnek, Steven. "Systemic Approaches to Literature: An Introduction with Selected Bibliographies." *Canadian Review of Comparative Literature/Revue Canadienne de Littérature Comparée,* 19.1–2 (1992): 21–93.

——*Comparative Literature. Theory, Method, Application.* Amsterdam–Atlanta, Rodopi, 1998.

——ed. *Comparative Central European Culture.* West Lafayette: Purdue University Press, 2002.

——*Comparative Literature and Comparative Cultural Studies.* West Lafayette: Purdue University Press, 2003.

Tötösy de Zepetnek, Steven and Irene Sywenky, eds. *The Systemic and Empirical Approach to Literature and Culture as Theory and Application.* Edmonton: University of Alberta, 1997.

Toury, Gideon. *In Search of a Theory of Translation.* Tel Aviv: The Porter Institute for Poetics and Semiotics, 1980.

——*Descriptive Translation Studies and Beyond.* Philadelphia: Benjamins, 1995.

Trousson, Raymond. *Un Problème de littérature comparée: les études des thèmes.* Paris: Lettres Modernes, 1965.

Tylor, Edward B. *Anthropology: An Introduction to the Study of Man and Civilisation.* London: Macmillan, 1881.

Vajdová, Libuša and Róbert Gáfrik, eds. *New Imagined Communities. Identity Making in Eastern and South-Eastern Europe.* Bratislava: Kalligram – Ústav Svetovej Literatúry, SAV, 2010.

Valdés, Mario J. "From Geography to Poetry: A Braudelian Comparative Literary History of Latin America." *Canadian Review of Comparative Literature/Revue Canadienne de Littérature Comparée* 23.1 (1996): 199–205.

——"Rethinking the History of Literary History." *Rethinking Literary History. A Dialogue on Theory.* Ed. Linda Hutcheon and Mario J. Valdés. Oxford: Oxford University Press, 2002. 63–115.

——"Preface by the General Editor of the Literary History Project." *History of the Literary Cultures of East-Central Europe: Junctures and Disjunctures in the 19th and 20th Centuries.* Ed. Marcel Cornis-Pope and John Neubauer. Vol. 1. Amsterdam: John Benjamins, 2004. xiii–xvi.

Valdés, Mario J. and Djelal Kadir, eds. *Literary Cultures of Latin America: A Comparative History.* 3 vols. Oxford: Oxford University Press, 2004.

Van Tieghem, Paul. *La Littérature comparée.* 3rd edn. Paris: Armand Colin, 1946.

Vargas Llosa, Mario. "Lisbeth Salander debe vivir". *El País* 6 September, 2009.

Venuti, Lawrence. *The Translator's Invisibility: A History of Translation.* London: Routledge, 1995.

——ed. *The Translation Studies Reader.* 3rd edn. London: Routledge, 2012.

Veselovsky, Aleksandr N. *Poetica storica.* Trans. Claudia Giustini. Rome: Edizioni e/0, 1981.

——"Envisioning World Literature in 1863: From the Reports on a Mission Abroad." Ed. Boris Rodin Maslov. Trans. Jennifer Flaherty. *PMLA* 128.2 (2013): 439–51.

Villanueva, Darío. *El polen de ideas. Teoría, Crítica, Historia y Literatura comparada,* Barcelona: PPU, 1991.

Villemain, [Abel-François]. *Tableau de la littérature au Moyen Âge en France, en Italie, en Espagne et en Angleterre.* 2 vols. Paris: Didier, 1875.

Wallerstein, Immanuel. *The Modern World-System.* 4 vols. Berkeley: University of California Press, 2011.

Weinberger, Eliot, ed. *The New Directions Anthology of Classical Chinese Poetry.* New York: New Directions, 2003.

Weisgerber, Jean. "Écrire l'histoire. L'exemple de l'*Histoire comparée des littératures de langues européennes*. Principes et organisation." Marc Angenot et al, *Théorie littéraire: problèmes et perspectives*. Paris: Presses Universitaires de France, 1989. 353–58.

Weisstein, Ulrich. "Literature and the Visual Arts." *Interrelations of Literature*. Ed. Jean-Pierre Barricelli and Joseph Gibaldi. New York: The Modern Language Association of America, 1978. 251–77.

——ed. *Expressionism as an International Literary Phenomenon*. Budapest: Akadémiai Kiadó, 1973.

Wellek, René. "The Parallelism between Literature and the Arts." *English Institute Annual* (1941): 29–63.

——"The Crisis of Comparative Literature." *The Princeton Sourcebook in Comparative Literature*. Ed. David Damrosch, Natalie Melas, and Mbongiseni Buthelezi: Princeton: Princeton University Press, 2009. 162–72 [originally 1958].

Wellek, René and Austin Warren. *Theory of Literature*. New York: Harcourt Brace, 1949.

Whitney, William Dwight. *Language and the Study of Language*. New York: Charles Scribner & Company, 1868.

Wienold, Götz. *Semiotik der Literatur*. Frankfurt: Athenäum, 1972.

——"Vorüberlegungen zur Rolle des Konzepts der Textverarbeitung beim Aufbau einer empirischen Sprachtheorie." *Text Processing/Textverarbeitung*. Ed. Wolfgang Burghardt and Klaus Hölker. Berlin: De Gruyter, 1979. 20–48.

Williams, Raymond. *Television. Technology and Cultural Form*. London: Routledge, 2003.

Winkler, Karen J. "Scholars Mark the Beginning of the Age of Post-Theory." *The Chronicle of Higher Education* October 13 (1993): A8–A9, A16–A17.

Wolf, Maryanne. *Proust and the Squid: The Story and Science of the Reading Brain*. New York: HarperCollins, 2007.

Woolf, Virginia. *The Common Reader*. Ed. Andrew McNeillie. San Diego: Harcourt, 1984.

Zaid, Gabriel. *Los demasiados libros*. Barcelona: Anagrama, 1996.

Zhang Tingyu, chief ed. *Ming shi* ["The History of the Ming Dynasty"]. Vol. 10 of *Ershiwu shi* [*The Twenty-five Dynastic Histories*]. Reprinted in 12 vols. Shanghai: Guji, 1991.

Zunshine, Lisa. *Introduction to Cognitive Cultural Studies*. Baltimore, MD: Johns Hopkins University Press, 2010.

INDEX

eBooks
from Taylor & Francis

Helping you to choose the right eBooks for your Library

Add to your library's digital collection today with Taylor & Francis eBooks. We have over 50,000 eBooks in the Humanities, Social Sciences, Behavioural Sciences, Built Environment and Law, from leading imprints, including Routledge, Focal Press and Psychology Press.

Choose from a range of subject packages or create your own!

Benefits for you
- Free MARC records
- COUNTER-compliant usage statistics
- Flexible purchase and pricing options
- 70% approx of our eBooks are now DRM-free.

Benefits for your user
- Off-site, anytime access via Athens or referring URL
- Print or copy pages or chapters
- Full content search
- Bookmark, highlight and annotate text
- Access to thousands of pages of quality research at the click of a button.

ORDER YOUR
FREE
INSTITUTIONAL
TRIAL TODAY

Free Trials Available

We offer free trials to qualifying academic, corporate and government customers.

eCollections

Choose from 20 different subject eCollections, including:

Asian Studies

Economics

Health Studies

Law

Middle East Studies

eFocus

We have 16 cutting-edge interdisciplinary collections, including:

Development Studies

The Environment

Islam

Korea

Urban Studies

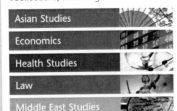

For more information, pricing enquiries or to order a free trial, please contact your local sales team:

UK/Rest of World: **online.sales@tandf.co.uk**
USA/Canada/Latin America: **e-reference@taylorandfrancis.com**
East/Southeast Asia: **martin.jack@tandf.com.sg**
India: **journalsales@tandfindia.com**

www.tandfebooks.com